D1518926

Bad Logic

Bad Logic

REASONING ABOUT DESIRE

IN THE

VICTORIAN NOVEL

❧

DANIEL WRIGHT

Johns Hopkins University Press

Baltimore

© 2018 Johns Hopkins University Press
All rights reserved. Published 2018
Printed in the United States of America on acid-free paper
2 4 6 8 9 7 5 3 1

Johns Hopkins University Press
2715 North Charles Street
Baltimore, Maryland 21218-4363
www.press.jhu.edu

Library of Congress Cataloging-in-Publication Data

Names: Wright, Daniel, 1983– author.
Title: Bad logic : reasoning about desire in the Victorian novel / Daniel Wright.
Description: Baltimore : Johns Hopkins University Press, 2018. | Includes
bibliographical references and index.
Identifiers: LCCN 2017035214| ISBN 9781421425177 (hardcover : acid-free
paper) | ISBN 9781421425184 (electronic) | ISBN 1421425173 (hardcover :
acid-free paper) | ISBN 1421425181 (electronic)
Subjects: LCSH: English fiction—19th century—History and criticism. |
Desire in literature. | Gender identity in literature. | Sex in
literature. | Narration (Rhetoric)
Classification: LCC PR878.D394 W75 2018 | DDC 823/.809353—dc23
LC record available at https://lccn.loc.gov/2017035214

A catalog record for this book is available from the British Library.

*Special discounts are available for bulk purchases of this book. For more information,
please contact Special Sales at 410-516-6936 or specialsales@press.jhu.edu.*

Johns Hopkins University Press uses environmentally friendly book materials, including recycled
text paper that is composed of at least 30 percent post-consumer waste, whenever possible.

CONTENTS

It's a pleasure to narrate the biography of this little book by expressing my gratitude to all of those who have shaped it along the way. *Bad Logic* began as a doctoral dissertation written at Columbia University, where Sharon Marcus's teaching converted me to the study of the Victorian novel before she became the chair of my dissertation committee. I continue to feel immensely thankful to her for having guided me with such intellectual rigor, humor, and warmth through the complicated journey of graduate school. A question about tautology, posed by Nick Dames to a group of students in a graduate seminar on Trollope and Eliot, was the first germ of this project: I'm grateful for that small but life-changing question, and for his intense and kind intelligence. Jim Adams arrived at Columbia just in time, and his care and thoroughness as a reader, his encyclopedic expertise, and his compassion and good cheer helped sustain and improve my work. I thank this fabulous trio for all they have done to make me into a scholar.

During those years of graduate school, I was lucky also to have the support and mentorship of several people beyond my dissertation committee, and I offer warmest thanks to Amanda Claybaugh, Sarah Cole, Susan Crane, Jenny Davidson, Eileen Gillooly, Erik Gray, Anahid Nersessian, Victoria Rosner, Gauri Viswanathan, and Nicole Wallack. Bruce Robbins and Heather Love served as outside readers at my dissertation defense, and I am so grateful for their engagement and encouragement. My graduate school comrades Jamie Parra and Christine Smallwood were cherished interlocutors in the early stages of this project: their readiness to ask big, difficult, thrilling questions helped shape many of the ideas in this book.

After graduate school, I was lucky to find a professional and intellectual home at the University of Toronto, and I am especially thankful to those wonderful colleagues who read and commented on various chapters in draft form: Liza Blake, Denise Cruz, Josh Gang, Kara Gaston, Audrey Jaffe, Mark Knight, Deidre Lynch, Terry Robinson, Cannon Schmitt, Dana Seitler, and Matt Sergi.

I owe Josh Gang special gratitude for countless conversations about this book and the ideas that inspire and surround it. Cannon Schmitt offered to read the entire manuscript at a critical juncture, and he commented on it with his characteristic (yet still astounding) generosity, acuteness, and wisdom. My gratitude for that reading is profound. For many different kinds of mentorship, professional advice, and support both personal and monetary in my first years at the University of Toronto, I thank Alan Bewell, Denise Cruz, Alex Gillespie, Audrey Jaffe, Deidre Lynch, Cannon Schmitt, Dana Seitler, Paul Stevens, Holger Syme, David Taylor, and Dan White.

I had the opportunity to present portions of this project to lively, engaged audiences at the Victorian Studies Association of Ontario, the Princeton Victorian Colloquium, the Work in Nineteenth-Century Studies group at the University of Toronto, the Trollope Bicentennial Conference, two ACLA seminars, the "Logic and Literary Form" conference at Berkeley, and several NAVSA conferences, and I thank Letitia Henville, Alison Syme, Beatrice Sanford Russell, Mark Knight, Terry Robinson, Nick Dames, Frederik van Dam, Anne-Lise François, Anahid Nersessian, Josh Gang, Daniel Williams, Jeff Blevins, Charles Altieri, and Rachel Ablow for extending invitations and facilitating those conversations. Chapter three was immeasurably improved by the careful reading of an article-length version by Andrew Miller, Ivan Kreilkamp, and an anonymous reader for *Victorian Studies*. I thank them for their sympathetic engagement with my work. For generous professional advice and camaraderie from colleagues beyond the University of Toronto, I thank Elaine Auyoung, Ayelet Ben-Yishai, Elisha Cohn, Rae Greiner, Devin Griffiths, Nathan Hensley, Claire Jarvis, Heather Love, Anahid Nersessian, and Emily Steinlight.

My work on this book was supported by (and would not have been completed without) a Connaught New Researcher Award from the University of Toronto, as well as generous research funding and a semester-long teaching release from the Department of English and Drama at the University of Toronto Mississauga. Portions of chapter two appeared in an earlier form as "Because I Do: Trollope, Tautology, and Desire," © Johns Hopkins University Press, 2013, in *ELH* 80, no. 4 (Winter 2013): 1121–43. Portions of chapter three appeared in an earlier form as "George Eliot's Vagueness," © Indiana University Press, 2014, in *Victorian Studies* 56, no. 4 (Summer 2014): 625–48. I am grateful to both presses for permission to reprint.

At Johns Hopkins University Press, I've been so lucky to work with the brilliant Catherine Goldstead, who shepherded this book through the peer review and publication process with such efficiency and good humor. Thanks also to Julia Ridley Smith, who expertly copyedited the manuscript; to managing editor Juliana McCarthy; and to the entire team at the press. I'm especially grateful to the two anonymous readers for the press who read the manuscript with amazing acuity and offered detailed, challenging, inspiring suggestions for improvement.

Finally, without my parents, Brian and Lisa Wright, I would never have become the kind of person who could write a book, since they are the ones who showed me the big wide world, who taught me to love to learn, and who allowed me to quit so many sports teams and flourish instead as an indoors kid. And without my husband, Jeff Campanelli, I'd never have finished this book, because my life wouldn't have had all his revitalizing love and laughter in it, all the warm tones of vinyl records, all his vivacity. For the many ways that he has supported me in my work, for the many ways he makes our life a joy, and for much more, I dedicate this book to him.

Bad Logic

To Give a Form to Formless Things

It can seem a kind of magic to put into language the vagaries of desire. We seek, and so often fail to find, those concepts and entailments that would make clear how the imperatives of desire press upon us, sometimes pleasurably and sometimes painfully. It may be that we need elegant models to teach us how to use the untapped resources of reasoned language, to put the pieces of desire together in unusual articulations. Dorian Gray's erotic awakening, for example, is occasioned not by a caress, a kiss, or even a charged look but by an argument. In the opening scene of Oscar Wilde's *The Picture of Dorian Gray* (1891), as Dorian listens to the stylish Lord Henry Wotton elaborate an argument on behalf of reasoned hedonism, he marvels at the power of words to become "articulate," to join themselves together in the service of a thrilling clarity about the life of desire:

> He was dimly conscious that entirely fresh impulses were at work within him, and that they seemed to him to have come really from himself. The few words that [Lord Henry] had said to him—words spoken by chance, no doubt, and with willful paradox in them—had touched some secret chord that had never been touched before, but that he felt was now vibrating and throbbing to curious pulses.
>
> Music had stirred him like that. Music had troubled him many times. But music was not articulate. It was not a new world, but rather a new chaos, that it created in us. Words! Mere words! How terrible they were! How clear, and vivid, and cruel! One could not escape from them. And yet what a subtle magic there was in them! They seemed to be able to give a plastic form to formless things.[1]

Lord Henry's deliberately bad logic—the "willful paradox" that shapes his line of thinking into a knot of contradiction—solicits the mind, but it also touches the body and makes it throb; as Eve Kosofsky Sedgwick points out, the goal of his speech is "less persuasion than seduction."[2] His reasoning about desire makes new worlds in place of what has been for Dorian only a chaos, but it is also "terrible," a "cruel" magic by which nothing is allowed to remain obscure, to escape from the sharp glare of language. While Lord Henry's ability "to give a plastic form to formless things" is dangerous—in its indifference to secrecy and evasion, to the feeling that some things are better left unsaid, that some desires dare not speak their names—for Dorian the danger is worth the risk. He is seduced, set humming by a language that helps him to know himself, spoken by another yet seeming to echo a voice that arises from within.

This book considers four forms of bad logic—contradiction, tautology, vagueness, and generality—that appear in the Victorian novel as mechanisms for giving form to the formless thing that is erotic desire, for putting into language desire's force, its opacity, its fuzziness, and its uncertain scope. These are not slippery slopes or begged questions, those logical fallacies that make for spurious arguments; rather, they're a set of logical problem-cases that are particularly good at revealing the hidden foundations and limit points of logic. In this book, I take erotic desire to be a particularly difficult object of knowledge (regardless of our historical period) and an even more difficult object of representation. Our erotic impulses, desires, feelings, and convictions seem especially resistant to being given intelligible form in language, or, at the very least, being given linguistic form threatens to impoverish desire, to mechanize it, or to hollow it out by making it socially useful and meaningful above all. But this worry does not necessarily relieve us of the imperative of ethical accountability when it comes to erotic life—it is only that we need to seek out more sensitive or labile models of accountability in trying to make "clear" and "vivid" our desire, both for ourselves and for others.

In the chapters that follow, I argue that in a century of intensive philosophical debate over the nature and scope of logic, novelists such as Charlotte Brontë, Anthony Trollope, George Meredith, George Eliot, and Henry James—concerned as they were with the careful investigation of ordinary language and the forms of intimate recognition it might allow—were in a unique position to linger with these problem-cases of language, showing us where language might find its limitations as an interface between the individual and the social world. But even despite its limitations, in the novelistic plot of desire, logic is necessary to characters called upon to make the idiosyncratic impulses of erotic life intelligible—to give them form—for others, for better or for worse. For better or for worse: the ambivalent qualification is essential. As we'll see, the novelists I consider often remain poised, like Dorian Gray, between a commitment to the form-giving magic promised by articulate language and a trepidation at how those forms might bind us to a particular ideal of clarity, becoming insidious and inescapable, allowing no room for dark places and for the different kind of pleasure associated with a murky, inchoate, ineffable desire. If ethical life often seems to be motivated, challenged, or shaped by the force of the erotic as well as the force of logical norms of reason, then it seems important that we understand how the erotic might become an object of the rational mind in the first place or, conversely, how the rational mind might be made into an object or mechanism of the erotic self.

What Is Bad Logic?

Each of the book's four chapters takes one form of bad logic and one Victorian novelist as its focus. The structure by which one novelist is linked to one form functions in this book as a heuristic that is meant to be provisional and riddled with exceptions, helping us to see how the questions associated with one particular kind of bad logic can come to dominate the work of a particular novelist, although not necessarily to the exclusion of all other questions. As I first began to conceptualize this book, I wanted to understand, for example, the moment in Henry James's *The Golden Bowl* (1904) when Prince Amerigo asks his friend Fanny Assingham if his old flame Charlotte Stant is still as beautiful as he remembers, and Fanny tries to describe Charlotte's irresistible charisma with a gnomic circularity: "one admires her," Fanny says, "if one doesn't happen not to."[3] It's easy to stumble over the Jamesian flourish of syntax before recognizing the tautology. Fanny asserts the general truth that "one admires" Charlotte before qualifying it with an accidental exception, the person who would "happen not to" admire her. The more clearly tautological paraphrase of the conditional is "if one admires her, then one admires her"; by making this tautology more highly wrought, Fanny hints into existence an impossible person whose desires are unpredictable, singular, botched. There's a wry comedy to Fanny's observation, because tautology is funny, aggressively obvious, even stupid—she uses the emptiness of the circular assertion to evade Amerigo's question, with its illicit hint of adulterous desire. But there's also something else at work in the creative indirection of Fanny's conditional tautology. It allows her to address the complex shape of erotic desire, as if tautology could ever be merely provisional, could ever allow exceptions or an escape from its unbroken circle.

I wanted also to understand a much blunter kind of tautology, less well crafted and more clichéd: the conviction that "I am what I am," which, like Fanny's tautology, promises an imposing clarity about identity while also threatening to trap us in its never-ending circuit. This phrase is everywhere, eminently detachable from context and yet so often situated in the Victorian novel in or around scenes in which erotic desire becomes an object of reason and ethical scrutiny. In *The Picture of Dorian Gray*, for example, Dorian arrives at this phrase, late in the novel, as an argumentative full stop, a forbidding conclusion as he attempts to account for a newly elaborated erotic identity that his friend Basil Hallward worries is damaging to Dorian and to others, the "new passions, new thoughts, new ideas" opened up to Dorian in his life of hedonism: "I am what I am," Dorian says finally, exasperated. "There is nothing more to be said" (95). The self-evidence of tautology acts in this case as a kind of punctuation and also as a means of escape. It rejects the terms of the debate by claiming an exemption, marking the place of a deep kernel of identity that in its feeling of absolute certainty must not be subject to rational argument but can only serve as a formal precondition for such an argument. There is, of course, a deep irony to Dorian's tautology, since he is not entirely what he is—in the world of this novel, he is both himself and a painting of himself, a person deeply riven into two. "I am what I am," encountered at this angle, is a desperate attempt to repair this rift, to insist upon desire as the foundation for absolute self-identity in place of desire as the occasion for a profound dislocation of the self.[4] Dorian's "I am what I am" offers a mirror image, moreover, to a similar tautology at which he has arrived only a few pages earlier, as he gives up trying to explain scientifically the supernatural properties that inhere in his portrait, thinking to himself, "If the picture was to alter, it was to alter. That was all. Why inquire too closely into it?" (91). I am what I am, and it is what it is: this pair of opaque, circular claims is the deflating final result of Dorian's complex experiments in erotic indulgence. And yet we might also understand these hard, seemingly indifferent tautologies as emblems of the cool detachment that Dorian requires of himself as he begins to accept the necessity, and indeed the pleasure, of taking his own erotic life as an object of rational scrutiny: "For there would be a real pleasure," he continues, "in watching it. He would be able to follow his mind into its secret places. This portrait would be to him the most magical of mirrors. As it had revealed to him his own body, so it would reveal to him his own soul" (91). In that pair of tautologies—"I am what I am" and "it is what it is"—there is a germinal worldview that sees the truths of the body as analogous to the truths of the soul. Some of those embodied truths may even claim an apodictic certainty, as clear and undeniable as mathematical axioms, or as the marks that emerge on Dorian's portrait, revealing to him the "secret places" of his mind. The unexpected meaningfulness of tautology, and its status in the Victorian novel as a resource for thinking about the opacity and conviction of desire, is the focus of chapter two of this book, which explores Trollope's profound ambivalence toward the kind of ideal clarity about desire that is so often formalized by the circular claim. I argue that novelistic and philosophical explorations of the logic and the erotics of unconditional conviction, in the nineteenth century and beyond, are divided into two camps: the *tautologophobic* reaction, which is suspicious of the easiness of tautological certainty and its valorization of an impossible kind of consistency; and the *tautologophilic* reaction, which sees in circular reasoning an opportunity to give form to the real ethical force of sexuality by claiming for it a place outside the jurisdiction of rational debate. Tautology is often understood as the stupidest, most lazily irrational kind of argumentation, and yet Trollope, along with his contemporaries George Meredith and John Henry Newman, asks us to attend to its complexity, its capaciousness, and its power as a mechanism of essentialism, and to revisit the question of where essence fits in our conceptualization of sexuality, sexual identity, and their social claims.

My research on tautology soon led me to its opposite: contradiction. If tautology formalizes a self-evident truth, contradiction formalizes a self-evident falsity, and it seemed to me that just as with tautology, the novel might use contradiction to reveal with great self-consciousness the limits, in this case the outer edges, of logic. Lord Henry, after all, is dubbed "Prince Paradox" by Dorian Gray (163), and as we've seen, it's the "willful paradox" of his argumentation that both attracts Dorian and bewilders him. Lord Henry claims in his first speech to Dorian, for example, that "Every impulse that we strive to strangle broods in the mind, and poisons us. The body sins once, and has done with its sin, for action is a mode of purification" (19). Dorian is right to pause: shouldn't a flagrant contradiction—the sinful action that purifies us of sin—disqualify this line of reasoning? On the contrary, Lord Henry shows Dorian in the wrenching shape of the contradiction the similarly wrenching shape of an illicit desire struggling for expression. Like tautology, contradiction makes visible the kinds of meanings that logic has trouble formalizing, the "secret places" to which its mathematics cannot lead us.

Contradiction and tautology are empty forms, but are necessary for establishing the twinned axioms around which logic organizes itself: the law of identity, which says that x must be x, and the law of noncontradiction, which says that x can never be not-x. As Alexander Bain puts it in his mid-Victorian account, to deny these two laws would be "intellectual suicide," even despite the important fact that neither contradictions nor tautologies contain any "information." Rather, they represent formal axioms that we simply cannot deny.[5] Ludwig Wittgenstein would later argue, along similar lines, that contradiction establishes an outer limit, and tautology a strangely vapid foundation, for logic as a system. While they seem entirely empty, he insists that they are not in fact "nonsensical":

> Propositions show what they say: tautologies and contradictions show that they say nothing.
>
> A tautology has no truth conditions, since it is unconditionally true: and a contradiction is true on no condition.
>
> Tautologies and contradictions lack sense.
>
> (Like a point from which two arrows go out in opposite directions to one another.) . . .
>
> Tautologies and contradictions are not, however, nonsensical. They are part of the symbolism, much as "0" is part of the symbolism of arithmetic.[6]

Tautology flees from meaning in one direction as it zeroes out truth, shearing it of its contingencies, reminding us what it looks like as a form without content. Contradiction moves away from meaning in the opposite direction, and functions as a zeroing mechanism in a different way, providing a formal resting place where we might pause before tipping over from positive to negative integers, able to look both ways from the perspective of the limit point.

Early in *The Picture of Dorian Gray*, we encounter a resonant way of describing the contradiction as a balancing act that offers a new and vital perspective upon the truths of the body. As Lord Henry debates the value of paradox with a group of lunch guests at his aunt's table, he finds support from the arch Mr. Erskine, who insists that "the way of paradoxes is the way of truth. To test reality we must see it on the tight rope. When the verities become acrobats, we can judge them" (36). Mr. Erskine sees in Lord Henry's "willful paradox" an athleticism, in which truth itself is strengthened by the difficult exercise of contradiction. The paradox is also a kind of acrobatic stunt: in this view, the badness we see in contradiction arises out of its status as an unnecessarily elaborate flourish, a way toward the truth that tumbles, spins, and flips. Finally, and perhaps most importantly, Mr. Erskine points out that Lord Henry's paradoxes make truth into an object of spectatorship—they allow us to stand back and see the "verities" that make up "reality" from outside. Later, in *De Profundis*, Wilde would be more explicit about the erotics of paradox: "What the paradox was to me in the sphere of thought," he writes, "perversity became to me in the sphere of passion."[7] The hurting form of contradiction, its way of linking thought and passion by formalizing the kind of self-negation that we often associate with reasoning about desire, as we stand back from our own bodies to occupy a third-person position of logical objectivity, is the subject of chapter one of this book, which traces the vexed relationship between what W. V. O. Quine called the "logical point of view" and the embodied, first-personal particularity of what I call the erotic point of view in Charlotte Brontë's major first-person novels, *Jane Eyre* (1847) and *Villette* (1853).[8] Desire is essentially idiosyncratic, while logic's mode of ethical reasoning is essentially impersonal, and we tend to think of ethical life as bound up with both of these points of view. On the one hand, my way of moving through the world has something to do with my own personal investments, attachments, feelings, erotic affinities, and intimacies, or with what psychoanalysis would call more generally my libidinal cathexes. On the other hand, to be reasonable about ethical life seems also to require an act of at least temporary self-negation by which I take on the perspective of omniscience and impersonality to which the rule of good logic appeals. This is the problem of what the philosopher Thomas Nagel calls "the view from nowhere," that is, the fundamental ethical question of "how to combine the perspective of a particular person inside the world with an objective view of that same world, the person and his viewpoint included."[9] In other words, when desire comes into play as an object of reasoning, we become caught in a basic contradiction by which one must be able to say "I am not I" or, perhaps, "I should not be I, at least for a moment," and therefore to waver painfully between the singularity of desire and the abstraction of logic.

But what about those other dimensions of logic, beyond the internal form of propositions and arguments, which structure our reasoning by organizing our language into sets? We can often forget that logic is as concerned with set theory as with syllogisms, and as I tried to move beyond the opaque force of contradiction and tautology, seeking out other kinds of bad logic, I encountered the blurred forms of vagueness. We can see the erotics of vagueness at work when Lord Henry invokes the metaphor of the vague boundary that has long been a problem for logic in his owns reflections on the scientific analysis of erotic life: "To note the curious hard logic of passion, and the emotional coloured life of the intellect—to observe where they met, and where they separated, at what point they were in unison, and at what point they were at discord—there was a delight in that!" (51). Lord Henry admits here that there is no sharp line separating what we call "passion" from what we call "intellect." Each is "coloured" by the other; they bleed into each other across vulnerable points in the line by which we try to separate them. Lord Henry finds the set of borderline cases generated by this vague boundary thrilling. That passion and intellect might be formally analogous—both of them vaguely outlined, porous, fuzzy—opens up for him a kind of microscopic scale for the study of erotic life and its relationship to reason, mapping out with ever greater precision the vague borderlands between them. He draws as well upon a long history of thinking about vagueness as a problem for binary logic, a history that originates, appropriately enough, in a set of ancient paradoxes. These paradoxes are the impetus for chapter three of this book, which examines George Eliot's treatment in *The Mill on the Floss* (1860) and *Middlemarch* (1871–72) of the vagueness intrinsic to both reason and desire, two fuzzy categories that meet and overlap as often as they separate. Eliot represents vagueness as the linguistic manifestation of an affective mood in which desire and reason can be understood as overlapping or interchangeable, but this does not mean that she celebrates erotic desire as the fundamental basis of our practices of ethical reasoning. Eliot is above all ambivalent about the productivity of vagueness. It is necessary, her novels suggest again and again, to understand vagueness and to remain open to it, aware of its consequences and of its implications for our strivings toward logical clarity. And yet at the same time, our social and ethical life, and indeed our erotic life, is dependent upon the boundedness of form, upon intelligibility, and finally upon the sharing of meaning. What is most important is that we make use of vagueness, always returning from its murky depths to the forms and categories that we need in order to get by and in order not merely to give in to what Maggie Tulliver in *The Mill on the Floss* calls "the seductive guidance of illimitable wants," those desires that seem never to find clearly defined limits.[10]

As I considered the problem of the set and its often indeterminate boundaries as a model for the problems we encounter when we try to give form to the formlessness of desire, I began to wonder about the circulation of "everything" as a particularly strange kind of set, the biggest of all, and also as a strange object of erotic investment. The problem of whether we can speak meaningfully about "absolutely everything there is," or whether such an "all-inclusive domain" can even be said to exist in the first place, since none of us has the capacity to see it or to know it, has been named by philosophers as the problem of "absolute generality."[11] Because the domain of absolute generality seems so unavailable, we often feel that when we speak of "everything," we might as well mean "nothing," as when Basil Hallward, the painter of Dorian Gray's portrait, uses generality as a technique of the closet, or what Sedgwick describes as "the alibi of abstraction."[12] "Dorian Gray is to me," Basil insists in a conversation with Lord Henry, "simply a motive in art. You might see nothing in him. I see everything in him. He is never more present than when no image of him is there. He is a suggestion, as I have said, of a new manner. I find him in the curves of certain lines, in the loveliness and subtleties of certain colours. That is all" (13). Basil's dilution of Dorian's embodied specificity is encoded here in the evasiveness of "everything," a generality of reference that, as I've suggested, fails to distinguish itself clearly from the "nothing" to which Basil opposes it. We can see here the way in which "everything" often functions as a ruse—offered up only to be qualified and narrowed into something more comprehensible, like the list of "certain" formal features of art that Basil enumerates. Dorian himself, however, is pointedly excluded from this list of objects—we might paraphrase Basil as saying, "I see everything in him except *himself*," the "present" image of Dorian that Basil insists is more of a hindrance to his attachment than an impetus.

Absolute generality can function as a strategy of evasiveness in which the object of erotic desire thins out to an "everything" so nonspecific that it feels like nothing, but it can also function as an object of genuine erotic investment that captures desire's enormous and diffuse extension, its resistance to any form that would circumscribe it. In James's *The Wings of the Dove* (1902), for example, Kate Croy takes "everything" as the sign of an all-encompassing erotic energy as she recalls her first meeting with her lover Merton Densher: "She had had originally her full apprehension of his coerced, certainly of his vague, condition . . . ; then she had had her equal consciousness that within five minutes something between them had—well, she couldn't call it anything but *come*. It was nothing to look at or to handle, but was somehow everything to feel and to know; it was that something for each of them had happened."[13] The "something" of erotic connection, the "something" that can only be described as coming, somehow becomes everything, so impossible is it to see its outlines or to fit it in the palm of one's hand. Densher's "vague" relation to Kate opens out into a wildly expansive generality of feeling that is as thrilling as it is diffuse—an object of feeling and of knowledge rather than of vision and touch. The confusion of "everything" when it claims for erotic desire an impossibly wide extension is the subject of chapter four, which follows the erotic vertigo of absolute generality through James's fiction, with a focus on *The Portrait of a Lady* (1881) and *The Golden Bowl* (1904).

That both Wilde and James, the objects of my readings so far, were gay men, and that both often engage the possibilities of bad logic as modes of reasoning about desire in the specialized sense of reasoning *around* desire, is of course significant, especially because this book goes on to consider most closely the representation of heterosexual desire in the Victorian novel. That choice is to some extent a nonchoice, dictated by my focus on the literary techniques of thinking and speaking that attach to erotic life insofar as it is represented in Victorian fiction, in which examples like *Dorian Gray* are few, and examples of fictional representations of speech and thought, whether intimate or public, about heterosexual desire and courtship are numerous. But I frame the project with representations of queer desire—both in this introduction and in the afterword on E. M. Forster and Radclyffe Hall and their early twentieth-century forays into a more candid kind of queer fiction than Wilde's—in order to insist upon a connection between queer people and heterosexual women as the subjects of fictional representations of desire in the nineteenth and early twentieth centuries. In both cases, the attempt to announce desire, to think about it and speak about it clearly, so that one might be understood as a being whose desire is not only real but also makes an ethical claim, can be fraught with risk. It's important to make clear that although bad logic can function as a logic of the closet, as I've already implied, generating an encrypted expression of desire that waits for the right reader to decode its meaning, it is not primarily a technique of repression—not, in other words, a way of moralizing sexuality or ignoring the real pressures it exerts. Dustin Friedman, for example, has recently argued that "in crafting a distinct literary voice that expresses the subject's boundaries while at the same time gesturing beyond them, Wilde shows us a form of homoerotic desire that creatively refuses its entrapment within the inevitable limitations of language," and in this way the symphony of bad logic that we've seen at work in Wilde's writing may be a special case prompted by the specific pressures of queerness.[14] But Friedman's point also helps us to link Wilde's creative refusal of language's limitations to broader Victorian questions about language and erotic life. Rather than a way of avoiding the expression of desire, bad logic is a way of pursuing that expression along very particular lines and under the pressure of very particular social norms, with the feeling that something is at stake ethically in our ability to give form to a desire that seems resistant to such formalization, or that seems at least as if such formalization would sap it of its energy.

Going Bad

If making intelligible the meaning of our erotic lives seems to Victorian novelists to require an embrace of contradiction or a wielding of opaque tautological propositions, or if heeding the ethical claims of our desire seems to lead us only into the murkiness of vagueness or the evasiveness of generality, then we and the Victorians might evaluate these entanglements of desire and language quite differently. To us there is little surprise in the idea that erotic desire wouldn't be fully amenable to logical syllogism, or at a more fundamental level, we wouldn't be surprised to hear that erotic desire isn't "truth-functional" at all. What is surprising about the bad logic that Victorian novelists use to represent erotic desire isn't its "badness" at all, as I've already implied, but its tenuous and lingering attachment to logic itself. Or, to put it differently, the "badness" I'm after isn't that of rebellion—the "negativity, risk of aesthetic failure, and bad behavior" that Douglas Mao and Rebecca L. Walkowitz, for example, recuperate as a feature of literary modernism in their introduction to *Bad Modernisms*. Nor, as I've already suggested, is it the badness of fallacy or error—something like the embarrassing social mistakes that Kent Puckett locates at the heart of the realist novel's project in *Bad Form*. Nor, finally, is it the badness of negativity—those "negative affects," for example, that Sianne Ngai analyzes in *Ugly Feelings*, addressing "the predicaments posed by a general state of obstructed agency," or the strains of negative feeling that have become central to queer theory after the work of such thinkers as Leo Bersani, Ann Cvetkovich, Lee Edelman, Heather Love, and Jack Halberstam.[15] Instead, I mean to invoke other registers of the word: the badness, for instance, of the bad penny—the counterfeit that somehow passes for the real thing. Or the badness of decay—the fruit going bad, its shape softening at the edges and becoming susceptible to impression and manipulation.

This sense of badness as decay is what Wittgenstein senses in his *Philosophical Investigations* when he presses upon a weak point in the structure of logic. He worries that a logic gone soft might be a logic that has lost its essence: "But what becomes of logic now? Its rigour seems to be giving way here.—But in that case doesn't logic altogether disappear?—For how can it lose its rigour?"[16] Wittgenstein imagines a logical rigor in the process of going bad, giving way under external pressure, like the finger bruising the piece of fruit about to turn from ripe to rotten. Judith Butler would later insist that the structures of symbolic meaning that seem to regulate the intelligibility of gender identities and sexualities contain within themselves similar points of softness, blooming bruises of badness, that provide opportunities for subversion. Butler famously argues in *Gender Trouble* that gender identities that appear to us as "developmental failures or logical impossibilities . . . provide critical opportunities to expose the limits and regulatory aims of that domain of intelligibility and, hence, to open up within the very terms of that matrix of intelligibility rival and subversive matrices of gender disorder."[17] Of course, while Butler imagines a subversion pursued from "within," an act of exposure, of opening up, and of inversion, Wittgenstein imagines the point of weakness as something *here* on the outside or on the surface, that we might point to, giving way under the external pressure of the skeptical philosopher. He also imagines it as a soft spot stumbled upon almost accidentally—and pressed upon or probed only with great trepidation. For him, logic is not a disciplinary force to be subverted with purpose and pleasure but a system of intelligibility that is only melancholically exposed as soft, incomplete, limited in its formal rigor—bad.

Here, I argue that Victorian novelists, long before Wittgenstein and Butler, were fascinated by the strange interaction between the ideal formalism of logic and the disordering forms of language that cause logical models to go bad, to lose the mathematical rigor that is their defining feature. But before proceeding, it's important to clarify what will already appear as a murky relationship among this book's central terms: language, logic, reason, and desire. Although this cluster of terms sometimes rearranges itself as I trace the historical trajectory of logic and its place within the philosophy of language, and as I set Victorian novelistic representations of desire against psychoanalytic, queer, and feminist theories of erotic life, we can begin with a set of provisional definitions. In these pages, *reason* almost always designates practical reasoning—the rational faculties and processes by which we decide what's best to do in a given situation; form intentions and turn them into actions; reflect upon our own status as ethical agents; and account for our motivations, desires, and decisions to others. To reason about desire requires, first, that desire be put into logical language, since language is the medium of the kind of practical reason I am to invoke here, and logical argument is therefore its form, whatever that logic may look like. While today we often understand *logic* to be synonymous with *symbolic logic*, a mathematical enterprise, I often use *logic* and *language* somewhat capaciously and interchangeably, in order to recover the flexible relationship between these two terms that characterized their use before the twentieth-century entrenchment of logic as a distinctive field of academic philosophy rooted in mathematical expertise. I use *logic* to designate the norms that determine the form of language and its intelligibility when we use it to pursue a reasoned argument, to persuade oneself or another that something is true. As we'll see in greater detail, philosophers of language can disagree profoundly about what "reasoned argument" includes and excludes: while a modern logician may include only those kinds of argument reducible to mathematical operations and equations, the ordinary-language philosopher J. L. Austin famously responded to such claims by arguing that performative language operates according to its own distinct formal logic, a logic of success and failure rather than truth and falsehood. Stanley Cavell later built upon Austin's work to argue for "passionate exchange" as a structure of argument determined by yet a different kind of logic, in this case a logic shaped by the erotic.[18] In the philosophy of language, *logic* can be (and has been) plural, and it's this plurality that I try to capture by taking *language* and *logic* as intimately connected (and often interchangeable) terms.

I argue, then, that the longing to give desire the rational form of logical language is most acute in situations where desire presses upon us as an ethical consideration or where we're called upon to make our erotic impulses intelligible to others or to ourselves. The novel's plots of desire, courtship, and marriage are riddled with such situations of characters expected to account for their erotic impulses, and so novelists develop complex strategies of representation in order to give intelligible form to erotic desire without diminishing or mechanizing it. Of course, the Victorian period is replete with unruffled accounts of sex and sexuality outside of the novel, in the then-burgeoning disciplines of psychology and sexology, and so the relative absence of these fields from this book may seem conspicuous. Victorian scholars of psychology and sexology, however, took sexual desire primarily as an object of scientific and/or historical inquiry. They taxonomized and categorized sex acts, catalogued examples, and mapped erogenous zones, but they were only rarely interested in the language of desire and the epistemological and ethical problems produced by the messy interaction between practical reason and erotic feeling. In his *Mental and Moral Science* (1868), Bain offers a clear biological account of sex as an "appetite that brings the sexes together" and is "founded on peculiar secretions, periodically arising in the system after puberty, and creating an uneasiness until discharged or absorbed." He carefully distinguishes the "sexual excitement" produced by "the contact and movement of the inferior parts of the body" from the loving emotion of "tenderness" brought about by the touching of other erogenous zones—"the breast, the neck, the mouth, and the hand." He notes that biological appetites and tender emotions, when they become the object of "verbal expression," require us to have at our command "shades of very great delicacy" in language.[19] But he doesn't go much further than this in considering the epistemological and ethical problems of reasoning about desire, because his mode of scientific analysis presumes that sexual appetites and erotic attachments are relatively universal, consistent, and predictable—that we might learn how to describe the operations of sexual desire from his textbook and thereby arrive at a shared scientific vocabulary of sex.

Havelock Ellis's anthropological method, on the other hand, leads him to include in his influential account of homosexuality a stunning array of first-person autobiographical accounts as case studies in sexual inversion. Ellis's method allows for a greater attentiveness to the idiosyncrasies of sexual identity, appetite, and fantasy than that of someone like Bain, offering a small hint of what a different approach to the language of sexuality might look like. As pieces of life-writing these accounts are often richly literary—they offer to us a trove of narratives of queer erotic *bildung*, and as Ellis puts it in introducing this collection of autobiographies, they demonstrate the sensitivity required to give a public form to the privacy of desire: "I am assured that many of the inverts I have met not only possess a rare power of intellectual self-analysis (stimulated by the constant and inevitable contrast between their own feelings and those of the world around them), but an unsparing sincerity in that self-analysis not so very often attained by normal people." Moreover, it seems to him that a desire for the expression of idiosyncrasy—an attraction to that intractable "contrast" between self and other rather than a desire for total identification—is what motivates his subjects to tell their own stories: "there is no doubt," he writes, "that inverts have frequently been stimulated to set down the narrative of their own experiences through reading those written by others. But the stimulation has, as often as not, lain in the fact that their own experiences have seemed different, not that they have seemed identical."[20] Ellis is right that when we reason out desire, trying to give it intelligible shape, it's often because we want to close a painful gap between self and world, to be recognized, and to share what we know about ourselves with others; he's also right that erotic life tends to function as an emblem of the idiosyncratic self. When I account for my queer desire, for example, even to another queer person, I do so in order to find understanding, to make clear what is deep and opaque in myself. But I do so also to maintain and emphasize my idiosyncrasy, my sense that my desire is no one else's yet must nevertheless be reckoned with by others.

Ellis is sensitive to these kinds of ethical and epistemological questions, particularly when it comes to the moralization and legal prohibition of queer sexualities. Here, I aim to think more expansively about how the novel, in the several decades preceding Ellis's work, addresses similar questions about the "unsparing sincerity" and nuanced "intellectual self-analysis" necessary to reasoning about desire, and deploys an ethics and epistemology of desire that would refuse simple moralization. Like Ellis, many Victorian novelists who narrated the experience of desire and traced plots of erotic *bildung* sought ways to register the meaning, intensity, and ethical force of such desire without falling into a binary morality of right and wrong sexualities. The problem of queer sexuality and its violently enforced closeting—the ways in which to speak it aloud in the nineteenth century requires a hypersensitivity to the shapes of language that give desire public form—might also extend its reach, then, into the heterosexual plots of desire and courtship that structure so many Victorian novels, in which desire is not the object of legal prohibition, but a nevertheless fragile object that must be handled carefully, by a language flexible enough not to shatter what it shapes. Victorian novelists, whether representing in fiction the desires of queer men or of heterosexual women, address a set of metaethical questions (what counts as an ethical consideration in the first place, and how if at all should we distinguish between erotic impulse and rational intention when it comes to ethical life?) rather than only ethical questions about whether particular desires are good or bad. The novelists I consider address these difficult ethical, epistemological, and finally representational questions about language and desire in quite various ways: at best, they share a profound ambivalence about the efficacy of language for making desire audible and intelligible. Can our relation to the truth of desire ever be what we would call rationally "articulate," let alone logical? Why would we want it to be, and why might novelists treat it as if it were? Desire is a pang, not a proposition; it's an electric shock, not a structured circuit. Or to attempt a better electrical metaphor: the system of desire would seem designed to carry a higher voltage than logic, so that to open a connection between these two systems would be to create a short circuit, in which the excessive energy of desire would disrupt and burn out the delicate filaments that sustain logical form.

We might say that the forms of bad logic that are the focus of this book arise from what Sigmund Freud would call compromise formations, that particular kind of symptom that manages a bad connection between conflicting systems, in this case the bad connection between desire and logical argument. For Freud, for the novelists that this book considers, and maybe for all of us, this bad connection must be sustained or repaired against all odds in order to make desire socially and ethically meaningful. And so bad logic tries to have it both ways: it allows desire to resist logic to some extent, or to press against its limits, but it also maintains a connection to its mechanisms of intelligibility, its formal guarantees of truth and validity. As Freud puts it in his own electrical metaphor, by which he explains the functioning of the compromise formation, all symptoms "are the products of a compromise and arise from the mutual interference between two opposing currents; they represent not only the repressed but also the repressing force which had a share in their origin."[21] In what follows, however, I don't take repression to be the default state against which desire struggles for expression, nor do I take the authority of "good logic" as a surrogate for the ego-ideal that both creates and maintains the repression of desire. Desire often hides from view in the Victorian novel only partially, not because its exposure would be bad, but because the forms of our language appear not to make an obviously comfortable fit with the unwieldy, fleshy, buzzing insistences of desire. The compromise formations of bad logic are not symptoms in the Freudian sense, but conscious, strategic compromises in a real sense. In the novels I analyze here, desire does not (always) hide from view as a potential object of rebuke, struggling to make itself rational and therefore intelligible in obedience to the disciplinary force of logical language, destined to botch the attempt and leave it half finished or only halfway logical. Certainly, desire can seem buried, opaque, and rationally inscrutable in the Victorian novel, but not necessarily because desire and language run in entirely opposite directions, as Freud might have it. Rather, we might simply say that desire and language share an odd, often uncomfortable, easily broken connection, yet they tend toward similar goals, and their default setting is cooperation. Desire and language cooperate in extending the self beyond the self; desire and language cooperate in cultivating intimacy and the feelings of recognition and social belonging that it allows; desire and language, although they falter in their mutual commerce, cannot be said to clash.

Psychoanalysis, in all of its many historical developments and instantiations from Freud to Jacques Lacan to contemporary literary theory, persists as our dominant model for the ways in which erotic desire takes shape in language, and it often provides me with an important theoretical vocabulary in what follows. But its "talking cure" and its organization of erotic *bildung* into a teleological series of developmental stages often prevents psychoanalytic theory from registering the vibrant obstinacy of erotic desire and the way that that very obstinacy, that muddle and that blur, can be given form or meaning. Consider the scenes of suspension, reverie, and trance that Elisha Cohn identifies as moments of much-needed escape from "the demands of vigilance and self-culture" often associated with the narrative of *bildung*, in which novelists make briefly visible "alternative configurations of intimacy, nature, and community."[22] Claire Jarvis traces through Victorian and modernist fiction a different kind of suspended animation in scenes of what she calls "exquisite masochism": "refined aesthetic vignettes" that formalize sex by stilling it, transferring its energies into elaborately staged tableaux of nongenital, masochistic sexuality in which we as readers can see sex made into form.[23] Like Cohn's and Jarvis's productive scenes of stalled movement, the novelistic plots of erotic *bildung* that are the focus of this book help us to find a nonpathological alternative to the Freudian model. As Bersani has argued in his own critique of psychoanalytic models of desire as fundamentally pathological, "Psychoanalysis has conceptualized desire as the mistaken reaction to a loss; it has been unable to think desire as the confirmation of a community of being."[24] Ordinary language philosophy provides one kind of remedy for this blind spot in psychoanalytic accounts of the idiosyncrasy of desire, and so does the realist novel, with its challenging and complex representations of the problems of ordinary language and intimate recognition.[25] I therefore draw upon ordinary language philosophy frequently as a theoretical frame, often in concert with psychoanalytic accounts of language and desire and queer and feminist approaches to the ordinary. As the editors of a recent special issue of *New Literary History* on ordinary language philosophy (OLP) as a tool for feminist thought argue in their introduction to the volume, "OLP helps feminists to understand everyday experience in transformative ways. In their attunement to the ordinary, the philosophers in the OLP tradition offer us a chance to rethink the everyday contexts in which normative relations of gender and sexuality are reproduced."[26] We might say that this feminist argument adds to Cavell's similar suggestion, in *The Claim of Reason*, that the philosophical pursuit of ordinary language, like Bersani's model of the psychoanalytic pursuit of desire, aims for the discovery of community and its foundations:

> The philosophical appeal to what we say, and the search for our criteria on the basis of which we say what we say, are claims to community. And the claim to community is always a search for the basis upon which it can or has been established. I have nothing more to go on than my conviction, my sense that I make sense. It may prove to be the case that I am wrong, that my conviction isolates me, from all others, from myself. That will not be the same as a discovery that I am dogmatic or egomaniacal. The wish and search for a community are the wish and search for reason.[27]

Cavell insists that even if our uses of language are often based upon nothing more than a sense of "conviction" rather than a knowledge of laws and formal axioms—a vague feeling or a "sense that I make sense"—such a conviction is not antisocial or solipsistic. It is a conviction about what *we* say, and a conviction that when I seem not to make sense—when, as Ellis would have it, there appears to be a forbidding "contrast" between my idiosyncratic self and the world around me—or when my conviction about what we say is met with perplexity, it must be because we haven't worked out what we say about this particular unforeseen reality yet. It must be that we are still searching for shared criteria, for mutually intelligible standards of meaning, and perhaps striving against the "normative relations" that are the coercive dimension of community and its claims to the definition of the ordinary. Desire, as Bersani insists, can represent a similar kind of searching for community or social cohesion, rather than only representing the alienating opacity of others.

Rather than understanding bad logic as essentially symptomatic—as an epiphenomenon of the Victorian novel's repression of sexuality—I try to think through its varied and messy (but intentional and strategic) uses as novelists work to feel out the capacities and incapacities of language for representing character. In the novelistic representations of erotic confusion, indecision, passion, or attraction that this book analyzes, repression is rarely what's at stake; in place of repression we find a yearning to make desire meaningful, to understand it better, and to give it a form that nonetheless respects its electric charge, its disorienting effects, and its throbbing pulse. While the work of Lacan represents in many ways the apotheosis of psychoanalysis as a kind of symbolic logic of desire, invested as it is in the full interconnection of sexuality and the mathematical symbolization of logic, he captures the general problem best in his own description of the kind of self-knowledge for which psychoanalysis aims:

Kern unseres Wesen, "the core of our being"—it is not so much that Freud commands us to target this, as so many others have done with the futile adage "Know
thyself," as that he asks us to reconsider the pathways that lead to it.

Or, rather, the "this" which he proposes we attain is not a this which can be
the object of knowledge, but a this—doesn't he say as much?—which constitutes
my being and to which, as he teaches us, I bear witness as much and more in
my whims, aberrations, phobias, and fetishes, than in my more or less civilized
personage.[28]

Whereas Lacan (by way of Freud) directs our attention to pathological symptoms or careless, thoughtless "whims," bad logic directs our attention to other
ways of "bearing witness" to desire. These strange "pathways" around and behind the clear forms of logical language are still indirect, or they seem to become
covered over with dust as soon as we've followed them. They aren't accidental or
mistaken, however, not logical "fallacies" but rather logical problem-cases, not
phobic or exceptional but rather intimate and ordinary. We don't need to look
behind them for the repressed causes that would give them clear, narrative (logical) form; they have their own meanings, as opaque and hazy and empty and
"bad" as those meanings may be.

In other words, these bad logical forms aren't in need of solutions; rather,
they're in need of attention, or at least a different kind of attention than we
usually offer to forms of language that appear to us as tormented or purposively
opaque, blurred or wildly imprecise. We might accomplish this by thinking
of bad logic as having unexpected "affordances," a term that Caroline Levine
borrows from the theory of design in order to capture "both the peculiar constraints and possibilities that different forms afford," and indeed to explain how
"form can do so many different, even contradictory things." But even Levine's
capacious model of form would potentially exclude the forms of bad logic I
analyze here. In order to avoid the charge that her argument excludes nothing
from the rubric of "form," she allows that "there are many events and experiences that do not count as forms" such as "fissures and interstices, vagueness
and indeterminacy, boundary-crossing and dissolution," and goes on to argue
that "these formless or antiformal experiences have actually drawn *too much* attention from literary and cultural critics in the past few decades."[29] I hope to
make a complementary case that questions Levine's particular way of pruning
the domain of form, by showing that even many "bad" forms (vagueness and
the "boundary-crossing" of contradiction included) shape and order erotic life
in Victorian culture and beyond. Levine is right that we've given an excess of
our critical attention to the breakdown of form, but I read this excess somewhat

differently than she does, wondering whether it has even led us to find break-downs where they don't exist, to the point perhaps that we can no longer see the formal and formalizing operations intrinsic to the vague boundary or the piercing contradiction.

A Melancholy Language of the Future

I have laid out some provisional definitions for the philosophical terms that are central to this book—language, logic, and reason—and the relationship of these concepts to desire. In this section, I turn to some of the debates over these terms that characterized the tumultuous fields of logic and the philosophy of language in the Victorian period. At the heart of these debates were the relationship between these two fields and their relative scope. On one side, thinkers such as Augustus De Morgan and George Boole published pioneering works of mathematical logic (what we call "symbolic logic") and argued that, given their mathematical discoveries, logic should become a specific subfield of the philosophy of language, theorizing only those forms of argument that concern positivistic knowledge and can therefore be translated into the algebraic language of variables, operations, and equations. On the other side of the debate, thinkers such as John Stuart Mill maintained that such a distinction would be impoverishing; they wanted to maintain the traditional, Aristotelian understanding of logic that tied it more intimately to our ordinary ways of speaking and thinking in words and sentences, rather than in symbols and equations.[30] This latter conception of logic allowed it to maintain a more intuitive and messily entangled relationship to other domains of thought such as ethics, epistemology, the philosophy of education, and psychology, all of which relied on kinds of language, argument, and reason not comfortably translatable into algebraic equations. Mill and his proponents, of course, lost out, as symbolic logic came to dominate the academic philosophy of language and our broader conception of what "logic" means in the first place. It wasn't until the middle of the twentieth century, with the advent of the Anglo-American movement of ordinary language philosophy pioneered by Ludwig Wittgenstein and J. L. Austin, that a real sense of debate and uncertainty about the relationship between the clear forms of logic and the opacities of ordinary language—a sense that the drastically narrowed scope of logic had left us unable to theorize the form of huge regions of argument and language—would return to the heart of academic philosophy. This historical overview is familiar to philosophers but less familiar to literary scholars—and as I've already made clear, one of this book's central claims is that within this history we must include a consideration of the realist novel as the nineteenth century's dominant discourse of ordinary language.[31]

From the Renaissance to the nineteenth century, logic had been dominated by what we call the "textbook tradition," in which works on logic explicated the principles of Aristotelian syllogism in different ways but never challenged the idea that the syllogism is the basic structuring form of propositional logic.[32] Mathematical logic—the first real challenge to the centrality of syllogism—began to take its distinctive shape as a philosophical project in England in the middle of the nineteenth century with De Morgan's *Formal Logic* and Boole's pamphlet, "The Mathematical Analysis of Logic," both published in 1847. These field-shifting works did not, of course, arise out of a vacuum. Rather, they developed out of a growing spirit of experimentation and fierce debate in the fields of mathematics and logic inspired at least in part by the work of G. W. Leibniz, who in his unpublished writings often speculated about the possibility of applying his algebraic calculus to the study of logic: "I have contrived a device, quite elegant," he writes, "by which I can show that it is possible to corroborate reasoning through numbers. . . . At last, without any mental effort or danger of error, we will be able to judge whether arguments are indeed materially sound and draw the right conclusions."[33] Effortlessness and the impossibility of error or unclarity would remain the keynote concepts of mathematical logic throughout its long history. The search for a mathematical form behind language was also the search for a realm of perfect lucidity within language.

This mathematical device remained a mere hypothesis for Leibniz, but by 1814 we see it resurface in the work of the Scottish Enlightenment philosopher and mathematician Dugald Stewart, who worries that Leibniz's dream of uniting mathematics and logic would make even moral thought subject to the workings of mathematical axioms and algorithms. Stewart points out that in mathematics "the solution of a problem may be reduced to something resembling the operation of a mill." Thomas Carlyle echoes Stewart's industrial metaphor—mathematics as a mill—in *Sartor Resartus* (1833–34), when his fictional philosopher Diogenes Teufelsdröckh asks of his culture, which seems to be losing its capacity for wonder in favor of the precisions of pure reason, "Shall your Science . . . proceed in the small chink-lighted, or even oil-lighted, underground workshop of Logic alone; and man's mind become an Arithmetical Mill?"[34] For Stewart, and for Carlyle's Teufelsdröckh, language's potential for vagueness and imprecision is something we want to maintain, engage with, and investigate, not something we should dream of expunging from our use of language, as Leibniz does in his fantasy of testing arguments "without any mental effort or danger of error," feeding everything into a mathematical mill that reduces rough edges and unique shapes into a uniform pulp.

Antoine Arnauld and Pierre Nicole's popular French logic textbook of 1662, which remained in print in England throughout the nineteenth century, was called *Logic, or the Art of Thinking*, and we might say that debates over the scope of logic as a field revolved around the question of whether we should imagine logic as an art closely akin to rhetoric or as a science closely akin to mathematics—in other words, the question of whether the field could make the transition from Arnauld and Nicole's "art of thinking" to Boole's "laws of thought."[35] In 1835, for example, William Whewell argued in his defense of the role of mathematics in a liberal education that "to cultivate logic as an art . . . appears to resemble learning horsemanship by book." It teaches us to reason, in other words, according to "precept," whereas in studying mathematics we learn to reason "by practice."[36] In the 1830s this was far from accepted wisdom, and the pamphlet prompted an anonymous and scathing review by William Hamilton in the January 1836 number of the *Edinburgh Review*, in which he insisted that mathematics was threatening to displace logic rather than strengthening our understanding of its formal mechanisms. "The tendency of a too exclusive study of these [mathematical] sciences is, absolutely," he writes, "to disqualify the mind for observation and common reasoning."[37] Mathematics deals with a shadowy realm of abstractions, Hamilton insists, and so it strains credulity to think that it could prepare us for the logical reasoning appropriate to everyday life. This metaethical question, about whether logic structures ethical decision making and the formation of intentions in the first place, let alone an algebraic logic, would not be solved in the nineteenth century. As I argue in chapter three, it's the same question that interested George Eliot later in the century. In *Middlemarch* her narrator insists that "formal reasons" are a very "artificial, inexact way of representing" the "indefinable movements" of our mind as we form intentions and turn them into actions; Eliot's narrator rejects any logical model, even the more traditional syllogistic form, as a stilted way of representing the "tingling" of ethical feeling and deliberation.[38] The mathematician-logicians Boole and De Morgan, however, concurred with Whewell in his sense that mathematics captured something of the essence of logical reasoning—its pure formalism, its deductive precision, and the self-evident truth of its basic axioms—in a way that Hamilton's idea of "common reasoning," or Stewart's model of holistic understanding and context-sensitive language, could never do. But unlike Hamilton, they believed that one could practice both kinds of reasoning—the mathematics of logic and the more ordinary reasoning of everyday life, without the study of one "disqualifying" the mind for the consideration of the other.

In other words, these thinkers seemed to disagree over the potential of logic for dealing with ordinary practices of rationality, and with the shapes and structures of what we would call ordinary language. Would logic be understood as a science of "common sense" that could formalize and regularize all kinds of deductive and inductive language and thought, including ethical reasoning? Or would logic be a purely mathematical enterprise, less tightly connected to the actual content or context of language and more narrowly focused on the mathematical laws that ground deductive reasoning in cases of objective or scientific knowledge? If logic as a field of inquiry and education suddenly narrows its scope to the purely mathematical forms of thought, then we seem to be left floundering, without a way to account for the truth of all those other kinds of thinking and knowing (the ethical, the affective, the erotic, etc.) that now seem to fall outside the purview of logic. We might imagine that it was precisely because of these reservations that despite major innovations in mathematical logic in the mid-nineteenth century, John Stuart Mill's more traditional 1843 text, *A System of Logic, Ratiocinative and Inductive*, remained immensely popular throughout the Victorian period. Mill insists on the absolute capaciousness of logic as an empirical science linked to ethics, epistemology, and theories of education: "By far the greatest portion of our knowledge, . . . being avowedly matter of inference," he claims, "nearly the whole, not only of science, but of human conduct, is amenable to the authority of logic."[39] In other words, any kind of knowledge gained by a process of inference falls under the domain of logic, and so the only kind of knowledge excluded from this domain is that gained from primary empirical experience, that is, from sensation and perception. Mill's proliferation of the form of logical inference through every imaginable domain of human personality is not necessarily an insidious project. His liberal individualism relies to some extent upon a reliable theory of right reasoning, and logic as a highly capacious theory of reasoning that covers the ethical, the political, the psychological, and on and on—provides the guarantee that a philosophy of individual freedom is not the same thing as a philosophy of "anything goes." As far as restraints on liberty go, logic seems less controversial and more inevitable than, say, government legislation. It can be understood as a normative structure intrinsic to human consciousness, a kind of benign shaping and delimiting principle for individual development, rather than an unnatural limitation imposed from without. Logic also fits seamlessly into the liberal ideal of reflective, rational self-cultivation that Mill championed elsewhere in his work.

However, despite its affinities with the goals of rational exchange and debate, Mill's account of the rational self in *A System of Logic* is also eerily solipsistic. Mill realizes that logic is untenable as a science of rational clarity and soundness unless it is to some extent abstract, ethereal, and impersonal rather than context sensitive, social, and concrete, and yet his desire to link logic to ethics and the philosophy of education make this admission difficult for him. "If there were but one rational being in the universe," he argues, "that being might be a perfect logician; and the science and art of logic would be the same for that one person as for the whole human race."[40] The sentence is strained by its accommodation of two contradictory impulses, one toward the pure abstraction of logic and the other toward the idea of logic as a mechanism of social intelligibility and collective truth seeking. Mill's contradiction here encapsulates the practice of Victorian liberalism that Elaine Hadley has named "abstract embodiment," "a purposefully paradoxical neologism," as she describes it, "that seeks to encompass liberalism's desire for a political subject who is abstract (and capable of abstract thought) but also individual, abstract and yet concretely materialized, 'free' though in its place."[41] Mill's point in this passage is that logic is a "science and art" of interior, contemplative reasoning, not of the messier, more literary enterprise of rhetoric; it is entirely abstract, in Hadley's terms, and not dependent upon an individual body "in its place." Even in the absence of other people, logic would still exist as a structuring principle for my own thought, and would be complete and perfect. And yet the universality of logic—mine is necessarily the same as yours—can only be a really useful or explanatory fact in the context of a social world where truths might need to be shared and communicated, as Hadley helps us to remember. The perfect logician, alone in the universe, would still be doing logic, but to what end, and with what materials? In the end, his status as the perfect logician relies upon his being no one in particular or, more accurately, both someone and potentially anyone. Similarly, Mill's utilitarianism founds itself on the idea that we must follow the same rules of ethical deliberation "whether we are considering our own good or that of other people," my own particular pleasure or the pleasure of "all mankind," even "the whole sentient creation."[42] Mill was concerned above all with maintaining the connection between logic and the kind of "common reasoning" by which we could deduce, for example, the truths of ethics, but that connection seems to threaten logic's status as a pure science. It introduces too many variables that we find ourselves unable to account for, and of course our nagging desire for freedom and individuality tends to make us turn up our noses at the idea that we're bound to the rules of logic even in the kinds of thinking and reasoning that seem most personal, private, or pleasurably irrational.

De Morgan's and Boole's most important challenges to Mill arise out of their assumption that logic deals with a particular kind of positive knowledge that is not clearly linked to practical reason, affect, desire, and so on. De Morgan, for example, argues that Mill and the thinkers who follow him are much too interested in the content of logical propositions, at the expense of their capacity to understand their form:

The study of logic . . . considered relatively to human knowledge, stands in as low a place as that of the humble rules of arithmetic, with reference to the vast extent of mathematics and their physical applications. Neither is the less important for its lowliness: but it is not everyone who can see that. Writers on the subject frequently take a scope which entitles them to claim for logic one of the highest places: they do not confine themselves to the connexion of premises and conclusion, but enter upon the . . . formation of the premises themselves. In the hands of Mr. Mill, . . . logic is the science of distinguishing truth from falsehood, so as both to judge the premises and draw the conclusion, to compare name with name, not only as to identity and difference, but in all those varied associations of thought which arise out of this comparison.[43]

If Mill looks to logic as the master form organizing all of our approaches to the understanding of ethics, human character, and psychology, De Morgan's aim is to make logic "humble," to confine it to its proper object, the form of rational thought, and to remove from the field all that confuses and misdirects that enterprise. Boole follows De Morgan in this conviction, imagining a highly organized network of different kinds of knowledge, some of which overlap with or illuminate one another but not predictably or consistently. It is something like what Richard Rorty would later describe in pragmatist terms as "the 'contingency of language'—the fact that there is no way to step outside of the various vocabularies we have employed and find a metavocabulary which somehow takes account of all possible vocabularies, all possible ways of judging and feeling."[44] Rorty's argument has other Victorian precedents in addition to Boole. In *Methods of Ethics* (1874), Henry Sidgwick contends that one never chooses a single ethical method to follow consistently but rather is guided by "a mixture of different methods, more or less disguised under ambiguities of language," which can be understood as "alternatives" between which we constantly choose, so that a clarification of the complex relationship between these various ethical methods and their vocabularies might be more useful than a rigorous polemical argument on behalf of only one of them.[45] And in the final volume of his *Problems of Life and Mind* (1879), completed and published posthumously by his partner George Eliot, George Henry Lewes takes a similarly pragmatic approach in trying to find the analogy between what he calls the "logic of feeling," which takes as its object particular sensations and experiences, and the more familiar "logic of thought" or of "signs," which takes as its objects abstractions, ideas, and variables: "the Logic of Signs is to the Logic of Feeling very much what Algebra is to Arithmetic. Algebra is only Arithmetic under another and more generalized form, which operates on general symbols instead of particular numbers, substituting *relations* for *values*."[46] Even in his attempt to discover the very laws of thought, Boole anticipates these later thinkers in imagining the mind as an articulated network of vocabularies, a domain over which logic might exert a privileged, enlightened, but by no means exclusive power.

Although mathematical logic may fare more poorly in describing the messy, subjective forms of ethical deliberation, in other words, Boole insists that an acknowledgment of the limited scope of logic does not preclude the conviction that logic can shed light upon other forms and vocabularies of the mind, albeit in partial and unpredictable ways. He describes the extension of logic's illuminating reach in a metaphor that we will return to in chapter three as we consider the problem of the vague boundary: "As the realms of day and night are not strictly coterminous, but are separated by a crepuscular zone, through which the light of the one fades gradually off into the darkness of the other, so it may be said that every region of positive knowledge lies surrounded by a debateable and speculative territory, over which it in some degree extends its influence and light" (400). Boole's specialization of logic allows him to disentangle it from what he and Mill both agree to call "common reasoning," or what I have been describing more specifically as the problem of practical or ethical reasoning, particularly when it comes to erotic desire. Yet Boole remains enamored of that shadowy realm, the "crepuscular zone" in which logical reasoning and other kinds of thinking are difficult to tell apart. One thing is certain for him: this zone should remain somewhat shadowy, left undetermined by his work on logic itself, primarily in order to avoid the charge that the mathematical logician wishes to translate all kinds of thought and feeling into algebraic variables. "To supersede the employment of common reasoning," Boole insists, "or to subject it to the rigour of technical forms, would be the last desire of one who knows the value of that intellectual toil and warfare which imparts to the mind an athletic vigour, and teaches it to contend with difficulties, and to rely upon itself in emergencies" (12). Boole imagines common reasoning as something of the body—muscular, vigorous, and improvisatory—and echoes Whewell's sense that practicing mathematics is like practicing horsemanship, while learning traditional logic is like learning the sport out of a book. Later in the century, Lewis Carroll would echo Whewell and Boole in insisting that learning and practicing symbolic logic is primarily a form of "mental recreation," an activity that "we all of us need for our mental health."[47] We can see now how Wilde's Mr. Erskine echoes all of these thinkers with his image of reason balancing on the tightrope of paradox. Boole's "athletic" mind, like Carroll's recreational mind and Mr. Erskine's acrobatic mind, is an object not of precise knowledge but of *use*, of strengthening exercise and repeated practice. The gendering of this athletic, muscular mind is significant, of course, particularly since the places where logical systems seem to go bad or soft—to "lose their rigor" as Wittgenstein puts it—are the major focus of this book.

As Andrea Henderson argues, the advent of symbolic logic in the nineteenth century, by posing these intractable questions, also had wide-ranging implications for literature. In reimagining the relationship between logical symbols and the words and sentences they stand for, Henderson shows that symbolic logic leads to a major shift in aesthetic theories of the symbol and its status as a referential sign, since this new kind of logic represented "a symbolism that frankly confessed its nonreferentiality even as it proclaimed its almost hieratic capacity to order the world." She takes Carroll's novel *Sylvie and Bruno* to be "exemplary of an impulse in Victorian logic and late Victorian literature to discover in the formal perfectibility of sign systems some recompense for the ungroundedness of representation and the moral relativism that ungroundedness seemed to imply."[48] I would add that the bad logic of the realist novel often seeks to recover something of the referential meaningfulness of form itself. As Anna Kornbluh has recently claimed, we might imagine a "nonmimetic realism" that "takes place, makes space, composes shape, inaugurates contour," that "negates and exceeds what exists," as opposed to the realism that would only "represent, depict, denote, or refer."[49] While Kornbluh's model is the structural drafting of the architectural blueprint, her terms resonate with logic, also a modeler of abstract forms with a strangely contingent relationship to embodied reality. Contradiction, tautology, vagueness, and generality: all of these are logical problem-cases that highlight the formal limitations, blurs, and incoherencies of the logical laws of thought, while also trying to make those limited, opaque forms meaningful, reorienting them away from mathematical abstraction and back toward reference and communication. As J. L. Austin puts it in "A Plea for Excuses," one of the founding documents of ordinary language philosophy, "Words are not (except in their own little corner) facts or things: we need therefore to prise them off the world, to hold them apart from and against it, so that we can realise their inadequacies and arbitrarinesses, and can re-look at the world without blinkers."[50] Austin's ordinary language philosophy does not separate word from world in order to find a purely formal approach to language, unconcerned with the clunky, vague materiality of world and self; rather, it performs a different kind of detachment, by which words are reimagined as pictures of the world more or less adequate, more or less precise. Austin detaches language from world in order to make language strange but does so only with the goal of resituating it as a particular kind of interface between self and world or between self and other. "When we examine what we should say when, what words we should use in what situations," Austin insists, "we are looking again not *merely* at words (or 'meanings,' whatever they may be) but also at the realities we use the words to talk about." Or, as Viktor Shklovsky would say in the early decades of the twentieth century in describing what we have come to know as the defamiliarizing quality of mimesis: "By 'enstranging' objects and complicating form, the device of art makes perception long and 'laborious.' The perceptual process in art has a purpose all its own and ought to be extended to the fullest."[51] The bad logic of the realist novel might be one way of "complicating form" and extending the perceptual process by foregrounding the difficulty of language itself, even in all its ordinariness.

The forms of symbolic logic were, on the other hand, intended to simplify rather than to make difficult, to replace the imprecisions of ordinary language with the lucidity of mathematics, and Boole was right to anticipate a major criticism of his algebraic logic—that its mathematical equations are simply too far removed from our everyday lives and our everyday thoughts to be recognizable and persuasive as formal models. Upon its publication, a brief notice of *The Laws of Thought* in the *Westminster Review* worried that systems such as Boole's are "psychologically false" and that they fundamentally "misrepresent reality" to such an extent that our very consciousness automatically rebels against his account of the meaning of language.[52] This review would have been published under the editorial supervision of George Eliot, who would launch her own scathing condemnation of the pursuit of algebraic logic in the same periodical two years later, in her essay "The Natural History of German Life" (1856). Eliot rightly points out that the impulse toward an ideal symbolic language represents a desire to escape the murkiness of ordinary language, with its "subtle shades of meaning, and still subtler echoes of association."[53] But she warns us that a world in which language is transparent is far from utopian:

> Suppose, then, that the effort which has been again and again made to construct a universal language on a rational basis has at length succeeded, and that you have a language which has no uncertainty, no whims of idiom, no cumbrous forms, no fitful shimmer of many-hued significance . . . —a patent deodorized and non-resonant language, which effects the purpose of communication as perfectly and rapidly as algebraic signs. Your language may be a perfect medium of expression to science, but will never express *life*, which is a great deal more than science. With the anomalies and inconveniences of historical language you will have parted with its music and its passions, and its vital qualities as an expression of individual character, with its subtle capabilities of wit, with everything that gives it power over the imagination; and the next step in simplification will be the invention of a

talking watch, which will achieve the utmost facility and despatch in the communication of ideas by a graduated adjustment of ticks, to be represented in writing by a corresponding arrangement of dots. A melancholy "language of the future"![54]

Eliot imagines the drive toward perfect, rapid communication as a drive toward the mechanization and even deodorization of social life—toward a world in which one is not an "individual character" but nothing more than a scentless, predictably ticking machine, a world in which language is not a "many-hued" and "resonant" kind of music but a two-dimensional Morse code.

Eliot insists that the relationship between form and content, or the relationship between language and the intractable complexity of "individual character," is not (indeed *should* not be) an easy one. Several decades later, however, Anthony Trollope would issue an indirect rejoinder to Eliot's denigration of symbolic logic as reducing language to a kind of automated Morse code. The goal of a great novelist, Trollope insists in *An Autobiography* (1883), is that language "must come from him as music comes from the rapid touch of a great performer's fingers; as words come from the mouth of the indignant orator; as letters fly from the fingers of the trained compositor; as the syllables tinkled out by little bells form themselves to the ear of the telegraphist."[55] While the idea of literary language as virtuoso musical performance or impassioned oration aligns with Eliot's desire for a resonant, historically contextualized language, Trollope's second pair of examples takes a sharp turn. To him, ease and directness of communication are the paramount virtues of good novel writing, and so he feels perfectly comfortable comparing the novelist's deployment of language to the work of the compositor arranging type or the telegrapher translating the dots and dashes of Morse code. Perhaps, then, the "deodorized" language of symbolic logic is not always as far afield from Eliot's redolent "historical language" as she would insist; perhaps it isn't so absurd to see the tapping telegrapher, the nimble-fingered pianist, and the realist novelist as pursuing similar arts—making use of a system of written notations in order to make something known about the self. Symbolic logic is limited in its capacities for representing character, but even Eliot allows that ordinary language is, in its own way, inconvenient, cumbersome, and unpredictable. We may tend to side with Eliot's view of the superior power of ordinary language, particularly when it comes to novel writing, but this wasn't necessarily a settled question for nineteenth-century novelists situated in the midst of intense philosophical debate over the nature of logic, its forms, and its potential futures. By so starkly opposing the formal clarity of symbolic logic to the formal murkiness of "historical language," Eliot may overstate her case, and may in fact underestimate the extent to which our ordinary language must always reckon with the fantasies of clarity that come attached to any theory of form, from logic to the novel.

The longing to accommodate desire to logic and to its mechanisms of social intelligibility, a longing that often seems to be implicit in the forms of "bad logic" that I analyze, does not necessarily equate, in other words, to a longing for rationalization, mechanization, or, in Eliot's terms, deodorization—not what Michel Foucault famously describes in the first volume of *The History of Sexuality* as an insidious "Logic of Sex" or a search for the "truth of sex." Rather, bad logic pursues an open-ended, pragmatic, and intimate reasoning *about* sex and desire that invokes logic without fully participating in its systematization of reason or its binary conception of truth.[56] In his later career, Foucault turned to the theorization of the philosophical, religious, political, and erotic practices that shape what he described as "the care of the self." I argue that thinking and speaking about our erotic lives, and representing those lives as part of a fictionalized interiority, need not always lead us into a harmful or impoverishing abstraction of sexuality, even if these practices necessarily invoke the abstractions of language: the forms and laws, in other words, of entailment, validity, and truth. Rather, these practices of reasoning about desire might themselves be part of an ethos of sexuality or, more specifically, an ethos of erotic self-understanding. Indeed, Foucault allowed that the care of the self, imagined as an embodied and erotic practice, had an inextricable relationship with the more familiar ancient imperative to "know yourself," an imperative often imagined in its historical reception as having to do only with rational or ethical self-understanding. As Foucault puts it, over the course of centuries "the principle that one must take care of oneself became the principle of all rational conduct in all forms of active life that would truly conform to the principle of moral rationality." Moreover, Foucault points out that the project of accessing the "truth" of the self involves various forms of mediation; in other words, the idea of a technique or "a technology of the self" (such as, I would suggest, logic, ordinary language, or the realist novel) becomes paramount in Foucault's history of the hermeneutics of the subject.[57] While the model of literary and cultural theory derived from Foucault's method in *The History of Sexuality* is always wary to some extent of connecting sex to formalizing or rationalizing systems of knowledge, I suggest that an attention to the variety of ways in which that connection might be drawn—or indeed the variety of ways in which we might imagine the drawing of that connection as difficult or disorienting or even painful—might help us to better understand the history of erotic self-understanding rather than foreclose such a study as an insidious project of turning sex into discourse.

In this book, I therefore pursue an implicit claim about practices of detachment, irony, or critical self-reflexivity in relation to erotic life. To what extent, after all, can we ever get outside of our desires in order to be able to reason about them, or even to *know* that they might be reasoned about, if they are so deep, so idiosyncratic, so irreducibly *there*? Amanda Anderson's *The Powers of Distance* helped to inaugurate a critical interest in the tenuous relationship in Victorian culture, particularly in the novel, between the practices of abstraction or critical detachment associated with Victorian ideologies of liberalism and cosmopolitanism, on the one hand, and, on the other, the practices of particularity or idiosyncrasy that may seem to limit our potential for detachment. We can see that this set of problems extended to debates over the nature and scope of logic and its abstract, objective model of the laws of thought. Despite the "polemical thrust" of Anderson's defense of detachment as politically viable and enabling, we often forget that her argument focuses largely on detachment in the Victorian period as an unsteady, temporary, and ambivalent state of mind that represents "the *aspiration* to a distant view," rather than a claim that anyone ever "fully or finally inhabits any given practice of detachment."[58] In her acknowledgment of "the characterological dimensions of detachment" as a limit to genuine or achieved impartiality, Anderson's argument invokes a long history of novel theory that understands the genre as attempting to control or contain or even shatter (with varying degrees of success or failure) the idiosyncratic and antisocial desires of individual characters in the service of some abstract model of bourgeois subjectivity (often seen to be epitomized by the distant, totalizing, omniscient perspective of high novelistic realism).[59] Anderson argues, against the grain of this tradition, that for the Victorians the development and representation of individual character was often bound up with a capacity for moments of critical detachment, and that idiosyncrasy and detachment exist in a dialectical rather than an antagonistic relationship.

Indeed, an interest in clarifying this dialectical (or perhaps productively paradoxical) relationship between abstraction and embodiment characterizes much recent work on liberalism, ethics, and sexuality in Victorian literature. Elaine Hadley, as we've already seen, points our attention to the practices through which the Victorians managed the difficult link between a politics of critical detachment and the embodied acts and spaces (the ballot box, for example) that sustain it as a lived politics—the ways in which "midcentury liberalism's core political techniques preserve abstracted traces of the bodily, at times an insistently situated body."[60] And recently, Kathleen Frederickson has argued for the concept of "instinct" as a surprisingly powerful link between Victorian ideas about sexuality and about liberal governance, pointing out that instinct was at the root of a host of "unsettling" questions for liberal philosophers: "How

rational are choices? What does 'wanting' something signify if you are biologi-
cally compelled toward your desire? . . . Can will and instinct be distinguished
from each other?" Frederickson argues that we have too often produced "rigid
binaristic accounts of reason and its others that do not do justice to how modes
of unreason also enliven liberal governmentality."[61] In *The Burdens of Perfection*,
Andrew H. Miller demonstrates the ethical dimensions of this kind of problem, in which embodied impulses and abstract ideas commingle, as he traces a
Victorian "moral perfectionism" grounded upon everyday practices of intimacy,
particularly through eroticized relationships of mentorship and identification.
In *Good Form*, Jesse Rosenthal imagines the novel as helping to cultivate a self-
consciousness about ethical intuition, the ways in which a narrative or an ethical conclusion "feels right," and argues that "when Victorians discussed . . . the
moral dimensions of novel reading, . . . they were being a good deal more attentive to the formal properties of the novel than we have tended to give them
credit for."[62] In *Empty Houses*, David Kurnick points our attention to the failed
theatrical ambitions of several important novelists to argue that "when we recognize the role of the theater in the creation of the novel of interiority, that novel
emerges as a record of the discontents historically sedimented in interiority—
less propaganda for the inwardly focused, socially atomized individual than a
rigorous account-book of interiority's exclusions."[63] Only by seeing the novel
of interiority from the point of view of the lost theatricality that it melancholically absorbs, Kurnick suggests, can we get a clear view of what "interiority"
really means for Victorian literary innovation. In a pair of earlier essays, moreover, Kurnick thinks through the tense relationship in Eliot's fiction between
forms of erotic investment and forms of abstraction or detachment.[64] And as
we've already seen, Claire Jarvis's *Exquisite Masochism* has demonstrated how
the Victorian novel develops formal strategies for the arrangement and masochistic suspension of sex, making of it an object for the reader's detached and
pleasurable examination. In this book, I draw upon the insights of these critics
into the complex relationship in Victorian literature between idiosyncrasy and
detachment, embodiment and abstraction, interiority and theatricality, sex and
form. But as in the work of the critics I have surveyed here, my aim in this study
is not entirely to "personalize" structures and ideologies that would seem to be
abstract, impersonal, or quintessentially public: liberalism, cosmopolitan detachment, ethical norms, spectatorship, and so on. Rather, I want to show how
these ideological apparatuses (logic included) are in the first place too enmeshed
with what we call "the personal" to make the distinction meaningful at all, at
least if the distinction is imagined as a punishing or disciplinary opposition. We
do more than sustain or reproduce a social structure like logic through our per-

sonal, everyday, or literary engagements with it—we also contest its demands, experiment with the kinds of affordances it unexpectedly offers, and through our idiosyncrasies try to make it elastic or forgiving.

Stanley Cavell argues, along similar lines to Eliot, that to linger with the difficulties of ordinary language serves an important ethical function, because even our ordinary utterances obey pragmatic rules of entailment, analogous to the formal rules of logic, to which we're constantly held accountable in social life. As he puts it, "we are . . . exactly as responsible for the specific implications of our utterances as we are for their explicit factual claims."[65] The difficulty, however, is that we sometimes seem not to know, or not to be able to know in the first place, what the rules are that govern the implications of our ordinary language. They seem elusive and vague in a way that logical rules of entailment can never be, or it may be that whatever it is we are trying to express seems to exceed the scope of the rules as they currently exist. And this failure to know often prompts in us a kind of improvisatory process of talking things out, trying to find our way back to what we do know in order to expand its reach:

> It sometimes happens that we know everything there is to know about a situation—what all of the words in a question mean, what all of the relevant facts are; and everything is in front of our eyes. And yet we feel we don't know something, don't understand something. . . . Socrates says that in such a situation we need to remind ourselves of something. So does the philosopher who proceeds from ordinary language: we need to remind ourselves of *what we should say when.* . . . And the point of the question is this: answering it is sometimes the only way to tell—tell others and tell for ourselves—what the situation *is.* . . . When you have more facts than you know what to make of, or when you do not know what new facts would show. When, that is, you need a clear view of what you already know.[66]

"Tell others and tell for ourselves": there is an intimate codependence here. Indeed, it seems that telling for ourselves is a prerequisite for telling others. Or it might be that telling others is a way of telling it for ourselves out loud and then awaiting either approval or rejection, the nod of recognition or the furrowed brow of failed meaning. Cavell insists that both goals are worthy and tightly interconnected. Telling for ourselves and telling others "what the situation *is*" does not equate for Cavell with already *knowing* what the situation is. It is, rather, a process of "reminding" ourselves what it is by connecting it to what we do know, getting "a clear view" of those hard-won rules of language in order to apply them to what we do not or cannot yet know. Telling "for" myself: it is as if I am meant to speak on behalf of someone who cannot yet speak for himself, or on behalf of some part of myself, buried very deeply, that is struggling to make itself heard.

CHAPTER ONE

Charlotte Brontë's Contradictions

For an example of the power of contradiction to represent erotic desire in the Victorian novel, we need look no further than one of the most famous lines of dialogue in all of fiction: the moment in Emily Brontë's *Wuthering Heights* (1847) when Catherine Earnshaw attempts to explain her love for the foundling Heathcliff by declaring to her friend Nelly Dean, "Nelly, I *am* Heathcliff."[1] We often remember and excerpt this protest as an exclamatory outburst—a spontaneous expression of passionate desire—rather than as a tentative assertion followed upon by explanations and reworkings of the original statement, punctuated by dashes rather than exclamation points: "Nelly, I *am* Heathcliff— he's always, always in my mind—not as a pleasure, any more than I am always a pleasure to myself—but as my own being; so don't talk of our separation again—it is impracticable; and— . . ." (82–83, ellipsis in original). We find this stuttering punctuation in the first edition, but one of Charlotte Brontë's several editorial changes for the novel's reissue following Emily's death was to radically alter this sentence, adding an exclamation point to punctuate the famous phrase and changing several dashes to colons or even periods. Indeed, if one compares the first edition to subsequent editions based on Charlotte's revised version, it becomes clear that Charlotte altered this passage much more thoroughly than any other. Perhaps she sensed something dangerous in that statement and desired to cordon it off from what surrounds it. In the first edition, now the standard for modern editors of the novel, the passage ends not with a bang but with a whimper, faltering upon the intrusion of the decidedly dispassionate question of impracticability. The force of the initial, bold, impossible contradiction— I am not in fact myself at all, I am another—takes on shades of meaning as Catherine tries to explain what she means. Is it that she's always thinking about Heathcliff, so that it feels to her as if he inhabits her entire mind? Or is it that his pleasures give her pleasure in a way that feels immediate rather than vicarious, as if his body were her own? This scene, after all, finds Catherine trying to explain an ethical decision made painful by the pressure of erotic attachment. She has decided to marry Edgar Linton, for what Nelly Dean insists are all the wrong reasons, not because she desires him but rather because through such a marriage she might indirectly improve Heathcliff's life and thereby do good to the man she truly loves. Earlier in the scene, in response to a perplexed Nelly, who wonders what draws Catherine to the rough and moody Heathcliff, Catherine says, "I'll explain it. I can't do it distinctly—but I'll give you a feeling of how I feel" (80). The contradiction in this case becomes a resource rather than an obstacle for meaning. Its very form seems to wrench, to hurt, to break, and so it allows Catherine to make herself clear feelingly, bringing into view the place where the rational clarity of logic finds its aching limit point.

On the one hand, "I *am* Heathcliff," spoken by someone who is in fact not Heathcliff, is literally a contradiction: "I am not I," or—to transform one of the tautologies that we've already seen in the introduction and that will lie at the heart of chapter two—"I am not what I am." On the other hand, Catherine's declaration is most intuitively read not as a rational proposition amenable to logical parsing but as a concise (if also blunt) metaphor for the feeling of loving someone as much as you love yourself: "I'll give you a feeling of how I feel." Of course Catherine isn't *really* Heathcliff, nor does she believe that she is; that emphatic "*am*" is simply a more aggressive, more expressive way of saying *it is as if I were* or *I feel as though I were* or *let us assume that I am*. Contradiction in this case enacts a particularly concise elaboration of a fictional world, only really meaningful if framed by the kind of implicit illocutionary speech act that must frame all fictional assertions, including the miniature thought experiment (or feeling experiment) that Catherine pursues: let's pretend; let's imagine; let's suppose. Even when we take this fictional frame into account, the contradiction remains. Can I be the omniscient narrator of my own life? Would I want to be? Nevertheless, the moral language of Catherine's speech prevents us from ignoring the rationalizing aims of the sentence. How else does "impracticable" enter into her train of thought? We cannot easily separate the two registers in which these lines are spoken (the erotic and the rational), and so we have to think more carefully about contradiction in order to understand what kind of experiment in moral accountability Catherine pursues here. What does it mean to account for a moral decision under an assumed identity? Our sense of the opacity of her speech arises out of an ideal of reflective rationality that assumes a person can and should occupy, if only temporarily or fitfully, the identity of the not-I.

In pursuit of this ideal, however, Catherine loses her way. She leaves the perceived selfishness of the first person behind, but replaces it with a doubled first person, echoing the fragmented first person generated by the novel's complex frame-narrative. In her preface to the 1850 edition of *Wuthering Heights*, Charlotte Brontë notes that Catherine's "honesty" shines through even "in the midst of perverted passion and passionate perversity," in a chiasmic turn of phrase that shows us the virtue of honesty caught between two warping libidinal impulses that pull it in opposite directions, an analog to the image from Wittgenstein that we encountered in the introduction, an image of tautology and contradiction as two arrows pointing in opposite directions away from meaning (liii). And this pulling apart of the self seems to lead us into tragedy rather than moral enlightenment: sacrificing oneself and one's own interests or imagining how a situation would look if one were not really, not only, oneself, is a moral good only if one does it properly—only if one doesn't get too mired in the sticky attachments of desire. If a novelist such as George Eliot seems to us to be devoted to the endless theorization of how one might occupy such a perspective responsibly or productively, as we see in greater depth in chapter three, then Emily Brontë seems equally committed to showing how excruciating—how difficult and disorienting—the attainment of such a perspective can be when our erotic lives enter into the picture.

This chapter argues that Charlotte Brontë charts a middle path between these two approaches, imagining the ethics of self-negation as bound up with the erotics of embodiment, attachment, and investment, rather than being at odds with the idiosyncrasy of erotic life. I don't intend to suggest that Emily is wrong in her representation of the psychic contradictions of erotic life and that Charlotte is right. Rather, together they help us to apprehend the variety of ways in which a basic contradiction between self-identity and self-negation might structure the novelistic representation of erotic desire, whether tortured or happy, unrequited or fulfilled, socially deviant or legally validated. Charlotte Brontë's use of first-person narration represents the contradictory imperatives of erotic and ethical experience—to be an embodied and idiosyncratic self with interests and desires and also to be a morally accountable and intelligible self, divested of those interests and desires—not as an impossible double bind but as a potentially productive opportunity to renegotiate the terms and the goals of social belonging. If Brontë's endings are famous for being at best dubiously happy, it's because they often involve a sense of diminished expectations. Her protagonists end not by acceding to the broad social community partly defined by logical, universal norms of reasonability and intelligibility, but by limiting themselves to small, intimate worlds defined by affection, emotional investment, and erotic affinity.[2]

This choice doesn't sound particularly surprising when described in this way—who would want to become an interchangeable face in a crowd rather than a loved, loving person defined by the comforts of intimacy? But in fact, this intimate mode of social belonging is often defined in Brontë's fiction by its very limitedness, the pointed refusal through which a protagonist closes herself off from the wide world in favor of a small one.[3] The final chapter of *Jane Eyre* (1847), for example, presents us with a scene of Jane in happy communion with her husband Rochester, in which she is, simultaneously and contradictorily, herself and not herself:

> No woman was ever nearer to her mate than I am: ever more absolutely bone of his bone and flesh of his flesh. I know no weariness of my Edward's society: he knows none of mine, any more than we each do of the pulsation of the heart that beats in our separate bosoms; consequently, we are ever together. To be together is for us to be at once as free as in solitude, as gay as in company. We talk, I believe, all day long: to talk to each other is but a more animated and an audible thinking. (519)

Jane describes a complex interplay of togetherness and separateness. She and Rochester have hearts that beat in "separate bosoms," and yet they are "ever together"; she is "bone of his bone and flesh of his flesh," and yet even in their togetherness they are "as free as in solitude." Finally, their dialogue is congruent with thought, but still different from thought in its substance, "animated" and "audible" rather than inward and silent. Jane goes so far as to imagine herself as "gazing for his behalf" as Rochester recovers from blindness: "I was then his vision, as I am still his right hand" (519). It is precisely because this relationship makes practices of self-negation erotic and intimately embodied that these practices become livable, intelligible, and knowable.

The ambiguous final chapter of *Villette* (1853) begins by describing a communion at a distance that is quite different from Jane and Rochester's intimate togetherness but that plays similarly upon the contradiction by which desire can seem like an unselfing of the self, as Lucy Snowe recounts in describing her long-distance relationship with M. Paul and the way it ascribes the functions of the body to another absent person: "The spring which moved my energies lay far away beyond seas, in an Indian isle. . . . His letters were real food that nourished, living water that refreshed."[4] This chapter ends with Lucy strongly hinting at M. Paul's death by shipwreck before concluding with a series of imperatives that bring into being a ghostly, abstract self who might have a happy ending after all: "Trouble no kind, quiet heart; leave sunny imaginations hope. Let it be theirs to conceive the delight of joy born again fresh out of great terror, the rapture of rescue from peril, the wondrous reprieve from dread, the fruition of return. Let them picture union and a happy succeeding life" (546). There is no person here, and certainly no Lucy Snowe, not even in the "picture" that she has consigned to us to "conceive." There are only feelings and events given over to us as readers: delight, terror, rapture, wonder, union, a happy life. In various ways, Lucy pictures the fulfillment of desire as both embodied and abstracted: M. Paul is the "spring" that moves Lucy and the source of "real food" and "living water" even across a great distance. Seen in this way, his death seems to be of little consequence. Their romance might continue just as well in imagination. Indeed, for Lucy that might be preferable.

If Brontë's picture of intimacy as a practice of self-negation doesn't actually resolve the troubling contradiction at the heart of erotic experience and its ethical dimensions, then what is its use? Why refuse one kind of impossible self-negation only to replace it with another? For Brontë, the culmination of the marriage plot often presents an opportunity to complicate the notion of self-negation and its role in sociability, as well as to elaborate its embodied, affective, and phenomenal dimensions. Brontë recognizes that we can't avoid the abstraction of the self (which we can also picture as the extension of the self beyond the self, or what I've called the unselfing of the self) when we want to become social beings, to see ourselves from the point of view of another in order to be able to account for our own desires and impulses clearly, and so she doesn't attempt to undo or foreclose such abstraction in depicting erotic relationships, as if such relationships could be a refuge of uncomplicatedly embodied, situated, subjective being. At the same time, she asks us to wonder about how the contradiction of self-negation might be made somewhat less painful and less ascetic.[5]

In the next section, I establish a philosophical and theoretical history for contradiction that ranges from logic and the philosophy of language to ethics and literary theory, while also beginning to set Brontë into that multifaceted history. I argue that the problems of the novel form, particularly those attached to point of view and first-person narration, offer ways of working through some of the persistent questions that have haunted the philosophical pursuit of contradiction. The Aristotelian law of noncontradiction in logic presumes a countervailing law of self-identity, and these two balanced logical axioms make it difficult to narrate the ordinary feeling of being divided between the self-identical position of the I (which Brontë associates with the immediacy of erotic life) and the self-negating position of the not-I (which Brontë associates with abstraction, the form of language, and the demands of ethical accountability). I then turn to readings of *Jane Eyre* and *Villette* that together show how Brontë's fiction represents and therapeutically manages this kind of contradiction, imagining it as a

structure for living and desiring rather than as a form of repression or a shattering of the self.

The Civic Status of a Contradiction

Logic, like justice, is supposed not to have a point of view. It is supposed to be
a set of immutable and objective laws of thought that ensures the predictable
and orderly production of sound reasoning and valid argument. It might be
more accurate, then, to say that logic is not absolutely without point of view,
since its normativity belies this claim. Logic polices an ethically charged boundary separating reasoning that is good, valid, and sound from reasoning that is
bad, spurious, or flimsy. Logic cannot, in fact, be blindfolded; rather, we might
imagine its point of view, to speak novelistically, as that of omniscience. Like
narrative omniscience, logic often feigns indifference—performing the neutral-
ity of description and mere formal containment instead of the normativity of
moral injunction and shaping intervention—and yet neither of these structures
can really escape interestedness. The rules of good logic require application, and
that application often requires interpretation. And indeed, the omniscient narrator is rarely *pure* in her omniscience, appearing to us more often than not as
a strangely human, limited, partial, minor divinity.[6] Rules are meant to be followed and obeyed, in other words, but they must also be used, or at least useful,
and their uses and applications tether them to specific points of view, and to
the specific shapes and textures of situations in which the rules seem insufficient
or ill equipped. This paradox about the logical structure of language—that it
seems both "metaphysical" or "ideal" in some broad sense and yet also must
govern our ordinary, messy, unpredictable uses of language—is at the heart of
W. V. O. Quine's cryptic title for his collection of essays *From a Logical Point of
View* (1953).[7] What, really, would that point of view consist of, and does it make
sense to wonder about *whose* point of view it might be? Part of Quine's project
in the essay that opens this collection, "On What There Is," is to criticize the
doctrine of the "meaninglessness of contradictions" (his example is "the round
square cupola on Berkeley College") as an outdated axiom that limits our ability
to evaluate accurately the meaningfulness of logical propositions. As he points
out, twentieth-century discoveries in mathematical logic show that there is "no
generally applicable test of contradictoriness" between strings of signs when we
begin to use computers to process highly complex logical arguments, so that
what may appear as a contradiction from one point of view may not in fact be
contradictory when reworked and clarified from a logical point of view.[8] Because the realist novel is often a study of shifting and precarious points of view,
it is well positioned to help us explore these questions about where we imagine

the "logical point of view" to be, whose we imagine it to be, and finally how that point of view might often be self-contradictory, both first person and third person, embodied and abstracted, erotic and rational.

We have already seen that these are the questions that fuel so much work in the philosophy of ordinary language, a field that returns again and again to those difficult moments at which, as Wittgenstein says, we become "entangled in our own rules" and must reassess the law-bound system that we have been following as if by rote.[9] For Wittgenstein, the contradiction represents the apotheosis of this kind of entanglement, the sticking point at which we seem to have run up against the impossibility of saying what we really mean and so fall into the meaninglessness of contradiction as if by accident. The contradiction appears in Wittgenstein as the ultimate failure of language or, at least, the failure of language to mean something. In the *Tractatus Logico-Philosophicus*, as we've already seen, he puts this plainly: "Propositions show what they say: tautologies and contradictions show that they say nothing."[10] Wittgenstein imagines a logical proposition as being, "in the negative sense, like a solid body that restricts the freedom of others, and, in the positive sense, like a space bounded by solid substance in which there is room for a body"; a contradiction, he says, "fills the whole of logical space leaving no point of it for reality" (42). Contradiction, in other words, blocks the connection between the world of logic and the world of reality: whatever "point" in logical space might make contact with the world that language aims to represent, contradiction obscures it. And so, in the end, "contradiction is the outer limit of propositions" (48). Later in his career, however, Wittgenstein begins to understand contradiction as a stumbling block that may serve a purpose in our groping attempts to make meaning in ordinary language as opposed to logical symbolism: "It is not the business of philosophy," he argues, "to resolve a contradiction by means of a mathematical or logico-mathematical discovery, but to render surveyable the state of mathematics that troubles us—the state of affairs *before* the contradiction is resolved. (And in doing this one is not sidestepping a difficulty.)"[11] Contradiction reveals to us an impasse that cannot simply be bulldozed away; instead, it requires us to retrace our steps and perhaps to find a different route.

It would be easy to replace "philosophy" here with "literary criticism," and "mathematical" with "formal" or "historical." Contradiction and the related concepts of paradox, aporia, and dialectical tension, are the bread and butter of huge swathes of literary theory, and all of the divergent uses of these concepts tend to draw upon a broadly conceived idea of the Hegelian dialectic, a form that we'll see is central to Hegel's own intervention into the field of logic. A brief representative survey of such work in literary theory, focusing most closely on theories of the nineteenth-century novel, would include Leo Bersani's psychoanalytic argument that the realist novel presents us with a contradiction between "structured desires" and "fragmented desires" and that the "psychic coherence" demanded by novelistic form "involves a serious crippling of desire"; Sandra Gilbert and Susan Gubar's foundational feminist argument that women novelists of the nineteenth century, including Charlotte Brontë, struggled to break out of a patriarchal, socially enforced "contradiction between their status as human beings and their vocation as females"; Fredric Jameson's structuralist Marxist argument that narrative represents "the imaginary resolution of a real contradiction," and his more recent argument that novelistic realism is based upon the "antinomy" between the moving temporality of "destiny" and the "eternal present" of affect; D. A. Miller's Foucauldian rejoinder to Marxist theory by which he stresses that "contradiction, . . . far from always marking the fissure of a social formation, may rather be one of the joints whereby such a formation is articulated," so that "contradiction may function not to expose, but to construct the ideology that has foreseen and contained it"; and finally, Eve Kosofsky Sedgwick's queer-theory argument that modern Western culture is structured by the long-developing "contradictions . . . internal to all the important twentieth-century understandings of homo/heterosexual definition."[12] Even from this schematic overview, we can see how contradiction has been mobilized in the history of contemporary literary theory in roughly two ways, and Miller explains this difference of approach best in his contrast between contradiction as "fissure" and contradiction as "joint." He insists that contradiction does not stand for a "fissure" in a social structure, artificially patched over by the unity of literary form, which the literary theorist must then expose to our view in order to erect warning signs around it lest we stumble into the chasm; rather, contradiction may be a "joint" in the social structure—often a structural articulation that is sensitively represented and reinforced by literary formalization—and in that case literary theorists should be anatomizing such joints in order to figure out how they work and what causes them to dislocate. Even Miller's sensitivity to contradiction as a complex, articulated form, however, remains alert to what he understands as its intrinsic deceptiveness and its role in habituating us to ideology.

Where are we now with respect to contradiction? Although these theories have said so many powerfully liberating things about the ways we're duped into believing in contradictions, the ways in which contradiction is covered over or repressed by the literary text or exacerbated by the literary text, or the ways in which we're blinded to the insidious worming of contradiction into our everyday lives, they might also leave us with a feeling that this project must be approaching exhaustion. We've so thoroughly debunked the contradictions that appear to structure our ideologies and our everyday lives, and indeed the literary representation of those everyday lives, that we're left yawning at the introduction of yet another aporia to be interrogated, yet another contradiction to be confronted and effectively dissolved. We have moved on, perhaps, to compiling these ideological contradictions in a kind of catalogue, since we as critics readily agree that contradiction is the basic form of power: the power of ideology, that is, simply to make contradictions work by naturalizing them and habituating us to them. The question for literary criticism today is, has contradiction run out of steam?[13] I don't believe it has, for reasons that this chapter aims to elucidate; at the same time, I argue for a more nuanced approach to contradiction as a form of reasoning that has its own meanings, textures, and possibilities, rather than a form that invariably shatters, or an unbearable tension that cries out for resolution or evasion, or that requires disciplinary containment. "Contradiction," after all, has a pragmatic sense in addition to its logical sense. It describes a strategic move in social interaction: simply saying no, disagreeing, or pointedly refusing.[14] In this sense, contradiction might stand for a way of moving through the world as an individual made up of contradictory aspects and contradictory points of view that is manageable even if painful, structuring even if sometimes terrifying.

As I've already suggested, contradiction has many meanings, not all of them logical (strictly speaking), but its logical meaning provides us a baseline definition, since the ultimate source of the taboo that surrounds contradiction is undoubtedly Aristotle's establishment of the law of noncontradiction as an axiom of logic and metaphysics. In its logical sense, contradiction describes a formulation of language that violates this axiom, which draws an outer limit to meaningfulness and intelligibility. But because of the force of the law of noncontradiction, people rarely speak and think in purely contradictory terms, and so the examples of genuine logical contradiction ($A \neq A$) in this chapter are quite sparse. Contradiction is most often anxiously and tentatively approached, as the precipice upon which one just barely balances, or a whirling reversal or revolution that links one moment to the incomprehensible next, as when Brontë's Jane Eyre stands rapt by the touch of the imperious St. John Rivers, the suitor whom until this point she has rebuked, and feels that "the Impossible—that is, my marriage with St John—was fast becoming the Possible."[15] In a moment such as this one, the self seems about to dissolve into thin air, and this sense of the precariousness of identity leads us to the specific and particularly vexed example of that technical definition of contradiction that concerns me in this chapter, that is, the contradiction at the heart of self-negation: "I am not I." The capacity to speak or imagine this kind of formulation and, more importantly, the mode in which one invests it (impossibly) with meaning emerge as crucial problems in linking together the embodied, "first-person" impulses of erotic desire with the abstract, "third-person" view of logical language.

It may appear as if the psychic or erotic feeling of a contradiction within the self doesn't properly belong to the domain of logic. The transparency of logical abstraction makes contradiction too fully meaningless for it to become an object of serious inquiry: "$A \neq A$," in other words, might appear to us as nothing more than a flagrant display of the impossible, and when I think or feel contradictorily, one might insist that this must be a symptom of some more profound psychic disorder rather than evidence for the meaningfulness of contradiction. Indeed, Aristotle's foundational explanation of the law of noncontradiction begins as an example of "a principle about which it is impossible to be mistaken" or, in other words, one of the self-evident axioms of reasoning that underlies any metaphysical inquiry: that "for the same thing to hold good and not to hold good simultaneously of the same thing and in the same respect is impossible."[16] A contradiction is not only forbidden because it doesn't make sense in the formal notation of the syllogism but because such a formulation of language would purport to describe something that isn't allowed in the first place by Aristotle's metaphysics: something cannot actually be x and not-x at the same time, and so to put into language "I am x and not-x" is not only formally but also substantively false in all cases. Aristotle goes on to insist that it is likewise "impossible for anyone to believe that the same thing is and is not," and yet at this point we may resist his line of reasoning: it may be the case that contradictions cannot inhere in the world, but couldn't I nonetheless *believe*, even if mistakenly, even if psychotically, that they do?[17] Aristotle can only maintain that such a belief is itself impossible—that a psychic contradiction is just as unimaginable as a metaphysical one—by defining a belief as an attribute of the self, something that "holds good" of a person. Just as an attribute cannot belong and not belong to a subject at the same time, a belief and its contradiction cannot belong to a person at the same time.[18] We might, however, insist that beliefs are not attributes—that the law of noncontradiction doesn't extend its policing force to the world of psychological interiority, or indeed to the domain of erotic life that is both psychic and embodied. We often *do* hold contradictory beliefs, or we hold a rational belief that contradicts an erotic impulse: things get murky where feeling, desire, and the body are involved. Even if we grant Aristotle's insistence that one may hold contradictory beliefs as long as they are not held *simultaneously*, we're confronted again by the problem of the tipping point: as we approach the moment at which impossible becomes possible, at which a belief becomes its opposite or sexual repulsion gives way to attraction, how do we reckon with the place at which these opposites must be conjoined or at least troublingly adjacent, translated from one into the other? Jane Eyre insists not that the Impossible dissolves and disappears before the Possible then shows up to usurp its former place; rather, in her formulation, the Impossible is "becoming" the Possible, and in that moment of becoming, contradiction is alive and painful, erotically charged and urgently meaningful. In its temporal extension, this is a narrative problem as much as it is a logical one, which is why the novel so often wants to zero in on such moments of painful self-contradiction.

Contradiction is a problem, then, for the temporality of narrative, which often wants to trace the moment at which, for example, repulsion "is becoming" attraction. This narrative problem has been an obstacle, however, even outside the realm of the novel for thinkers who seek alternatives to Aristotle's unbending law of noncontradiction. In his *Science of Logic*, Hegel reverses the Aristotelian rule by positing contradiction as the self-evident ground that structures thinking, insofar as thinking must always be imagined as a temporal process of "becoming" in which something constantly arises out of nothing. Indeed, part of the inadvertent comedy of Hegel's difficult writing to a contradiction-phobic sensibility is that he revels in contradictions at the most impossibly abstract level of thought, populates the bare idea of contradiction with meaning, and tries to show us that we can't in fact do without it. In writing an origin myth of thinking, for example, he describes the "beginning" in just this way: "As yet there is nothing, and something is supposed to become. The beginning is not pure nothing, but a nothing, rather, from which something is to proceed; also being, therefore, is already contained in the beginning. Therefore the beginning contains both, being and nothing; it is the unity of being and nothing, or is non-being which is at the same time being, and being which is at the same time non-being."[19] Hegel resolves contradiction through an incantatory practice of repetition and rearrangement—each of these sentences finds new ways to link being to non-being, or nothing to something, through a variety of syntactical and logical mechanisms: predication, causality, identity, tangency. There is not actually a coherent or conclusive model here of the relationship of being and non-being, aside from the intuitive assertion that they must be codependent in all kinds of ways; rather, there's a simple willingness to imagine the dimensions of this relationship as more complicated than the dualism of its terms.

Eve Kosofsky Sedgwick's critique of dualistic thinking from the perspective of affect theory operates along similar lines and echoes Hegel's *Science of Logic* in asking us to privilege spatial models in which concepts cluster in multiple and unpredictable ways "beside" one another rather than a system in which contradiction would imply a radical antifoundationalism. As she puts it, "*Beside* permits a spacious agnosticism about several of the linear logics that enforce dualistic thinking: noncontradiction or the law of the excluded middle, cause versus effect, subject versus object. Its interest does not, however, depend on a fantasy of metonymically egalitarian or even pacific relations, as any child knows who's shared a bed with siblings."[20] Sedgwick in fact directly echoes Hegel's sense (and that of British thinkers such as Boole) that logic is only one kind of "spiritual activity or faculty" that exists "*side by side* with others such as sensation, intuition, imagination, etc., desire, volition, etc."[21] Like Brontë, who questions the mutual exclusivity of desire and ethics, the axiom of noncontradiction is, for Hegel and for Sedgwick, an oversimplification when it comes to the living textures of thinking, affect, or erotic experience, in which power dynamics are often much more complicated than a simple antagonism of the dominant and the submissive.

This juxtaposition of Hegel and Sedgwick reminds us that the temporal problem of narrating contradiction (the problem of locating the tipping point at which nothing is becoming something, impossible is becoming possible) is inextricably linked to the spatial imaginary of narrative, which often wants to connect contradictory points of view, to link the situated point of view of the character or the first-person narrator to the unsituated point of view of narrative omniscience, or to identify Catherine's point of view with Heathcliff's. As Wittgenstein's argument about contradiction in *Philosophical Investigations* continues, he offers further insight into these kinds of "civic" questions about language, norms, and narrative points of view that contradictions compel us to ask:

> Here the fundamental fact is that we lay down rules, a technique, for playing a game, and that then, when we follow the rules, things don't turn out as we had assumed. So that we are, as it were, entangled in our own rules. . . .
>
> It throws light on our concept of meaning something. For in those cases, things turn out otherwise than we had meant, foreseen. That is just what we say when, for example, a contradiction appears: "That's not the way I meant it."
>
> The civic status of a contradiction, or its status in civic life—that is the philosophical problem.[22]

For Wittgenstein, a contradiction asks us to take a survey of the rules of the game, to step back for a moment for a wider view, and, most importantly, to negotiate the rules of the game with other people. If contradiction as an everyday act of thinking or speaking has a "civic status," it is only the result of a deeper problem in the philosophy of language, as long as we imagine that philosophy as fundamentally normative rather than descriptive or speculative.[23] We all, of course, make do with a language that operates according to a set of norms of rationality and intelligibility. At the same time, each of us contains something wildly unpredictable and unintelligible that presses against the limitations imposed by those norms and causes us to become "entangled in our own rules." We try to think and speak by the book, but there are always "those cases" in which "things turn out otherwise than we had meant, foreseen." And then we have to retrace our steps: if it's true that "That's not the way I meant it," then what, if anything, did I mean, and how can I communicate it to you in a form that can mean something to you? For Wittgenstein, the point might not always be to "resolve" contradiction by mathematically reworking our logical theory but to use contradiction as a way of keeping the structuring edges of that normative system in view, perhaps even locating the places where the drawing of those edges might be mistaken—where the boundaries must be more flexible than we at first imagined, or where they need to be broken and retraced. This interest in the particular case in which the rules seem no longer to work as we anticipated they would is, as Andrew H. Miller has pointed out in his study of Victorian moral perfectionism, the basic (and often unfairly devalued) insight underlying the ethical practice of casuistry. As Miller reminds us, for the Victorians, "casuistry" wasn't a pejorative; rather, it hewed closer to its original definition, by which it denotes "the practical reasoning that considers whether a particular act fits within an ethical paradigm and allows each—act and paradigm—to modify the other."[24] In other words, casuistry is one way to represent the ethical dimensions of the problem of point of view: what does it mean to try to shift between the rational, paradigmatic, logical point of view, on the one hand, and the situated, context-sensitive point of view on the other hand? If casuistry assumes that "act and paradigm" *can* exert a mutual influence, then it seems to cover over an important contradiction: the one that arises when I, in the first person, try to see things from the logical point of view.

The philosopher Thomas Nagel has famously described this difficulty of shuttling between the ideal and the concrete, between the objective and the immediate, between the clearness of logic and those unpredictable moments in which it nevertheless throws up snares, as the problem of locating and describing "the view from nowhere." He argues for various ways of reconciling the "personal" element of ethical deliberation to the countervailing ethical requirement of objectivity. Nagel argues that "there is no necessity . . . to abandon all values that do not correspond to anything desirable from an impersonal standpoint, even though this may be possible as a personal choice—a choice of self-transcendence."[25] We may have it in us to "transcend" the self and all of its attachments, but do we need to? Would we want to? Nagel insists that because the world is populated by many particular points of view, none of which is intrinsically or objectively the "center" of that world, it is actually important to wonder, "How *can* I be a particular person?"[26] The problem is not only how to be objective but also how to learn to be particular, how to occupy what I'm calling the erotic point of view, in the face of constant demands to see oneself from a "centerless" perspective. For Nagel, objectivity exists in a relatively harmonious relationship with subjectivity rather than contradicting it, and in fact our ability to occupy an objective point of view indicates to him that we have within us two aspects of the self, the particular and the nonparticular:

> Objectivity allows us to transcend our particular viewpoint and develop an expanded consciousness that takes in the world more fully. . . .
>
> Every objective advance creates a new conception of the world that includes oneself, and one's former conception, within its scope; so it inevitably poses the problem of what to do with the older, more subjective view, and how to combine it with the new one. (5)

There's a strange paradox in Nagel's spatial and temporal metaphors. On the one hand, the transcendence of my particular viewpoint leads to an *expansion* of consciousness. My whole consciousness widens so as to include more of the world, to make my particularity feel a little bit smaller and more insignificant. This expansion is also part of a temporal process, by which the accumulation of experience over time can be part of a sequence of "objective advance[s]" that situate my limited point of view in an ever-complicating and ever-widening context. But how can an "expansion" of the self still leave the self behind? This is a crude question to pose in response to Nagel's sensitive model of objective selfhood, and yet I think it's nevertheless an insistent question. Another way of asking it would be: why is the objective advance an expansion of the self rather than a shattering, effacement, or cancellation of the self? What if what I really want is to shrink my consciousness, or to *stop* its expansion at some point so as to hang on to those contingent erotic attachments to the world that seem to make me *me*?

Nagel imagines objectivity as expanding the particular self toward its fullest potential and its widest scope, with the goal of salvaging objectivity as a structural principle, making its relation to the self friendly (if potentially disorienting) rather than oppositional, but we might want to insist that the history of objectivity has in fact presupposed such an opposition. As Lorraine Daston and Peter Galison have argued in what I understand as an implicit rejoinder to Nagel, "objectivity is the suppression of some aspect of the self, the countering of subjectivity," rather than (or in addition to) allowing the expansion or widening of the subjective consciousness.[27] But Daston and Galison intensify this argument in their investigation of the concept of "structural objectivity" at the heart of symbolic logic and mathematics:

> A curious parallel between self and world governed conceptions of structural objectivity. On the side of the world, all that mattered were structures—not phenomena, not things, not even scientific theories about things. . . . On the side of the scientific self, only that small sliver of the thinking being counted, purified of all memories, sensory experience, excellences and shortcomings, individuality *tout court*. . . . Structural objectivity did not so much eliminate the self in order to better know the world as remake self and world over in each other's image. Both had been stripped down to skeletal relations, nodes in a network, knower and known admirably adapted to each other.[28]

Daston and Galison do not exactly refute Nagel's model; they argue, like him, that objectivity shapes and transforms the subjective self by forcing us to see that subjective self in the mirror of the subject-less point of view and to bring those "parallel" but incongruent images into alignment. Their central metaphor, however, is the reverse of Nagel's. While Nagel describes the shaping force of objectivity as a mechanism of the expansion and extension of consciousness, Daston and Galison describe that same shaping force in disciplinary terms, as a severe shrinking, narrowing, or purification of subjectivity—something akin to George Levine's problem of "dying to know," by which the possibility of perfectly objective knowledge seems in nineteenth-century literature and scientific writing to be bound up with a fantasy of death, which would finally cancel the "limits of the limiting self."[29] I invoke these two models of objectivity, one philosophical and one historical, in order to demonstrate that despite their different emphases, they share an interest in the unstable relationship between points of view, and the very different ways in which we can narrate our attempts to make such relationships amenable and enabling rather than tenuous and threatening. To return to D. A. Miller's terms, we might see the relation of objectivity to subjectivity as an articulating "joint" rather than a disruptive "fissure." This contradiction enables our interaction with a world rather than disciplining us as Miller might imagine, and yet it is nevertheless a joint that may be painful or uncomfortable to extend and flex.

Because the novel often negotiates similar problems of perspective and similarly difficult oppositions between particularity and omniscience, the first person and the third person, it seems ideally positioned as a way to formalize just such an adjoining of opposed perspectives, which is why the philosopher Bernard Williams reaches for a term of literary art in describing the "radically first-personal" perspective of moral reasoning: "How can an *I* that has taken on the perspective of impartiality be left with enough identity to live a life that respects its own interests? If morality is possible at all, does it leave anyone in particular for me to be?"[30] The idea that ethical impartiality threatens to drain me of "identity" is significant here: it helps us to see how adopting a third-person point of view might challenge the tautological rule of self-identity that will be the focus of chapter two, the idea that I am I, not some imaginary other, located elsewhere, who could view myself dispassionately. To leave this self-identical position, this "particular" self, behind, is to diminish that person, to make his boundaries uncertain. To follow Williams's literary metaphor even further, we can imagine this as a free indirect point of view, "an *I* that has taken on the perspective of impartiality," like a character who has taken on some features of omniscience without being able to leave her body behind.

Jane Eyre's Impossibilities

While Emily Brontë's Catherine Earnshaw looks for a way to leave the limitations of the first-person perspective behind, and Bernard Williams transposes the terms of narrative point of view into philosophy, wondering how the person who aspires to omniscience might thereby drain herself of her particularity and find herself mired in the indeterminacy of a free indirect style of existence, we might say that Charlotte Brontë is committed to reckoning with the limitations of the first-person perspective, which are after all the real limitations of everyone's particular, human point of view. We all remember Rochester's weirdly telepathic cry for help after he has been blinded during his wife's destruction of Thornfield by fire, Jane Eyre's tingling reception of his call, and her urgent response. We don't often think carefully about the connection of that scene to the scene that immediately precedes it (already cited earlier in this chapter), in which Jane stands momentarily on the point of giving in to St. John Rivers's beleaguering series of marriage proposals, which she has so far steadfastly refused. But then St. John touches Jane, and this touch is enough to set her moral compass spinning, in search of the path that might take her from "here" to "there," from "impossible" to "possible": "I stood motionless under my hierophant's touch. My refusals were forgotten—my fears overcome—my wrestlings paralysed. The Impossible—that is, my marriage with St John—was fast becoming the Possible. All was changing utterly with a sudden sweep. Religion called— Angels beckoned—God commanded—life rolled together like a scroll—death's gates opening, showed eternity beyond: it seemed, that for safety and bliss there, all here might be sacrificed in a second. The dim room was full of visions" (482). Brontë uses the past continuous tense to its full paradoxical effect here by combining it with the language of speed, punctuality, and completion. What seems to be happening "fast" and "utterly," "with a sudden sweep," is nonetheless never accomplished. The impossible doesn't become the possible, but it "was becoming"; all doesn't change in the end, but it "was changing." Indeed, time seems to collapse in the series of punctual, simple-past-tense religious images of the next sentence: Jane is "called," "beckoned," "commanded," and her life "rolled together like a scroll" rather than being laid out in sequence as it is in the novel we're now reading. It seems for a moment that a simple exchange might be possible—sacrifice "all here" for "bliss there" and resolve the set of contradictions that put Jane in a state of bad conscience. But how, after all, can one get from the "here" of profound doubt to the "there" of absolute certainty? "I could decide if I were but certain," Jane tells St. John, before crying to the heavens, "Show me, show me the path!" (482–83).

The scene neatly echoes the similar existential crises of Jane's adolescence, in which she faces a future about which she finds she is radically uncertain. As she awaits the morning on which she'll finally depart the cruel Lowood School to take up her post as a governess at Thornfield, she loses sleep in trying to observe the phenomenon of change itself: "A phase of my life was closing tonight, a new one opening to-morrow: impossible to slumber in the interval; I must watch feverishly while the change was being accomplished" (107). This wonder at the turning of new leaves develops out of an anxious certainty that nothing endures—that nothing remains certain. While still a student at Lowood, worrying about her dying friend, Helen Burns, Jane describes the process by which "my mind made its first earnest effort to comprehend what had been infused into it concerning heaven and hell: and for the first time, it recoiled, baffled: and for the first time glancing behind, on each side, and before it, it saw all round an unfathomed gulf: it felt the one point where it stood—the present; all the rest was formless cloud and vacant depth; and it shuddered at the thought of tottering, and plunging into that chaos" (94). In other words, one doesn't only totter and plunge on the brink of death; rather, the tottering and the plunging are happening all the time, if one would only take notice. What *is* now may *not be* in a moment, whether in heaven and hell, in impossible and possible, in repulsion and desire, or finally in right and wrong. Jane has fully taken on Helen Burns's grave insistence that "nobody can be sure of the future" (66). If that is true, then it does seem that one is constantly, anxiously tottering on the edge and plunging into chaos—what are the self-evident, transcendent forms and principles that bind "here and now" to "there and then"? We see in the next chapter several Victorian writers attempting to come to terms with the force of certainty; in Brontë, however, we find a rejection of such certainty—the certainty, for example, that "now" will always have arisen out of "then." The surprise of reading these scenes together—the scene of Jane's adolescent existential crisis and the scene of her adult struggle with the ethics of erotic life—is that so little seems to have changed. The "formless cloud" surrounding the present moment gives way to the adult Jane's "inward dimness of vision, before which clouds yet rolled" (482).

In the latter case, however, an answer does arrive. It is in response to Jane's morally anxious entreaty of Heaven—"Show me the path!"—that she hears Rochester's entreaty as if in her own mind. And yet in our tendency to remember Rochester's plea—"Jane! Jane! Jane!"—as a radio-transmission scene of telepathy, it's easy to forget how physical, erotic, even orgasmic this scene of communion is: "My heart beat fast and thick: I heard its throb. Suddenly it stood still to an inexpressible feeling that thrilled it through, and passed at once to my head and extremities. The feeling was not like an electric shock, but it was quite as sharp, as strange, as startling: it acted on my senses as if their utmost activity hitherto had been but torpor, from which they were now summoned and forced to wake. They rose expectant: eye and ear waited while the flesh quivered on my bones" (483). Even here, there's something of a repetition: we can't help but compare the young Jane who "must watch feverishly" as her life changes with the adult Jane who waits on Rochester's response with flesh quivering. The important difference is that in the moments between St. John's touch and Rochester's penetration, Jane has traded religious supplication for erotic conviction, and the inscrutable calls of angels and commands of God for the equally inscrutable imperatives of sexual desire.[31] It's not that those formless clouds have rolled away, in other words; it's that one conviction, about the force of transcendent rules that always seem uncertain and unknowable, has given way to another conviction, about the force of desire, that utmost "inexpressible feeling," as itself a rule.

In fact, Rochester has earlier figured marriage to Jane as a route to blissful isolation in a set of images that resonates with the radical antisociality of Catherine Earnshaw's moral community of two and Jane's heeding of the electric pulse of the body's desires. There is the image of the invisible "cord of communion" that Rochester feels attaching him to Jane, which he threatens may be "snapped" by too much distance (291), as well as Rochester teasing Jane that " 'once I have fairly seized you, to have and to hold, I'll just—figuratively speaking—attach you to a chain like this' (touching his watchguard). 'Yes, bonny wee thing, I'll wear you in my bosom' " (312). Later, in *Villette*, Brontë would rework this metaphor in Lucy's idea that her friend Ginevra Fanshawe's magnetic hold over Graham Bretton is like "an electric chord of sympathy between them, a fine chain of mutual understanding, sustaining union through a separation of hundreds of leagues" (175). Despite Lucy's consistent conviction of Ginevra's vapidity—Lucy has earlier said that "her liking and disliking, her love and hate, were mere cobweb and gossamer" (93)—she takes this model of distant communion to heart as an ideal: "Ginevra gradually became with me," Lucy says, "a sort of heroine" (175). But at the same time, these images insist upon linking mechanisms (the chain or the cord) and on metaphors of ownership (I'll keep you in my pocket like a watch) that emphasize the separateness of lover and beloved, and so they stop short of the kind of pure contradiction that underwrites Catherine's appeal or Jane's feeling of the tingling interpenetration of souls and bodies. These are images in which one person leashes another but not in which one person becomes another or is filled by another.

Rochester's images of cords and chains are, furthermore, far more jealously possessive than Lucy Snowe's, and in order to allay the anxiety roiling underneath these images of possessive desire—the anxiety that Jane might escape from him into the wide world—Rochester elaborates a fantasy in which they'll live as a married couple on the moon. This is the story he uses to explain their engagement to his ward Adèle: "I am to take mademoiselle with me to the moon, and there I shall seek a cave in one of the white valleys among the vulcano-tops, and mademoiselle shall live there with me, and only me" (308). Adèle is skeptical, and with a certainty very different from Jane's pleas to be shown a seemingly impossible path, insists, "But you can't get her there; there is no road to the moon: it is all air; and neither you nor she can fly," to which Rochester responds with a tall tale in which he meets a fairy in the woods who promises to fly him to the moon if only he puts a magical golden ring on the fourth finger of her left hand (308). There is, indeed, no road to the moon; Adèle penetrates to the heart of the matter by insisting on the impracticability of getting away from the world and the omnipresent pressure of its laws and moral norms, even in a story: it is all air. And Rochester dismisses her argument with an appeal to the power of the marriage ceremony which elevates it to a magical rite capable of bridging the impassable gap from *here* to *there*, earth to moon, social to antisocial. The paradox here is in the idea that a social and legal institution might itself effect one's release from the constraints of social and legal norms. If Catherine Earnshaw insists upon the "passionate perversity" of pure desire and its claim to ethical relevance even outside the bond of marriage, then Rochester imagines ways of elaborating the same kind of antisocial moral universe of two by experimenting with marriage, bending it to his will. This marriage would be, after all, an illegal, bigamous one, and yet Rochester believes that its validity can or should arise out of mutual desire rather than law. At least on the moon.

Although Rochester's allegory of marriage refers to the material symbols of the wedding vows (the ring and its placement on a particular finger) rather than to their enunciation, many of his earlier conversations with Jane exemplify the linguistic and dialogic dimensions of performativity, and in fact test the limitations of the power of the performative utterance to legislate ethical norms or to create ad hoc exceptions to preexisting moral rules—another way that this novel thinks through the problem of fusing the logical point of view to that of the individual's erotic impulses and attachments. In their first extended private conversation, Jane responds to Rochester's allusions to his moral failings and painful memories by insisting on an attitude of earnest self-improvement: "you said you were not as good as you should like to be, and that you regretted your own imperfection; . . . if from this day you began with resolution to correct your thoughts and actions, you would in a few years have laid up a new and stainless store of recollections, to which you might revert with pleasure" (161). Rochester responds with what seems a more liberated, if also a more radically antisocial, solution, effected through a simple performative utterance: "I don't doubt myself; I know what my aim is, what my motives are; and at this moment I pass a law, unalterable as that of the Medes and Persians, that both are right. . . . [U]nheard-of combinations of circumstances demand unheard-of rules" (161). The performative is, for Rochester, a mechanism with which to deal with the sheer unpredictability about the future that so worries Jane as a student at Lowood confronting the reality of death. It seems to him that moral thinking must be idiosyncratic, performative, and flexible if it is to accommodate this kind of unpredictability. Jane is more cautious, however, and her response to Rochester's legalistic performative is to modify it into a kind of supplication. "That sounds a dangerous maxim, sir," she says; "because one can see at once that it is liable to abuse. . . . The human and fallible should not arrogate a power with which the divine and perfect alone can safely be entrusted. . . . That of saying of any strange, unsanctioned line of action, 'Let it be right'" (161–62). Rochester teases Jane by invoking the apparently charmlike power of the performative utterance to effect its end simply by being spoken: "Let it be right," he responds, "the very words: you have pronounced them" (162). Jane corrects herself: "'*May* it be right then,' I said, . . . sensible that the character of my interlocutor was beyond my penetration; at least, beyond my present reach; and feeling the uncertainty, the vague sense of insecurity, which accompanies a conviction of ignorance" (162). But of course Rochester's "character" is only beyond Jane's "present reach," and her sense of "uncertainty," "insecurity," and "ignorance" help us to see that her response is not entirely moralizing, but perhaps merely hesitant and reflective. "*May* it be right" is at once a refusal to "arrogate" an authority that one is unequipped to wield—a humble prayer directed toward a transcendent moral authority, whether God or simply moral law—and at the same time retains the idea that moral norms are precisely *not* transcendent and stable. That they are subject to change Rochester and Jane agree, but their disagreement is over the nature and source of this changeability of norms: changed by whom? and from where? Both characters are aware that moral certainty involves the individual in a contradiction unless one is willing to abstract oneself entirely, for example, into a position of divine impartiality—and both experiment with ways of confronting that contradiction, jockeying for different kinds of moral authority in limited versions of self-transcendence.[32]

The self-centeredness and antisociality of Rochester's claim to authority is flagrant, but of course, we might also understand Jane's "uncertainty," "insecurity," and "ignorance" as defining characteristics of the first-person narrator confronting the limitations of her knowledge. Jane's inability to penetrate Rochester's character represents precisely her non-omniscience, in contrast to a third-person narrator who would be able to enter into the complex motivations behind Rochester's strange moral attitude. More importantly, Jane's discomfort does not spur her on to techniques of more forceful interrogation but instead prompts a religious tribute to an imagined omniscience whose authority she is loath to usurp. She utters a prayer that we can read as being directed either at God (may Rochester's new law be right, pending divine approval) or at an omniscient narrator (may Rochester's new law be right, pending the full exploration of his consciousness and/or the end of this novel). While Audrey Jaffe has argued that first-person narrators typically situate themselves "in epistemologically superior positions with regard to other characters" and thereby "reveal a desire for superior knowledge and power similar to that which an omniscient narrator possesses in relation to characters," moments like this one, in which performative rather than epistemic authority are in question, complicate Jaffe's picture.[33] Moreover, Jane-as-narrator knows a great deal about Rochester's motivations that she chooses not to disclose in the interest of both psychological realism and narrative suspense.

That questions about narrative omniscience are at heart epistemological questions—what are the mechanisms by which a narrator knows so much and by which she controls and disseminates that knowledge?—has often been taken for granted. But it is clear that one of the uses of performative utterance as a technique of narration (and especially of first-person narration) is to upset the centrality of knowledge and omniscience in our conception of the potential sources of a narrator's power, and thereby to destabilize the perspective from which ethical claims could be tested against logical norms of practical reason and impartial detachment. We might understand characters as beholden not to the knowledge of an impersonal omniscient narrator but only to the knowledge that they have at hand, a problem that becomes especially fraught when, as in the case of *Jane Eyre*, narrator and character are the same person, separated only by time and hindsight. Rochester's fantasy is one of ethical omnipotence rather than narrative omniscience, while Jane's supplicating performative expresses a desire for neither of these. Rather, her *"May* it be right" seems to capture the way in which ethical thinking depends upon a kind of creativity in trying to make one's immediate social world fit one's idiosyncratic desires and exceptional circumstances, rather than making one's desires match a static and universal set of moral rules.[34] Rochester is accustomed to ruling by fiat: upon first meeting Jane, he says, "Excuse my tone of command: I am used to say, 'Do this,' and it is done" (145). Jane, on the other hand, insists upon a negotiation between desire, with its limited intelligibility but insistent urging, and ethical account- ability, which may be more flexible in response to desire than one would at first imagine.

For Rochester, in other words, the answer to all of these questions about the individual's capacity to rework moral, logical, legal, or religious rules tends to be simple: norms should be determined by him and from his perspective. On the other hand, his protracted and teasing marriage proposal to Jane combines the authoritativeness of the command—"I summon you as my wife" (293); "I entreat you to accept me as my husband" (294)—with a troubled sense that individual feeling may not entirely trump moral norms. Rochester worries about whether his love for Jane can cancel out the illicitness of bigamy and his own mistreatment of his wife, as he murmurs to himself, "It will atone—it will atone. . . . Is there not love in my heart and constancy in my resolves? It will expiate at God's tribunal. I know my Maker sanctions what I do. For the world's judgment—I wash my hands thereof" (295). Rochester seems to have responded to Jane's *"May* it be right." Here, we see a moral reasoning that refers hopefully to a future time—"it *will* atone"; "it *will* expiate"—and to a divine au- thority higher than the human law against bigamy. Following the engagement, of course, we see Rochester try to effect a balance between the everyday life of a married couple and his need to get outside of earthly moral obligations in his fantasy of love on the moon.

All of these scenes present themselves as partial solutions to the problem of radical uncertainty about the future and about the nature of change (the problem of that contradictory moment in time at which the impossible "is be- coming" the possible), as well as a related uncertainty about the self-evident or third-person grounds of moral reasoning (the problem of how the impulses of individual desire might communicate with and meaningfully shape the pressures of the law and of ethical norms). It is terrifying to totter on the edge of the present, there is no road to the moon, and often we're left to our own devices in identifying the right course of action, unable to square our own peculiar circumstances with the rigidity of the law. Sedgwick's concept of the "periperformative" utterance, which merely refers to a performative and which can be "the site of powerful energies that often warp, transform, and displace, if they do not overthrow the supposed authorizing centrality of that same performative," may be clarifying here, as this concept helps us to see that performative authority is never seamless or absolute.[35] Rather, it is always a site of contest and often represents a situation in which various divergent points of view can destabilize the frame that would guarantee the efficacy of performative speech.

Stanley Cavell's concept of "passionate utterance" asks us to consider with even greater specificity how a narrow focus on performativity in the philosophy of ordinary language in fact obscures the affective and erotic dimensions of argumentation in language. We might say the same thing about the tradition of literary theorists' interest in ordinary language philosophy as a theoretical framework, which has tended to focus disproportionate attention on speech-act theory, actually only a small subfield of ordinary language philosophy.[36] Cavell distinguishes the passionate utterance from the performative by suggesting that "a performative utterance is an offer of participation in the order of the law," while "passionate utterance is an invitation to improvisation in the disorders of desire."[37] In other words, if philosophical questions about language often limit themselves to "what we should or ought to say" or "what we may and do say," then an account of passionate utterance would be equally rigorous in thinking about the social efficacy of "what we must and dare not say, or have it at heart to say, or are too confused or too tame or wild or terrorized to say or to think to say" (185). On the one hand, this is messy. These are, after all, the "disorders of desire." On the other hand, Cavell's argument expands our understanding of what kinds of experiences and what forms of language and argument can claim a position in the realm of the ethical and the intelligible. If we don't take passionate utterance seriously as a meaningful kind of communication, then "we are stopped short in the obligation to make our desires, hence our actions, intelligible (and to ourselves) and hampered in our demand and right to be found intelligible in those desires and actions, to ask residence in the shared realm of reason" (188). Cavell tends to take "passion" and "desire" in their most capacious senses—passion as any powerful feeling, desire as the root of the intentions that lead to action—and so the specificity of the erotic as an ethical pressure tends to be glossed over in his theory of passionate utterance. But his philosophical argument is nevertheless crucial to the project of this book—that is, his insistence that passion and desire might have a "demand and right to be found intelligible." We may be wrong to assume that passionate utterance is always mistaken, symptomatic, or unstructured—merely a failed attempt to make something happen with words. On the contrary, much of our "shared realm of reason" might be shaped by the form of the passionate.

Cavell's argument itself plays upon a set of contradictions in order to emphasize the opacity of passionate utterance, which, in its association with disorder and affective response, seems antithetical to the values of rational or logical intelligibility—another way in which Cavell's model deviates somewhat from the model of bad logic, which remains attached to these values. One way out of the contradiction between the first-person and third-person imperatives of ethical thinking, in other words, is simply to grant that the contradiction exists but to insist that contradiction might be a structure rather than a dissolution of structure—a joint rather than a fissure, to return to D. A. Miller's terms. More specifically, these two dimensions of ethical thinking might come together productively in the context of what Cavell calls "passionate exchange," a kind of conversation in which "there is no final word, no uptake or turndown, until a line is drawn, a withdrawal is effected, perhaps in turn to be revoked," rather than being conjoined by the disciplinary and ideological force imagined in Miller's model (183). In such a scene, the imagined third-person view of moral omniscience recedes in order to make way for a dynamic, intimate, and, most importantly, open-ended power play. Cavell's theory of passionate utterance asks us, in other words, to reconsider what a "shared realm of reason" might look like from a position on the ground. Rather than being structured by and beholden to an abstract, ordered set of logical norms, its goal of making our lives "intelligible" might require it to comprehend other dimensions of psychic life such as the idiosyncratic imperatives of erotic desire. It might also be a realm that changes shape, texture, and composition in response to demands for intimate recognition, not only in response to reasonable consensus. Indeed, even the clumsiest and most accidental of our expressions of desire or repulsion make us accountable in ways we do not intend. When Jane implies that she finds Rochester ugly, for example, she attempts to absolve herself: "it was only a blunder," she tells him. "Just so: I think so," he replies, "and you shall be answerable for it" (154).

Lucy Snowe's Intimate Abstraction

In *Villette*, Brontë imagines a very different solution to the problem of self-negation and the third-person point of view than those we find in *Jane Eyre*, particularly in its narrator Lucy Snowe's apparent achievement of the kind of detached rationality that would consider the idiosyncrasy of erotic life an irrelevance to ethical thinking. Critics have had much to say about the complexity of Lucy Snowe's position as a narrator. On the one hand, she seems to ape narrative omniscience: she is detached, socially withdrawn, self-effacing to the point of virtual invisibility, and has an interest in the cool and secretive practices of surveillance exemplified by the character of Mme. Beck, who becomes to Lucy both a nemesis and a kind of mentor. On the other hand, her evasions, withholdings, and fugue states mark her out as the apotheosis of the unreliable and limited first-person narrator. And no matter what her pretensions to detachment, she is, after all, a first-person narrator rather than an omniscient one. Amanda Anderson insists that we should be sensitive to this "rejection of omniscience," in order to understand the ways in which Brontë "uses the first-person narration of Lucy Snowe to stage a reflective engagement with questions of detachment."[38] Like Anderson, Nicholas Dames emphasizes the novel's tenuous balancing of the systematizing and scientific scrutiny of the "phrenological gaze" with the erotic energy implied by that practice of physical scrutiny. Phrenology models "a new kind of eros," he suggests, "one that is crucially not founded on childhood cathexes but rather on an adult process of reading, counter-reading, attribution, and denial."[39] Whereas these critics show us *Villette*'s rich middle ground between rational abstraction and situated engagement, John Kucich complicates matters by arguing that self-negation is not a tactic of omniscient detachment in *Villette*. Rather, he writes, Brontë's "eroticizing of repressive solitude is most fully expressed in the heightened inwardness of her reticent protagonist-narrators."[40] For Kucich, the first person becomes all encompassing as Lucy Snowe eroticizes interiority and expands it, and therefore Lucy and Brontë's other protagonists turn this kind of "self-enclosure" into a form of power "and formulate it as a bulwark of the self against others rather than as a means either of interpersonal unity or of complete self-negation."[41] Finally, Elisha Cohn has pointed to Lucy Snowe's frequent states of dream and reverie as allowing her to elaborate a strangely mindless kind of sensation—"abstract yet intense feelings that will not register as the thought of a consolidated self," as Cohn describes it, an "absorption in a bodied state that makes her feel disembodied." For Cohn, Lucy's contradictory states, those trances in which she "bodies forth non-being," raise a vexing question: if "felt pleasure" is "made available by the lack of a conscious mind to experience it," or, in other words, if sensation can only really be pleasurable when consciousness seems to go to sleep, then "whose pleasure is it?"[42] Despite their different approaches and methodologies, however, Anderson, Dames,

Kucich, and Cohn share the conviction that, in *Villette*, Brontë purposefully resists easy oppositions of first-person and third-person perspectives, abstraction and engagement, reason and affect, or self-effacement and erotic experience.

These arguments share a submerged line of thinking, which is worth teasing out, in their different ways of implying that the idiosyncrasy of erotic life might have some necessary relationship to what Cavell would call the "shared realm of reason." What varies among these critics is what precisely this relationship looks like. For Kucich it is an antagonistic relationship: Brontëan desire is essentially "solipsistic" on his view, and Cohn to some extent concurs by imagining Lucy's disembodied pleasures as made available by states of reverie rather than positions of rational detachment.[43] For Dames, the erotic potential of phrenological reading arises out of the fact that "Lucy and M. Paul share the phrenological language and can therefore reach a position of relative parity."[44] Anderson emphasizes Lucy's balancing of idiosyncrasy—"a detachment she can call her own"—with her interest in the socially intelligible models of detachment presented by characters such as Mrs. Bretton ("maternal impersonality") or Mme. Beck ("institutional and familial surveillance").[45] Although I group myself with Dames and Anderson here in insisting upon the importance of shared vocabularies and social intelligibility to erotic life, I also argue that for Brontë desire is often the impetus for, rather than an epiphenomenon of, this kind of community building. While Dames suggests that Brontë elaborates a "new kind of eros," I wonder whether we might also think of her as elaborating new kinds of practices for making eros socially viable or intelligible—practices that draw upon both first-person inwardness and intimacy and third-person detachment, self-negation, or abstraction.

Villette provides plentiful descriptions of Lucy Snowe as a cool and detached observer of the world around her. Early on in the novel, Lucy describes with arch disdain the young Paulina Home's emotional engagement in watching passersby through the window: "These sudden, dangerous natures—*sensitive* as they are called—offer many a curious spectacle to those whom a cooler temperament has secured from participation in their angular vagaries" (16, original emphasis). When she arrives in London she describes her "homeless, anchorless, unsupported mind" (57), and in recounting her early days at Mme. Beck's *pensionnat*, she emphasizes the purposeful self-splitting that is required to maintain such a position of social withdrawal and invisibility: "I seemed to hold two lives—the life of thought, and that of reality; and, provided the former was nourished with a sufficiency of the strange necromantic joys of fancy, the privileges of the latter might remain limited to daily bread, hourly work, and a roof of shelter" (85). Here we see that Lucy's status as a semi-omniscient observer of other people is actually far from being limited to direct observation. While Lucy often secretes herself in shadows and dark corners in order to observe unseen, such withdrawal can allow her to indulge those "strange necromantic joys of fancy" rather than scrutinizing the real and living world around her: "While wandering in solitude," she tells us, "I would sometimes picture the present probable position of others, my acquaintance" (175). Lucy's practices of withdrawal, then, take two different forms that sometimes overlap: literal moments of social and spatial withdrawal that are aligned with the exercise of visual scrutiny, as well as moments of withdrawal into the interior self that are aligned with the exercise of imagination and rigorous self-examination.

Although it often seems as if Lucy's powers of scrutiny are unrealistically omniscient, she is actually quick to admit their limitations. Despite her claim that Graham Bretton "laid himself open to my observation" (107), for example, Lucy goes on to make an important qualification as she puzzles over his attachment to Mme. Beck's establishment: "For what *he* waited I do not know, nor for what he watched; but the peculiarity of his manner, his expectant, vigilant, absorbed, eager look, never wore off: it rather intensified. He had never been quite within the compass of my penetration, and I think he ranged farther and farther beyond it" (112–13, original emphasis). Lucy does not make confident judgments based on her observations of his behavior; rather, her position of invisibility makes her "free to puzzle" and "wonder" about them. Imagination picks up for Lucy where the powers of observation and "penetration" meet their limitations. In other words, a focus on Lucy's detachment calls attention to the novel's preoccupation with visuality, scrutiny, and empirical data collection, but recognizing the limitations of that detachment points us to the interior psychic life that Lucy often exalts. It's easy to see Lucy's tendency to retreat into inwardness as the most deeply antisocial feature of her character, closely linked to her tendency toward self-seclusion and harsh asceticism. While Lucy figures "the life of thought" as a place of retreat from the "trial" that intimate social exchange represents to her, that life of thought also seems to be a place of virtual death, fueled by "necromantic joys" rather than living (and lived) experiences, at best cancelling out pain rather than cultivating pleasure. Lucy shapes her interior life according to an ideal of eremitic, melancholic, repressive self-discipline, but it seems that this inwardness often transforms from a tactic of phobic and antisocial avoidance into a source of pleasure. In other words, there's a difference between an unnoticed withdrawal—simply choosing to be alone, not being missed by anyone—and a positive or tactical refusal, in which one refuses the company of someone who might care. Indeed, later on, once Lucy has become somewhat accustomed to the intense and extended social interaction required of her as a teacher, we see her begin to represent the "life of thought" in a much different register: she describes a day spent wandering alone in the garden, "finding warmth in the sun, shelter among the trees, and a sort of companionship in my own thoughts. I well remember that I exchanged but two sentences that day with any living being: not that I felt solitary; I was glad to be quiet" (145). While it's tempting to condescend to Lucy's declarations of pleasure in solitude as mere defense mechanisms against acknowledging her depressive character, it seems more reasonable and productive to pay attention to the nuanced way in which her descriptions of solitude and of inwardness change in response to the "intimate trial" that she undergoes at Mme. Beck's. In going beyond herself, Lucy also learns to be a companion to herself, and a pleasure to herself. We can't help but hear echoes of Catherine Earnshaw and her description of the life of the mind: "I *am* Heathcliff—he's always, always in my mind—not as a pleasure, any more than I am always a pleasure to myself."

When Lucy does represent her "life of thought" directly, it's often as an allegorized duel between painfully divided aspects of the self—a psychomachia—rather than as productive intellectual reflection, but here too we should pay attention to these scenes as providing an important barometer of personal development. One of the most harrowing of these scenes arises out of Lucy's growing attraction to Graham Bretton and her intense desire that he write to her frequently. Allegorical "Reason" steps in to dampen these hopes and to exhort Lucy to reject any intimate relationship with Graham: "He may write once," warns Reason; "So kind is his nature, it may stimulate him for once to make the effort. But it *cannot* be continued—it *may* not be repeated. . . . [G]rant no expansion to feeling—give holiday to no single faculty: dally with no friendly exchange: foster no genial intercommunion" (255). But Lucy does not understand herself as freely submitting to the dictates of Reason. Indeed, she represents this allegorical character as monstrous and violently coercive: she is a "hag," "vindictive as a devil," and "envenomed as a step-mother"; she commands "the obedience of fear, not of love" and "she could not rest unless I were altogether crushed, cowed, broken-in, and broken-down." Lucy is the victim of Reason's "ill-usage: her stint, her chill, her barren board, her icy bed, her savage, ceaseless blows" (255–56). Reason's warm and loving opponent in this scene is "Feeling," "that kinder Power who," Lucy tells us, "holds my secret and sworn allegiance. . . . A spirit, softer and better than Human Reason, has descended with quiet flight to the waste—bringing all round her a sphere of air borrowed of eternal summer. . . . My hunger has this good angel appeased with food, sweet and strange" (256). Of course, the effect of the allegory is to spectralize and externalize what should be a deeply interior psychological contradiction; these are not voices in Lucy's own head as much as visitors who descend from another world to war for Lucy's "sworn allegiance." There's a set of complicated contradictions here. Lucy represents Reason as a distant and inscrutable agent of coercive power, which demands realism and asceticism in place of the eroticized pleasures of desire, longing, and imagination. But although reason seems to descend from without, it demands that Lucy retreat to the psychic realm within—the very interior realm that Lucy so often identifies with escape from reality and the cultivation of fantasy.

Somewhat counterintuitively, Lucy often understands abstraction—the projection of the self beyond the self—not as an activity of the rational mind, but rather as a risky, eroticized pleasure prohibited by reason. Lucy tells us, for example, that stormy weather "woke the being I was always lulling, and stirred up a craving cry I could not satisfy. . . . I did long, achingly, . . . for something to fetch me out of my present existence, and lead me upwards and onwards" (121). And yet this self-transcendence, the movement out of the self, "upwards and onwards," is always squelched, and a description of that squelching is the occasion of one of Brontë's most gruesome images: "This longing, and all of a similar kind, it was necessary to knock on the head; which I did, figuratively, after the manner of Jael to Sisera, driving a nail through their temples. Unlike Sisera, they did not die: they were but transiently stunned, and at intervals would turn on the nail with a rebellious wrench; then did the temples bleed, and the brain thrill to its core" (121). The extended simile turns on that obtrusive and redundant modifier, "figuratively." Of course figuratively—how else? The excessive marking of the metaphor deflates its brutality. Although the attempt to abstract oneself, to fly like a ghost, onward and upward, out of the body, is like the pain of twisting that impaled head on its stake, this is not literally a case of pain mortifying pleasure. It's a case of being nailed in place, stuck within one's head—within that brain that sits between those bleeding temples—and therefore grotesquely immobilized. This image recalls Andrew Miller's idea, following Kierkegaard, that I can feel "nailed to myself in being this person as opposed to being that person, being me as opposed to, say, being you. This line of implication stresses the incarnation: my having one body, only one; this one not that one; none other, however much I may want it."[46] In this case, however, Lucy doesn't want to occupy or to be a different body but pictures her "longing" as a body of its own, a strange parasite or appendage, a creature that she must nail to the earth in order to prevent its unpredictable movements, "upwards" and "onwards."

In short, Lucy upsets our expectations about the contradiction between abstraction and embodiment. It's reason that crushes and cows us bodily, and it's desire that tries to free us from the body. Reason keeps the self inside the self; desire carries the self beyond the self, not in the body touching another body, but in a limited form of self-abstraction. Theatrical performance and spectatorship provide one model for Lucy's navigation of erotic attachment at a distance. When M. Paul enlists Lucy to perform in the theatrical at Mme. Beck's fete, she discovers "a keen relish for dramatic expression," only to chastise herself that this kind of thrill is inappropriate for "a mere looker-on at life" (156). At the ball that follows the theatrical, Lucy reemphasizes the double movement of retreat in which withdrawal from the crowd aligns with withdrawal into the self: "it was time I retired into myself and my ordinary life. . . . Withdrawing to a quiet nook, whence unobserved I could observe—the ball, its splendours and its pleasures passed before me as a spectacle" (156). Once again, Lucy's escape into a dark corner is about the self-negation of invisibility and spectatorship, as well as the self-aggrandizement suggested by the idea of retiring "into" oneself, as Kucich might argue. But Lucy's retirement is fleeting. Full of the excitement of her dramatic performance, she is soon entering into the fray of conversation: "For the second time that night I was going beyond myself—venturing out of what I looked on as my natural habits—speaking in an unpremeditated, impulsive strain, which startled me strangely when I halted to reflect" (167). Lucy's discovery of the pleasure of "going beyond" herself in intimate social exchange, and the painful difficulty of sustaining this deviation from her "natural habits," foreshadows the mental breakdown that concludes the novel's first volume. Lucy, left nearly alone for the long summer vacation, devolves into a feverish fugue state that ends with her confession in a Catholic church, described once again in terms of a peculiarly limited and controlled self-abstraction: "the mere relief of communication in an ear which was human and sentient, yet consecrated— the mere pouring out of some portion of long accumulating, long pent-up pain into a vessel whence it could not again be diffused—had done me good" (179). Here Lucy finds a more nuanced image for the pleasure of communication— not merely a "going beyond" that threatens to dissolve the self, but a narrow, directed "pouring" of the self and its pains toward and into another, where it will remain safely contained. After her breakdown, as she awakens in the home of the Brettons, she describes the experience by which her soul "re-entered her prison with pain, with reluctance, with a moan and a long shiver. The divorced mates, Spirit and Substance, were hard to re-unite: they greeted each other, not in an embrace, but in a racking sort of struggle" (185). The metaphor of divorce and reconciliation signals the way in which all of these experiments in intimacy and solitude bear upon the development of this novel's marriage plot, which at this point begins to dominate: the second volume focuses on Lucy's unrequited attraction to Graham Bretton, and the third volume narrates her courtship with M. Paul.

These volumes also continue to account for Lucy's development of complex ideas about art, spectatorship, and theater—first in her account of a visit to an art museum and then in her passionate appraisal of the actress Vashti—and these episodes inform Lucy's negotiation of the complex entanglements of introspection with sociability, and materiality with abstraction.[47] At the art museum, left alone to ponder the paintings, Lucy describes yet another allegorized "misunderstanding and consequent struggle" between "Will" and "Power": "The former faculty exacted approbation of that which it was considered orthodox to admire; the latter groaned forth its utter inability to pay the tax; it was then self-sneered at, spurred up, goaded on to refine its taste, and whet its zest. The more it was chidden, however, the more it wouldn't praise" (222). Will mimics Reason, prodding and mocking Lucy coercively into submission to social consensus. But if that previous skirmish of Reason and Feeling seemed like an externalizing projection of interiority, this one ends differently, with a relaxation into a passive and unreflective pleasure in lived experience: "Discovering gradually that a wonderful sense of fatigue resulted from these conscientious efforts," Lucy continues, "I began to reflect whether I might not dispense with that great labour, and concluded eventually that I might, and so sank supine into a luxury of calm before ninety-nine out of the hundred of the exhibited frames" (222). No more shuttling back and forth between contradictory perspectives, or between the self and the not-myself; Lucy arrives at a practice of easy companionability with her own thoughts.

Later in the art museum scene, Lucy seems to search for a middle ground between the set of paintings depicting the ascetic "vie d'une femme" and the oversexed fleshiness of the "Cleopatra." The former depict women "grim and gray as burglars, and cold and vapid as ghosts. What women to live with! insincere, ill-humoured, bloodless, brainless nonentities!" (226). No one, of course, could "live with" these women, just as no one can live with the reclusive, withdrawn, ascetic Lucy. They barely exist, or at best they move in burglarish, ghostly stealth. But at the same time, these women are only "as bad in their way" as the "gipsy-giantess" Cleopatra (226), with her "wealth of muscle" and "affluence of flesh" (223). The magic of the actress Vashti's performance, on the other hand, lies in its aggressive and explosive holding together of the fleshliness of the body and the "vapidity" of abstraction. Vashti, to Lucy's eyes, so revels in the contradictory combination of muscle and abstraction that her example is impossible to process: "To her, what hurts becomes immediately embodied: she looks on it as a thing that can be attacked, worried down, torn in shreds. Scarcely a substance herself, she grapples to conflict with abstractions. . . . The strong magnetism of genius drew my heart out of its wonted orbit; the sunflower turned from the south to a fierce light, not solar—a rushing, red, cometary light—hot on vision and to sensation" (287). Again Lucy is pulled out of herself and out of the habit of her "wonted orbit" by an erotic "magnetism." Lucy finds in Vashti a perplexing but attractive combination of sensuality ("embodied," "thing," "torn in shreds," "grapples," "heart," "hot") and immateriality ("what hurts," "scarcely a substance," "abstractions," "light"). Vashti represents a distant spin out of orbit, toward a "cometary" light, and yet this rushing expansion somehow increases the heat on Lucy's "vision" and "sensation." The whirling and dizzying energy of the Vashti scene arises out of this fever-pitch litany of contradiction, which so densely exemplifies the painful feeling simply of existing with others, of going tentatively beyond oneself without disappearing into thin air.

And yet, as we've seen, Brontë's marriage plots tend not toward complete self-negation but rather toward a local and intimate kind of self-abstraction. Even when she finally acknowledges her desire for M. Paul, Lucy offers the caveat, "I knew what I was for *him*; and what I might be for the rest of the world, I ceased painfully to care" (533, original emphasis). Of course, as always in the world of Brontë, "painfully"—although the ambiguous placement of the adverb suggests that either the caring or the ceasing might have been the painful thing and that Lucy only trades the excruciating effort of social belonging for the excruciating effort of giving up that belonging in favor of something smaller. This is after all a purposeful self-containment within the kind of community of two that so fascinates both Emily and Charlotte Brontë, even while it's still an effacement of the self. Lucy now knows what she is "for *him*," which implies both that Lucy's self-knowledge is a prerequisite for romantic fulfillment (I am doing this for you) and also that her self-knowledge is ultimately routed *through* him (I know how to be the person you want). Lucy's romantic plot doesn't feature the sheer volume of scintillating and barbed conversation that we see in Jane Eyre's relationship with Rochester or even in her debates with St. John Rivers. M. Paul learns about Lucy largely through his surreptitious searches through her desk, and when he tries to persuade her to convert to Catholicism, she is pointed about her clumsiness at debate: "He pleaded, he argued. *I* could not argue—a fortunate incapacity; it needed but triumphant, logical opposition to effect all the director wished to be effected; but I could talk in my own way—the way

M. Paul was used to—and of which he could follow the meanderings and fill the hiatus, and pardon the strange stammering, strange to him no longer" (463). Lucy's achievement of intelligibility is intimate and also limited—she has not learned to reason logically and triumphantly about her religious investments, her idiosyncrasies, her desires, and yet she has learned how to do it "for *him*." This is a kind of communication that's as much about silence as it is about speech—M. Paul understands Lucy partly because he can "fill the hiatus" in her meandering account of herself, which neatly echoes the mysterious hiatuses of *Villette* itself, as the novel opens with Lucy's cryptic refusal to tell us the details of her own past and the loss of her immediate family.

And speech, moreover, isn't equipped for making love and desire intelligible. Even as Lucy confesses her love to M. Paul, stammering and incoherent, she tells us, "In such inadequate language my feelings struggled for expression: they could not get it; speech, brittle and unmalleable, and cold as ice, dissolved or shivered in the effort" (537). Lucy is unable even to use language to describe clearly how language fails her. In that final alternative—"dissolved or shivered"—lies an uncertainty about the unforgiving iciness of language. Of course, "shivered" has two meanings when it comes to things that are "cold as ice": Lucy's speech shatters into fragments, like a piece of ice cast against a wall, but her speech might also tremble at its own chill. It might finally dissolve, like a piece of ice melting into a pool of water. All of these connotations are at work here, but they exist in tension with one another. The shivered fragments might be pieced back together, but the dissolved ice can never reconstitute itself exactly as it was. Lucy's metaphors describe speech as a cold, brittle thing that either disappears or chatters its teeth or breaks to pieces, or perhaps a speech that does all of these things in turn. Lucy understands language as an inflexible vessel for the externalization of feeling, bound to destroy what it tries to convey. In other words, even at the supposed culmination of Lucy's transition into adulthood, we hear an echo of Jane Eyre's lament at the confusions of childhood as she narrates her efforts to tell the doctor what has caused her fit in the red room at Gateshead: "Children can feel, but they cannot analyse their feelings; and if the analysis is partially effected in thought, they know not how to express the result of the process in words. Fearful, however, of losing this first and only opportunity of relieving my grief by imparting it, I, after a disturbed pause, contrived to frame a meagre, though, as far as it went, true response" (29). It seems that this is not merely a childhood affliction but a lifelong struggle that one must learn to accommodate. To go beyond oneself and yet not to lose oneself along the way; to impart one's griefs, pains, and desires to another; to analyze what resists analysis; "to express the result of the process in words," in "speech, brittle and unmalleable"; to be oneself and another, or more accurately to be oneself *for* another: what more challenging set of contradictions could one imagine negotiating?[48]

Of course, it's ultimately marriage that comes to represent the fruition of this model of intimate abstraction for Brontë, and so we revisit Jane with Rochester, bone of his bone and flesh of his flesh; his right hand, seeing and feeling on his behalf; ever together; talking all day long. St. John Rivers ends the novel as a vexed cautionary tale, admirable in his religious dutifulness and his extreme self-sufficiency and yet somehow unspeakably tragic in his refusal of the kind of erotic intimacy that defines Jane's and Rochester's marriage: "St John is unmarried: he will never marry now. Himself has hitherto sufficed to the toil, and the toil draws nearer its close" (521). For St. John, what has been will always be— what "has hitherto" sufficed must continue to suffice as the end of his life "draws nearer." He represents a social withdrawal much more radical because much more determined and deterministic than Lucy Snowe's. She and Jane do not have uncomplicatedly happy endings, nor do they end by any gestures of radical rebellion. They end in a lived-in and comforting contradiction, simultaneously alone and in company; withdrawing and desiring; retreating within the self and venturing beyond the self, if only tentatively and with careful, feeling steps.

In the next chapter, we'll see that tautology offers us a different version of the antisocial "retreat" within the self, which may also represent an escape from language itself. While escapes from the social world of logical accountability in favor of the erotic point of view are often uneven or ambivalent, tautology helps us to see what happens when logical accountability is altogether refused, and when the shakiness of erotic point of view becomes the diamond-hard conviction of erotic essentialism.

CHAPTER TWO

Anthony Trollope's Tautologies

In Anthony Trollope's *Can You Forgive Her?* (1865), when Mrs. Greenow admonishes her maid Jeanette that "You shouldn't think about handsome men, child," Jeannette responds, "And I'm sure I don't. . . . Not no more than anybody else; but if a man is handsome, ma'am, why it stands to reason that he is handsome."[1] Jeannette's circular reasoning disarms the prohibition against her open expression of erotic interest; by framing it as a matter of reasoning so simple as to be tautologically irrefutable, Jeannette normalizes her desire ("Not no more than anybody else") and depersonalizes it ("it stands to reason"). If a thing is so inescapably certain (handsome is handsome), what could be the harm in speaking it aloud? Jeannette's apologia seems not entirely to belong to her, even while it announces her own desire, and shows how the self-evidence of tautology allows a safe way in which to perform an otherwise risky erotic disclosure. But this security comes at the cost of making erotic desire impersonal, *out there* (in reason, in the self-evident truths of logic) rather than *in here* (in the body, in the thrumming of libido). We can't help but react to Jeannette's perfect tautology with ambivalence—a sense that by rationalizing her desire, successfully sticking it to Mrs. Greenow, she has also muted that desire's particularity.

Jeannette is a minor character, but her tautology mirrors the problem at the heart of the novel's main plot, which follows Alice Vavasor's protracted erotic indecision. After becoming engaged to the beautiful but dull John Grey, she worries that she has made an error and that she should instead marry her dark and dangerous cousin, George Vavasor, a man to whom she is sexually indifferent but whose political connections may allow her to realize her own ambitions for political involvement, at least by proxy. The novel follows Alice through many changes of heart, and its title asks us whether we can absolve her for her inconsistency—for her apparent failure to remain true to the certainty of desire in the way Jeannette seems to do. While Alice is able to think of plenty of sensible reasons why she should marry George (with him she might "make herself useful,—useful in some sort that might gratify her ambition"), her desire to marry Grey does not seem as amenable to a rational account (342). It is presented as a self-evident truth that seems to arise from nowhere and to lead nowhere, and she is wary of the simplicity of desire's certainty: "She was not satisfied with herself in having loved him. In her many thoughts on the subject, she always admitted to herself that she had accepted him simply because she loved him;—that she had given her quick assent to his quick proposal simply because he had won her heart. But she was sometimes almost angry with herself that she had permitted her heart to be thus easily taken from her, and had rebuked herself for her girlish facility" (50). Alice's attraction to Grey is too easy, too unavailable to deeper inquiry—it is what it is—and she worries that to accept such a feeling is facile, immature, "girlish." Where Jeannette embraces tautology as a way to insist upon desire's self-evidence, Alice avoids tautology, even while experiencing the kind of certainty it would formalize. She remains suspicious of its opacity and its smooth contours. In place of its punctuality, its compulsion to "quick assent," she longs for dilation, complexity—narrative.

Indeed, to Roland Barthes, the circular, empty, opaque form of tautology represents just the kind of desperate escape attempt from language that Alice fears. "One takes refuge in tautology," he writes, "as one does in fear, or anger, or sadness, when one is at a loss for an explanation. . . . Tautology testifies to a profound distrust of language, which is rejected because it has failed. Now, any refusal of language is a death. Tautology creates a dead, a motionless world."[2] We've already seen a similar account of "failed" language in Wittgenstein's elaboration of what happens when we encounter a contradiction and feel as if we've become "entangled in our own rules," or when Jane Eyre and Rochester come to a profound disagreement about the individual's authority to legislate ethical norms through the use of performative speech. While the moment of impasse represents for Wittgenstein an opportunity to reevaluate the state of our language game, for Barthes tautology is what happens if we refuse that project of reevaluation and instead flee from the scene altogether, or simply curl up into a ball. We find a safe haven in the static, obstinate quality of tautology—its comfort in declaring in response to failure that "it is what it is." In another essay collected in *Mythologies*, entitled "Racine is Racine," Barthes describes tautological reasoning as a "petit-bourgeois predilection" and an insidious form of "anti-intellectualism" exemplified by the naïve mode of literary criticism which would, for example, attempt to find its way to the essential "truth" of the work of Racine or to locate "Racine degree zero."[3] And so it seems that, fundamentally, Barthes's suspicion of tautology arises out of a suspicion of the concept of "essence" as a model for truth. The lazy conviction that Racine is Racine narrows the truth of his work to an opaque kernel, foreclosing the kind of criticism that would find in Racine's work a plural and unpredictable set of truths.

This chapter challenges Barthes's dismissal of tautology but not Alice's. In other words, it refuses Barthes's idea that tautology is a dead form, unmoving and uncomplicated, while remaining attuned to Alice's sense that the neatness of tautology might also have costs. Through readings of *Can You Forgive Her?* and *The Way We Live Now* (1875), set against George Meredith's novel *The Egoist* (1879), I'll demonstrate Trollope's ambivalent approach to erotic certainty (the idea that erotic desire "is what it is") and erotic essentialism (the idea that a desire or complex of desires can ground the essentialist conviction that "I am what I am"). For Trollope, tautology can give shape—the shape of a circle, or a circuit—to the feeling of erotic certainty, simultaneously opaque and crystal clear, that is so often the focus of his fiction, but it can also coerce, reduce, flatten, and silence. Jeannette's tautology is both perfectly clear and perfectly unclear, as are so many of Trollope's characters who insist that they are who they are and that their desires are their desires. When Jeannette tells Mrs. Greenow that handsome is handsome, we're meant to feel, on the one hand, that she's right, that sexual attraction simply *is*. But, on the other hand, Trollope often laces his novel with moral lessons that warn against a pathologically intense devotion to certainty—to the idea that the meanings of words, acts, or identities are ever perfectly clear. Take Louis Trevelyan, whose descent into jealous madness provides the main plot of *He Knew He Was Right* (1869). His mistaken certainty of his wife's betrayal becomes a jealous delusion, a manufactured certainty that needs to be renewed again and again, held together in the face of the doubt that would interrupt its cycle and reveal its artificiality: "He told himself from hour to hour that he knew that he was right—but in very truth he was ever doubting his own conduct."[4] Trevelyan's is an artificial, second-order certainty—a certainty *about* the absolute lucidity of certainty: "he knew that he was right," he was *right* that he was right. A subplot of the same novel ends with the deeply conservative Jemima Stanbury realizing, with great regret, the long error of her own tenaciously held certainties: "There was ever present to her mind an idea of failure and a fear lest she had been mistaken in her views throughout her life. . . . [T]here was an idea present to herself that it could not be God's intention that things should really change for the worse, and that the fault must be in her, because she had been unable to move as others had moved."[5] Being *this* certain about what things mean, what the world means, can ruin a life, can lead to mad delusion, can distract us from confronting our own faults, our own errors, our neuroses; it is a certainty experienced as a desperate holding together of the self, or a holding of one's own ground against movement. Through this certainty, one prevents one's own body from falling to pieces, from breaking apart at the faults within.

The central argument of this chapter is that Trollope is a novelist invested in fantasies of absolute clarity but also, perhaps paradoxically, highly sensitive to the ways in which those fantasies are haunted by the opaque impulses and desires of the body. Trollope makes use of tautology, and engages with the feeling of deep certainty it represents, in order to demonstrate desire's simultaneous clarity and opacity. Just as tautology can seem both formally lucid and pragmatically inscrutable, desire insists upon its claims with perfect directness while also resisting the forms of rational intelligibility that would make it the subject of argument and debate. While this chapter takes Trollope's fiction as its central object, it also takes detours along the way. One of my goals in what follows is to establish tautology's natural promiscuity across periods and genres. Even as we try to take it as an object of some historical specificity or to root it in a reading of Trollope and the novel form, we find that because tautology is so neat and so formulaic, it's easy to repackage in other genres and historical moments. We might understand the formulaic quality intrinsic to tautology not as a shortcoming but rather as an opportunity for comparative thinking, a way of locating surprising resonances in the approach to desire, certainty, and identity across texts, periods, and discourses.

I begin by setting Trollope's theory of novel writing, with its goal of perfectly clear meaning, against a philosophical and theoretical history of approaches to tautology—from Kant to "surface reading"—that take up similar questions about lucidity and the instincts of the body. I then turn to *Can You Forgive Her?* and continue to develop my reading of that novel as resistant to the clarity of tautological certainty, constantly aware of the ease with which the expectation of erotic certainty can license sexual coercion. In an interlude, I consider the ways in which the problems of certainty and essence raised by Trollope migrate elsewhere through the formulaic tautological assertion "I am what I am," from George Meredith's *The Egoist* (1879) to queer and feminist thought in the twentieth century. This interlude allows an opening into what I call *tautologophilia*, the sense that the coerciveness of tautology can be and indeed has been turned to good use as a tactic of queer politics, an insistence that sexual identity is self-evident and beyond debate, not a question of approval or rejection but a question of certainty. Finally, I turn to a reading of *The Way We Live Now* (1875), in which Trollope represents erotic certainty as part of a strategic essentialism by which female characters position erotic impulse outside of the realm of rational debate in just the way that later queer thinkers would draw upon the power of "I am what I am." Tracing Trollope's ambivalence toward tautology (and the legacies of that ambivalence) will help us to pursue several big-picture questions through this chapter that arise when we try to take tautology as object or even as method: How do we use tautology as a way of approaching things, reading things, knowing things, despite its potentially flattening effects? What, after all, is so *bad* about self-evidence and self-identity, the principles that tautology formalizes in language? Our sense of tautology's status as bad logic—as empty, lazy, conservative, and superficial—is a legacy of our disavowal of essence, and we might use the more complex history of tautology as form that I present here in order to advocate for a renewed (even if modified, tempered, provisional) belief in the essentialism of desire.

I Am What I Am

Trollope's famous metaphor comparing the labor of a novelist to that of a shoemaker helps him to defend the workmanlike nature of his writing practice in *An Autobiography*, and it tells us a great deal about Trollope's theory of writing as craft.[6] But it doesn't tell us much about his theory of the novel form: that is, his theory of how a novel, once assembled like a shoe, communicates meaning—something that shoes don't do, especially the sensible kind that Trollope surely has in mind. I've long been fascinated by a different metaphor out of Trollope's *Autobiography*, by which he explains the kind of perfect intelligibility the novelist's art should aim to achieve:

> Any writer who has read even a little will know what is meant by the word intelligible. It is not sufficient that there be a meaning which may be hammered out of the sentence, but that the language should be so pellucid that the meaning should be rendered without an effort to the reader;—and not only some proportion of meaning, but the very sense, no more and no less, which the writer has intended to put into his words. . . . The language used should be as ready and as efficient a conductor of the mind of the writer to the mind of the reader as is the electric spark which passes from one battery to another battery. In all written matter the spark should carry everything.[7]

If the novel is a shoe, then the language of which it is made is electricity, and I and Trollope are two batteries. I plug myself in, and a circuit is formed. Meaning passes into me—the meaning intended, no more and no less—and, in a dimension of this metaphor that Trollope leaves mysterious, we can only assume that I pass that charge back and the circle continues. The language of the novel is decidedly *not* shoelike, not a solid sewn-together thing wrapped around a form and likewise, in the version presented here, not a hunk of stone out of which I hammer a meaningful shape.

This metaphor reveals that Trollope's deeply ambivalent theory of the novel form is a philosophy of language, even if it's elsewhere a philosophy of labor and commodification, and in this section I use this image as a point of access into a history of tautology and its fantasy of total clarity. In the figure of novel as battery, the novelist aims for language that is formally transparent, a mere conductor, the clear fluid through which that electric spark of meaning—*every-thing* in the meaning—is carried. And yet, of course, this is (flagrantly) a fantasy. It's never this easy. The narrator of *Can You Forgive Her?* admits as much in his description of Plantagenet Palliser's philosophy of perfect clarity in his political speechifying, which mirrors the stereotypical image of Trollope's transparent style: "He desired to use words for the purpose of teaching things which he knew and which others did not know; and he desired also to be honoured for his knowledge. But he had no desire to be honoured for the language in which his knowledge was conveyed" (268). Palliser, like Trollope, wants words to be transparent conductors of knowledge, but while the narrator casts Palliser's ideal of lucid speech as noble, it is, more importantly, "very dull" (267). Communication is not the only thing we do with language, and to assume it is would require an image of language that leaves us yawning, wanting more, or at least a language less dull in another sense—more finely honed, able to cut. Ruth apRoberts, however, understands the transparency of Trollope's language as crucial to the forcefulness of his psychological realism: "He *masters complexity*," she argues; "he makes us forget the words while we apprehend effortlessly the most tenuous delicacies of nuance in psychology, or social situations of the most extreme complexity."[8] The same paradox arises in apRoberts's description as in Trollope's own: how can one maintain a sense of solid "meaning" or the granularity of "extreme complexity," while also aiming for an ideal of language as an invisible "conductor" of significance or a vehicle of effortless apprehension? Trollope thinks of language as perfectly clear but also embodied—it is the spark that zaps and buzzes in the flesh even while remaining invisible to the naked eye.

For much of history, tautology was not a logical term but a rhetorical one, designating a kind of stylistic flourish at odds with the lucidity of style that Trollope advocates. In his *Orator's Education*, for example, Quintilian simply defines it as "the repetition of the same word or phrase" for superficial argumentative emphasis.[9] This rhetorical sense of the word has never quite disappeared: Trollope himself names such inelegant repetitions "tautologies" when he considers the sloppiness that can result from rapid writing.[10] But only in the nineteenth century, with Immanuel Kant's *Logic* (1800) and its concept of an analytic truth, did it also begin to take on a specialized sense in which it described a logical proposition that is necessarily true by virtue of its form. As Kant puts it, "Tautological propositions are virtually empty, or void of consequence; for they are of no use whatever. Such is, for instance, the tautological proposition, A man is a man. For if we can say nothing more of a man, than that he is a man, we know nothing more of him at all."[11] Kant gives us everything here that we usually associate with the tautology: circularity, uselessness, an incapacity to expand our knowledge about the actual world. But he also hints at something more in that admission that tautology is only "virtually" rather than literally empty—empty of *content*, perhaps, if not without a significant *form*.

While Kant defines tautology as a relatively vapid kind of proposition, Ludwig Wittgenstein would later argue for a more meaningful role for tautology in the mathematical foundation of logic. We've already seen, in the previous chapter, Wittgenstein's argument that contradiction fills the whole of what he calls "logical space," leaving no opening through which it can connect to reality. Tautology, on the other hand, "leaves open to reality the whole—the infinite whole—of logical space. . . . Tautology and contradiction are the limiting cases—indeed the disintegration—of the combination of signs" (42). If contradictions represent the outer limit of all "logical space" for Wittgenstein, since they are statements that can never follow from any ordinarily meaningful proposition, then "tautology is the unsubstantial point at their center" (48). All logical statements seem to run the risk of falling at any moment into tautology, since in leaving open the whole of "logical space," a tautological proposition allows any other proposition to follow from it logically. "Diamonds are diamonds" (a tautology we will encounter later in this chapter) as a statement about the world doesn't preclude or confirm the truth of any other proposition, and therefore it doesn't shape or narrow our knowledge about the world. No other meaningful sentence that I might use to describe the world could contradict it. Tautology is, in this sense, pure logical form: it fails to communicate anything; it collapses in on itself. And yet, somehow, it means something.

Wittgenstein's metaphor—of tautology as the black hole at the center of the galactic system of propositional logic, with contradiction as the void beyond its outer limit—helps to explain the function of tautology as a formal principle. Tautologies, Kant and Wittgenstein agree, are not meant to generate new knowledge. They tell us what we already know, or perhaps make us feel that we already know it by asserting that it cannot be otherwise than true. The fact that tautologies merely formalize the assertion of a priori truths helps to explain why they might have a powerful function in literary texts, particularly in realist novels, which are themselves formal systems for the representation of a world. But realist representation can never give us the full density and reality of an "actual world," and like tautology itself, we might understand the world of a realist novel as both empty and full (only an illusion, yet a densely populated one), both transparent and solid (something we see as if "through" the material existence of words on a page).[12] Of course, merely generating a tautology cannot actually *make* a truth self-evident, but we do need at least one self-evident truth in order to begin deducing others—an idea most famously proposed by René Descartes. Tautology is the performance of extreme confidence in a truth's self-evidence—I am thinking, therefore I think (therefore I exist)—and so its role in the ethical accounting that fills so many Victorian novels can be tricky. For Descartes, it is *thought* that provides us with the essence of our existence: I am, essentially and self-evidently, a thinking being. For many Victorian writers, it came to seem as if erotic desire was a kind of conviction similarly immune to doubt and that could therefore be exempted from social interrogation or debate. Tautology can trick us by making the actually refutable seem mathematically irrefutable, but it can also persuade us to include new kinds of propositions (such as "my desire is my desire") under the rubric of irrefutable knowledge.

And yet, it seems that this kind of "exemption" of the erotic from social life—its immunity to argument, debate, or accountability—threatens to *kill* desire, and then to embalm it for social display in the dispassionate, still form of the tautology.[13] Tautology is easy to understand, transparent, and accessible, but it is also difficult to parse, obdurate, and opaque. "It is what it is" strikes us as a phrase that is both meaningfully capacious and lazily meaningless: it could represent either resignation to the intractability of the status quo or a defiant attachment to a fact that one considers unquestionable. Barthes has already offered us the key to understanding the attitude of *tautologophobia* as linked to the death of language; he argues that the static circularity of tautology "creates a dead, a motionless world." If language fails to go anywhere, fails to move by the process of logical entailment from one proposition to the next, and instead falls back upon itself, it then appears to represent a world that is similarly arrested, unchanging, and dead. When tautology describes the self—I am what I am—it threatens similarly to impoverish identity, to make it into nothing more than an empty assertion that refers only to itself.

John Henry Newman, however, makes an attempt from within the complex field of Victorian logic to recuperate tautology as method in *An Essay in Aid of a Grammar of Assent* (1870), where he theorizes painstakingly the logical nature of assertions that we believe unconditionally to be true. His theory helps me to explain why I tend to take "tautology" and "certainty" as intimately related problems of bad logic and sometimes use these terms interchangeably or in combination. Where we find absolute certainty, we tend to find a shadow tautology, grounding that certainty and giving it the form of self-evidence. The epistemological problem of certainty is bound to the logical form of tautology not only in theory but in philosophical practice. Newman calls unconditional belief "assent," and for him, this was, as we might expect, a problem of religious faith. How can we describe the conviction of faith while still maintaining a sense that we must at some point be *persuaded* to believe, and that this persuasion is at least partially effected by logical argument? Newman's concept of assent is somewhat different than tautology in that it doesn't aim to describe a formally self-evident truth. Rather, it describes a kind of belief that we *once* held conditionally, contingent upon the truth of an entailed series of premises that would prove our belief as a conclusion, but it is a belief from which that contingency has, as it were, fallen away. Once I feel certain of a truth without condition or contingency, I can be said to assent to it rather than merely to infer it. Newman insists that in order to make a genuine "assertion," as opposed to a mere "argument," I must first assent to the truth that I assert: "An assertion is distinct from a conclusion, as a word of command is from a persuasion or recommendation. Command and assertion, as such, both of them, in their different ways, dispense with, discard, ignore, antecedents of any kind, though antecedents may have been a *sine qua non* of their being elicited. They both carry with them the pretension of being personal acts."[14] How to talk logically about that which is "personal"? This is one central question of Newman's *Grammar of Assent*, and it does away with some of the sheer arrogant obstinacy of tautological self-evidence. Tautology may, in fact, be one among several ways to formalize the affective experience of certainty that Newman associates with assent, even though that certainty may have arisen at some point out of a process of persuasion, education, or (in the terms of faith) conversion. Tautology may be one way, in other words, to assert—to lay claim to a certain truth shorn of its antecedent conditions. The certainty of assent is somewhat different, therefore, from what Andrew Miller has identified as the attitude of "knowingness" that Newman often critiques—the "jaded" attitude by which we communicate "that we know it already, have heard if before" and that "situates us as belated, as if we had somehow outlived ourselves, and were beached on the viewless aftermath of all our experiences."[15] The certainty of assent, while it represents a belief become irreversible, past refutation or debate, is always immediate and intensely alive rather than belated or blasé, a point to which one can return in order to begin again from something solid.

Newman's theory of assent presumes, indeed, that it is the real, the embodied, the concrete, that makes the greatest impact upon us and thus carries the fullest force of persuasion: "What is concrete," he argues, "exerts a force and makes an impression on the mind which nothing abstract can rival" (36). And this leads Newman into a powerful kind of essentialism, grounded in the tautological assertion "I am what I am," that finally links his theory of assent to the power of tautological assertion. Because we must begin somewhere in our practices of reasoning and belief, he argues, we might as well begin with the self, and the self-evident truth of our own subjective constitution: "I am what I am, or I am nothing. I cannot think, reflect, or judge about my being, without starting from the very point which I aim at concluding. My ideas are all assumptions, and I am ever moving in a circle. I cannot avoid being sufficient for myself, for I cannot make myself anything else, and to change me is to destroy me. If I do not use myself, I have no other self to use. My only business is to ascertain what I am, in order to put it to use" (347). In many ways, Newman's argument represents a radical rejection of traditional logic: he is committed to finding a place in logic for the many ways in which each of us is, fundamentally, defined by a set of assumptions, assents, or assertions, on which groundwork we build our rational lives. As Rachel Ablow has pointed out, his model of certainty as something deeply personal allows Oscar Wilde, for example, to draw from his work a powerful connection between the feeling of certitude and the pleasures of "both aesthetic taste and erotic desire." Through this connection certainty is made both private and strangely vicarious, something one absorbs from the object of one's desire.[16] We are certain of much more than the transparent, formal truth that "A is A," and it would be impossible to live as a particular person were we to divest ourselves of those more particular, less clearly axiomatic assumptions. Newman's model can also be understood as positioning the concrete, situated self as a limitation to the kinds of truths available to social intercourse or intelligibility. "Real assent," Newman insists, "is proper to the individual, and, as such, thwarts rather than promotes the intercourse of man with man. It shuts itself up, as it were, in its own home, or at least is its own witness and its own standard; and . . . it cannot be reckoned on, anticipated, accounted for."[17] This is one way to understand assent and its cousin tautology as sources of resistance or as modes of self-exception from the realm of intelligibility, debate, or good logic—and this idea will be important later on when we turn to *The Way We Live Now*. But it's also striking how Newman feminizes and domesticates assent, shut up in its own home, unavailable and invisible, the angel in the house of the mind. This quality of Newman's thinking about certainty, and his desire to claim for it a kind of power even in its profoundly eremitic quality, is perhaps what Thomas Hardy had in mind when he misogynistically dismissed Newman's "feminine nature, which first decides, & then finds reasons for having decided. He was an enthusiast with the absurd reputation of a logician and reasoner."[18] But as Gauri Viswanathan has argued, Newman's theory of assent, in its way of making belief so radically private, is also an epistemological and even political theory of "dissent," a mode of belief made available only by a "direct, unmediated relation to experience, . . . detached from an enclosed interpretive community that commands assent."[19] Precisely that which makes these forms of conviction limited in their social efficacy, in other words—their muteness, their unaccountability, their unpredictability—also makes them particularly powerful ways of "dropping out."

Wittgenstein makes a brief, indeterminate reference to Newman's *Grammar of Assent* in opening his *On Certainty*, an unfinished set of working notes published posthumously in 1969 ("On this a curious remark by H. Newman"), and his own meditation upon the problem of certainty and its relation to logical persuasion intensifies Newman's idea that our own embodiment constitutes a privileged ground of certainty.[20] My certainty that I have a body, that these are my hands, are Wittgenstein's constant touchstones in arguing that much of our ability to live, to make way in the world, to participate in life with others, rests upon our willingness to take an enormous number of truths for granted. These certain, undoubted bits of knowledge are for Wittgenstein "the axis around which a body rotates" or stable "hinges" on which other propositions turn (22, 44). Without them, we could do nothing, and yet Wittgenstein's urgency in wanting to get to the root of certainty—how it works, why we need it—comes from his sense that we could always imagine the world otherwise, that our certainties may be as fragile as Louis Trevelyan's mad, doubt-plagued jealousy, or Jemima Stanbury's antisocial obstinacy. What is certain for me, for anyone, is in fact contingent, accidental, a feature of my own human, animal existence. As Wittgenstein puts it, "I would like to regard this certainty, not as something akin to hastiness or superficiality"—the superficiality, perhaps, of the mere tautology—"but as a form of life. . . . But that means I want to conceive of it as something that lies beyond being justified or unjustified; as it were, something animal" (46–47). Certainty is the ground upon which one's life is built—its very form, its animal instinct, impervious to questioning or to persuasion—just as tautology is the very form of logical truth. But at the same time, we must come to some social consensus about the kinds of things one can be certain about in this way, about which truths we can hold to be self-evident. There is a social force to certainty, especially when the object of one's certainty is an unfamiliar or dubious idea to others. Wittgenstein, for example, tries at one point to formulate a satisfactory response to the hypothetical person who would assert, with certainty, that the earth did not exist before he was born. He might question this person, he says, "in order to find out which of my convictions he was at odds with. And then it *might* be that he was contradicting my fundamental attitudes, and if that were how it was, I should have to put up with it" (32). Wittgenstein arrives here at a model of mutual trust, "putting up" with the other whose certainty may be mistaken. Just as certainty forms my own life, makes it possible to be and to do in the world, trust in another's certainty forms a social life in which we frequently reevaluate what we are allowed to—even required to—take for granted: "What practical consequence has it if I give a piece of information and add that I can't be making a mistake about it? The other person might doubt my statement nonetheless. But if he trusts me he will not only accept my information, he will also draw definite conclusions from my conviction, as to how I shall behave" (88). Perhaps we can never make ourselves fully transparent to one another, Wittgenstein suggests, can never make visible to others the logical deduction that underlies our most deeply held convictions (because perhaps such deductions do not even take place in these cases), but we can nevertheless make our certainty understood, choose to trust the certainty of others, or merely to "put up" with those certainties we persist in thinking must be misguided. In Wittgenstein's terms, "adding something special to what is generally laid down"—putting forward some new kind of knowledge that we should all feel certain about, that we must all trust others' certainty about—is a powerful social action, and so even in something as opaque as assent, "there is something universal . . . not just something personal" (88, 57).

In many literary theorists' recent turn away from the hermeneutics of suspicion and toward a hermeneutics of the textual surface, we might detect a legacy of these philosophical considerations of certainty as method—as a way of approaching the world, other people, and texts in search of their meanings and truths. One theoretical aim of this chapter, in other words, is to pose the taking-seriously of tautology as a particularly powerful test case for the methodologies currently gaining traction under the name of "postcritique," "surface reading," the "descriptive turn," or the "new modesty."[21] Stephen Best and Sharon Marcus have argued for surface reading as an alternative to the methods of "symptomatic reading," which as we saw in chapter one are often based upon an interest in the discovery and resolution of contradiction rather than in the smooth and superficial form of tautology. As Best and Marcus point out, symptomatic reading was (and is) appealing because it understands literary criticism as a kind of political activism, and the forceful extraction of the "hidden" meanings of a text as a powerful practice of critique.[22] One potential argument for surface reading, however, is that the surface meanings of the text might themselves represent "an affective and ethical stance"; in other words, this "embrace" of superficiality—allowing ourselves to be *certain* of what texts say, if even as a provisional position—means "accepting texts, deferring to them instead of mastering or using them as objects, and refuses the depth model of truth, which dismisses surfaces as inessential and deceptive."[23] My reading of literary tautology extends this concept to its potential limit. Tautologies, so the conventional wisdom goes, are superficial and logically meaningless—logically meaningless *because* superficial. In a particularly compact way, they seem to present us with the apotheosis of surface meaning—we cannot even try to look to the "depth model," it would seem, because there is no linguistic depth there to be plumbed. My reading allows us to see the way in which texts can simultaneously represent ideology *and* its critique, perhaps even in the same kind of language. We simply need to notice the rich meaningfulness of the kinds of language we usually dismiss as hopelessly dumb.

Perhaps surprisingly, it's Roland Barthes, that most vocal critic of tautology, whose theory of descriptive criticism in *S/Z* (1970) is such an important point of reference for many advocates of surface reading. And this seeming inconsistency, of Barthes's being committed to "superficial" practices of description and taxonomy while also railing against the anti-intellectualism of the superficial form of tautology, exposes a kind of anxiety at the heart of surface reading. If we're simply describing what's already there in front of us, rewording it or repeating it or insisting upon the clear givenness of its meaning, but not rearranging or altering or indeed deconstructing it, are we doing anything more than insisting that "it is what it is"? The labor of detailed and inventive description might be important, and Barthes would likely want to insist that his carefully formulated system of literary description of Balzac's *Sarrasine* goes far beyond the thoughtless, fundamentally useless assertion that Balzac is Balzac. (I would say this is a fair distinction.) Nevertheless, there's something to the association of surface reading and tautological argumentation. As Cannon Schmitt has pointed out, many surface readings aim for a tautological obviousness, or an insistence that the text simply represents what it represents, but they also insist that "the value and necessity of seeing what lies in plain sight is given force by the assertion that what lies in plain sight has been overlooked or cannot easily be seen—has been obscured by habits of mind fostered by a certain critical approach and cannot be perceived without the aid of another, countervailing approach."[24] Tautology acts as a bad double for practices of descriptive reading—an image of what those practices would look like without the rigor and sensitivity that description and observation can still employ—and a double that the advocates of such methodologies, Barthes foremost among them, may be eager to disavow. But Schmitt also reminds us that tautology might sometimes be just what we need when our instinct is to distrust the surface and its certainties and burrow immediately to the depths. Against Barthes's suspicion that tautology can only be dead, anti-intellectual, and antisocial, I argue that it might represent a desire to reorient language and its potential social uses, to return to a zero point at which the establishment of apodictic truths is still an open question.

A deeper theoretical and methodological problem is at work, too, when we attempt to fall in love with the badness of tautology, to take it on as a model for the assertion of erotic truth rather than dismissing it as a tool of sexual and psychological coercion: the seeming anti-narrativity of tautology, its refusal to go anywhere, or its habit of ending precisely where it begins. In its model of the ongoing "work" of analysis through the process of the talking cure, for example, psychoanalysis empowers narrative as a tool for untangling the stubbornest knots of desire (compulsion, repetition, melancholia), while also to some extent emphasizing the way in which desire makes one partially opaque to oneself, and the related fact that the moralized labor of the psychoanalytic cure never ends. Indeed, for our classic psychoanalytic theories of the novel from René Girard to Peter Brooks to Eve Kosofsky Sedgwick, psychoanalysis is invested in both narrative circularity and narrative closure. On this account, the quest to make sense of one's libidinal cathexes is endless, except insofar as the movement toward closure actually mirrors the compulsion toward inanimacy represented by the death drive. Moreover, formal structures such as narrative, character, or *bildung* align with the formalized, law-bound energy of desire or libido as opposed to the messy, unnarratable energy of the drive. And yet narrative only ends, at least according to Brooks, because of our irrepressible and unaccountable desire to return to the beginning, to escape the repetitive oscillations of plot and to return to stasis—in short, to close the circle. As he puts it, "If the motor of narrative is desire, totalizing, building ever-larger units of meaning, the ultimate determinants of meaning lie *at the end*, and narrative desire is ultimately, *inexorably*, desire *for* the end."[25] Brooks's conception of plotting relies on the seemingly uncontroversial assumption that we want to reach the end of a narrative in order to know what it all means, and before him Girard described the same apparent yearning in even more moralistic terms that use logic as a rubric: "All types of structural thinking assume that human reality is intelligible; it is a *logos* and, as such, it is an incipient *logic*, or degrades itself into a logic. It can thus be systematized, at least up to a point, however unsystematic, irrational, and chaotic it may appear even to those, or rather especially to those who operate the system."[26] Both Girard and Brooks translate psychoanalytic concepts (particularly the concept of desire) into the vocabulary of structuralism in order to mobilize desire as a mechanism of narrative form. Both of these theories of the novel take desire as a structuring energy that can aid in the process by which narrative totalizes, systematizes, and orders meanings. And this is, in some sense, a reasonable use of psychoanalytic theory, which as I have suggested invests similar effort in the formalization of what is most chaotic in each of us.

The bad logic of tautology may in this sense represent a kernel of unintelligibility in the midst of a structuring system (the realist novel) that often values the systematization and totalization of meaning above all. Strangely, the circular form of tautology, in all its opacity, might insist that the narrative cannot come full circle, that some iota of truth will always remain unassimilated, opaque, and dumbly insistent. It's precisely this problem that seems to haunt Brooks: novels must complete the circuit in order to come to clarity and closure, but at the same time this clarity kills the desire that motivated our reading in the first place. Judith Butler has attempted one corrective to this paradox by insisting that the limitations of self-knowledge (for her built into the terms of psychoanalytic theory) could actually ground a revised version of moral accountability rather than leading us on a never-ending search after clarity. As Butler puts it, in language that explicitly registers our love-hate relationship with tautology, "Suspending the demand for self-identity or, more particularly, for complete coherence seems to me to counter a certain ethical violence, which demands that we manifest and maintain self-identity at all times and require that others do the same."[27] Butler names the kind of "ethical violence" that Trollope sometimes associates with the bad logic of tautology: its painfully coercive demand for consistency of oneself with oneself at all costs, its transformation of desire into an unbreakable promise. This turn against ethical violence represents a simultaneous turn against narrative closure or revelation: "By not pursuing satisfaction," Butler insists, "and by letting the question remain open, even enduring, we let the other live, since life might be understood as precisely that which exceeds any account we may try to give of it." Like Barthes, Butler argues that the tautology of self-identity represents a death, or at least a movement towards deathlike stasis. It is a restrictive and strangling refusal to "let the other live."

Tautologophobia and *Can You Forgive Her?*

The claims of erotic certainty, then, can be opaque, suspicious, and constraining because tautological, but also easy because tautological, as long as one is willing to accept their circular terms. The circuitous pursuit of "forgiveness" in *Can You Forgive Her?* (our forgiveness, the narrator's, John Grey's), always oriented toward "her," the potential object of redemption (whether the inconsistent Alice or the too-consistent Jeannette), helps us to see what is at stake, then, in the triangulated relationship between tautology, sexuality, and moral accountability. Taking desire as certain, essential, undoubtable, allows us an easy rebuke to those who would moralize it, who would take its sudden swerves and deep-felt pulls and repulsions as objects of guilt or absolution. But it also reduces our capacity to narrate desire, to talk about it, or to understand it as open-ended. As apRoberts might say, tautology masters complexity—but it's unclear whether we want the complexity of desire to be overpowered in this way. John Grey, for example, is described again and again by the novel's narrator and characters as mesmerizingly good-looking, but the easiness of his appeal is always coupled with the reality of Alice's potential to lose herself in marriage to him. With the acceptance of his desirability comes the end of Alice's complexity, her vacillation, and therefore her story.[28] While George offers her a vicarious political life, Grey offers her—what? Lady Macleod, one of Alice's many advisors, seizes upon the strangely repellent aspect of Grey's literally stunning good looks: "She was overawed by him after the first three minutes. Indeed her first glance at him had awed her. He was so handsome,—and then, in his beauty, he had so quiet and almost saddened an air! Strange to say that after she had seen him, Lady Macleod entertained for him an infinitely higher admiration than before, and yet she was less surprised than she had been at Alice's refusal of him" (186). Lady Macleod is unable to identify the quality that makes her simultaneously attracted to Grey and indifferent to him, but in the scene that follows, Alice seems to decipher the problem as she stares into his face, "serene in all its manly beauty" (188). Unlike George, who "if he were moved to strong feeling, showed it at once in his eyes,—in his mouth, in the whole visage of his countenance," Grey "when speaking of the happiness of his entire life, . . . had no more sign of passion in his face than if he were telling his gardener to move a rose tree" (188). Grey's beauty is easy to comprehend, "awe" inspiring, "serene," and "quiet," but it is boring—it's not enough. His attractiveness simply *is*, but this self-evidence—this absolute easiness—also offers grounds for suspicion. Isn't there more to desire than there is to gardening? Indeed, Alice later connects the forcefulness of Grey's appeal to his placid occupation of the kind of self-identity we've already analyzed elsewhere (a self-identity formalized by tautology) as opposed to her own profound inconsistency. She says of him that "no possible position in life would put him beside himself" (655), whereas at the height of her indecision she sees herself as a split personality, both object and subject, both a fiction and its reader: "She sat there, thinking of her fate, as though it belonged to some other one,—not to herself; as though it were a tale that she had read" (396). The textual metaphor makes it clear that Alice's self-analysis is partly about a confrontation with narrative itself: what do we gain and lose by keeping the story of desire going rather than opting for the neat closure of erotic certainty?

Tautology poses a danger, then, when it is understood as the apotheosis of lucidity: it can function as a form of deceit by which elusive erotic feelings are made to seem suspiciously straightforward. Yet as reasonable as this position might be, Alice, who wishes to attend to the vicissitudes of erotic feeling rather than trust it as self-evident, has often been made into an object of strangely intense derision. In Robert Polhemus's aggressive evaluation, she is "tedious," "a hard-hearted, boring prude," and a "self-righteous, conscientious, passive, sexless 'good girl.' "[29] And as one anonymous early reviewer of *Can You Forgive Her?* put it in a formulation that empties out Alice's development as a protagonist with a flip tautology: "Alice wins our forgiveness because she is Alice."[30] Tautology requires a relaxed acceptance that its meaning is simply given as a smooth surface, with no depths to plumb—as opposed to George Vavasor's (and indeed Alice's) sense that difficulty and complexity are the qualities that characterize the truest, realest meanings. As George puts it, "In this world things are beautiful only because they are not quite seen, or not perfectly understood" (79). Tautology, on the other hand, is easy to understand. And so tautology causes Alice—who wants to "make herself useful," to "gratify her ambition," for the purposes of which erotic attraction seems utterly "vain and futile" (50)—to feel as if she is committing an act of submission in capitulating to her desire for John Grey. Grey believes that his task is to turn this feeling toward an acceptance of easiness, and Alice does begin to come around to Grey's way of seeing things almost immediately after accepting George's proposal, a decision that finalizes the split between Alice's material, desiring self and the abstract, contractual self represented by her money.[31] When she offers George her money but not her passion, she puts it succinctly: "my money shall be less cross-grained than myself" (355). Money has no texture, but Alice's self does, and a rough one at that. We then get Alice's expression of repentance: "Her acceptance of her cousin's offer had not come of love;—nor had it, in truth, come chiefly of ambition. She had not so much asked herself why she should do this thing, as why she should not do it" (373). *Why not?* is not a tautology. It is, however, a form of double negative—"there is no reason not to do this"—which bears some of the same features as tautology. It threatens to make a lack of evidence against a particular claim equivalent to positive evidence in support of the opposite claim. Rather than being a closed circle, then, the double negative endlessly refers away from itself, proving its opposite by its own irrational mathematics. The threat of the double negative is the threat of losing one's self.[32]

It's important to note that the novel frames Alice's choice as binary (there are two suitors here but no more) and that both choices represent to her different versions of a loss of self, so that in this case neither erotic attraction nor political opportunity seem to offer any real possibility of self-affirmation or development, let alone fulfillment. This feature of the novel might explain its phobic response to tautology and the erotic certainty it represents. Both of Alice's choices threaten to smooth her "cross-grained" texture or to empty her out. As Claire Jarvis has pointed out, we can only imagine what this novel would look like if Trollope wasn't obligated to represent erotic choice as so terribly singular and final that it appears to be a "foregone conclusion."[33] Alice and her cousin Kate both describe, for example, the ways in which marriage to Grey would represent a kind of living death. In a letter to Grey, Alice laments that while his life can continue normally after marriage, in the same house and with the same day-to-day pursuits, for her it would be "as though I were passing through the grave to a new world" (136). Kate, advocating on behalf of her brother George, amplifies Alice's concern when she compares a marriage to Grey to death and imprisonment: "You would have been as much lost to me, had you become Mrs Grey of Nethercoats, Cambridgeshire, as though you had gone to heaven. . . . But such an Eden is not tempting to me, nor, as I think, to you. I can fancy you stretching your poor neck over the dyke, longing to fly away that you might cease to be at rest, but knowing the matrimonial dragon was too strong for any such flight. If ever bird banged his wings to pieces against gilded bars, you would have banged yours to pieces in that cage" (167). The equation between absolute pleasure—this is heaven, or even Eden—and life-denying imprisonment becomes crystallized in Kate's pile-up of metaphors. Grey's desirability is easy and undeniable, but marriage, and the finality of desire it represents, cannot help but squelch personhood and restrict movement. Even erotic life cannot be all, especially when it becomes subsumed and irrevocably contained by marriage. All of this reaches its sad culmination in Alice's perfunctory reappearance in a party scene in *Phineas Finn* (1867–68), the subsequent novel of the Palliser series. Grey is listed among the Members of Parliament and other political power players in attendance, and then we get a passing afterthought: "Mr Grey had also brought his wife" (342). Alice's indecision as to her object choice allows her a voice and a narrative role as the protagonist of a long and complex novel, but after her choice is made and the marriage finalized, she all but disappears from the ongoing plot of the Palliser novels.

Forgiveness in this novel is often, as Sharon Marcus argues, "violently coercive," and the reconciliation of Alice and Grey is no exception.[34] The reinstatement of certainty means forcing Alice to reinhabit a body whose impulses she has been unwilling to trust as self-evident, and Grey's physical and argumentative coercion mimics the violent intimidation that is George Vavasor's favored mode of persuasion. Importantly, John Grey softens the aggression of his demands by cloaking them in political and ethical language. "I have a right," he declares, "to demand your hand. My happiness requires it, and I have a right to expect your compliance. I do demand it. If you love me, Alice, I tell you that you dare not refuse me. If you do so, you will fail hereafter to reconcile it to your conscience before God" (771). Here we discover the important caveat of John Grey's trust in tautological self-evidence, lest we begin to think that his primary goal is the empowerment of women's erotic desire. Grey uses bad logic *as though* it were an irrefutable form of logical argumentation; he dissimulates by transforming the difficult problem of erotic attraction into the sharpness of the ideologically laden imperative. Louis Althusser's influential account of ideology, for example, emphasizes its relationship to the "primary 'obviousness'" of the idea that "you and I are subjects (free, ethical, etc. . . .)." On an unreflective account, obviousness might appear uncomplicated and uncontroversial, but Althusser argues that ideology feeds upon the tautological force of the obvious: it "imposes (without appearing to do so, since these are 'obviousnesses') obviousnesses as obviousnesses, which we cannot *fail to recognize* and before which we have the inevitable and natural reaction of crying out (aloud, or in the 'still, small voice of conscience'): 'That's obvious! That's right! That's true!' "[35] Far from being seamless and easily assimilable, obviousness—and even the embodied, certain, insistent obviousness of erotic desire—can be a particularly dense manifestation of ideological coercion.

In the scene that follows Grey's ethically charged set of demands, Grey makes the jump from argumentative trickery to physical aggression, and the sheer rapidity of this leap reminds us that in Trollope's fiction, tautology has a close connection to the language of embodiment, a language of surfaces, opacity, and sheer force. The connection is made explicit in the description of Grey's physical intimidation of Alice: "She shrank from him, back against the stonework of the embrasure, but she could not shrink away from his grasp. She put up her hand to impede his, but his hand, like his character and his words, was full of power. It would not be impeded" (772). For Grey, irrefutability is a weapon, a hand with a mind of its own that cannot be held at bay, and Alice's submission to irrefutability comes to seem more like imprisonment than liberation. Grey's final words raise the stakes: "the battle is over now, and I have won it." When Alice responds, "You win everything—always," the narrator tells us that "she still shrank from his embrace" (772). Tautological certainty, or obviousness, can disguise itself among the rationalistic language of rights, ethics, and religious duty in order to distract from the spuriousness of its own irrefutability. Indeed, Marcus suggests that the coerciveness of forgiveness in the novel is made all the more effective by the dissimulation of that coercion. The interrogative of Trollope's "hectoring title," she argues, "encapsulates the novel's recoding of force as ethics, commands as questions: not 'you must forgive her,' but 'can you forgive her?' "[36] Marcus's observation helps us to see how the power of tautology might be wielded in a different way and to different ends: what if tautology were not "recoded" and were instead embraced in all its aggressive opacity and antisociality? Later on, I suggest some answers to this question as they are elaborated upon by Trollope in *The Way We Live Now* (1875), returning to the power of embodied tautological certainty that we encountered in Newman, Wittgenstein, and Trollope's theory of novelistic clarity. But even in the final chapters of *Can You Forgive Her?*, as Alice Vavasor's plot draws to a pained resolution, Trollope continues to remind us that while tautology can be easy and penetrable, it can also be as hard as a diamond.

Can You Forgive Her? ends on a mixed note. We conclude with Alice having accepted the easiness of her love for Grey and with their engagement finally settled. But even once the marriage is decided, we and Alice are left with an uncomfortable feeling. The importance of tautology is reemphasized in the title of one of the final chapters, "Diamonds are Diamonds," and the chapter itself reemphasizes the mixed possibilities of tautology. Lady Midlothian, a wealthy relation of Alice's who has advocated for her marriage to Grey, finally reconciles with her by giving her a gift of diamonds. Alice, still resentful of Lady Midlothian's meddling, declares, "I don't care for diamonds," and explains that in comparison to all the other jewels she has received, "to me they are just as good as the others." Alice's friend Lady Glencora responds with a pair of tautologies: "Diamonds are diamonds, and garnets are garnets; and I am not so romantic but that I know the difference" (824–25). To the end, Alice resists the possibility that anything can be this simple, this glaringly manifest, and clings to the "romantic," to George Vavasor's insistence that the least intelligible states of mind are the most beautiful. Glencora's pithy demonstration of the pellucidity of tautology, however, has the unintended effect of shuttling aside the powerful symbolism of the diamonds. Glencora herself complains earlier in the novel that her choices in romance were constrained because she was "terribly weighted with her wealth" (254). Lady Midlothian, Alice's nemesis, has won the day and is weighing Alice down with jewels in much the same way. The gift attempts to concretize the finality of Alice's marital decision and to prevent the continued wavering of her desire. We can't help but think of Jane Eyre's famous rejection of Rochester's gift of jewels: "Jewels for Jane Eyre sounds unnatural and strange: I would rather not have them," a formulation in which the preposition "for" doubles as a sign of substitution: jewels threaten to take the place of Jane Eyre (311). In a similar way, diamonds, presented here as the example par excellence of the close connection between tautology and hardness, threaten to make Alice vanish altogether because they come at her as an attack from without.[37]

I Wish I Were Able to Tell What I Am

George Meredith's novel *The Egoist* revolves around the badness of that tautological cliché, "I am what I am," and I turn to it now to serve as an object of comparison, with the idea that reading Meredith with and against Trollope helps us toward a clearer understanding of the questions about tautology and desire that they share, and also the ways in which they diverge. Both *The Egoist* and Trollope's *Can You Forgive Her?* consider the dark side of tautology as the form of erotic certainty, and both oppose it to the narrative energy of erotic indecision, and yet they pursue this problem in different ways. Meredith connects tautology to the impossible expectation of erotic consistency, summed up in the tautological idea that a promise is a promise, and Trollope links tautology to a suspicious easiness that flattens desire's nuances and stills its vacillating movements. *The Egoist* tells the story of Clara Middleton, who is pressured by those around her into accepting the marriage proposal of Sir Willoughby Patterne, whose very name indicates his attachment to formulaic thinking, and spends much of the novel trying to find a way out of the terrifying bind of her promise. At one point, Willoughby defends himself against Clara's accusation that he is overly prideful by way of our all-purpose tautology of personal identity. "I am what I am," he says: "It might be demonstrated to you mathematically that [my pridefulness] is corrected by equivalents or substitutions in my character. If it be a failing—assuming that."[38] For Willoughby, "I am what I am" is far from a neutral assertion of something essential about his identity; instead, he leaps from the grammatical symmetry of tautology to a morally charged image of an arithmetically precise balance of character, in which "I am (prideful)" can be cancelled out by "I am (some quality that is as good as pridefulness is bad)."

Later on, even as Clara seeks a mechanism by which to escape the engagement, she seems to have internalized Willoughby's coercive bad logic. Trying to resign herself to a future she can't change, she looks for comfort in tautology: "She had accepted Willoughby, therefore she accepted him. The fact became a matter of the past, past debating" (242). Tautology takes on its mummifying function here, turning the temporally extended act of promising (an open-ended ethical concept, which would allow that some promises might reasonably be broken when circumstances or indeed minds change) into a buried corpse, dead and past and out of reach. Meredith's novel could not be clearer: tautology is bad precisely because of the insidiousness of its irrefutability, because of its egotistical essentialism of identity and its concomitant moral absolutism. Willoughby disguises his aggression in the form of that classic moralistic truism: a promise is a promise. It's easy to see how the most apt response to such intimidation might be another tautologically inflected plea: no means no. Indeed, if Clara becomes trapped in the bind of the promise, unable to find a way out of its demands for consistency, Alice Vavasor is stuck in a different way by the time we meet her, caught between a broken promise and a new one that contradicts it, already made to seem inconsistent and trying to find her way back to the kind of erotic truth that might signal which promise is the right one.

Clara's increasing desperation to be released from her engagement leads Willoughby to adopt an increasingly obstinate, and increasingly tautological, moral code. "Plighted faith," he insists, "signifies plighted faith, as much as an iron cable to hold by. . . . Bride is bride, and wife is wife, and *affianced* is, in honour, *wedded*" (195, original emphasis). This is, of course, the really bad version of bad logic. The subsidiary clause, "in honour," is deemphasized into invisibility, and again, the temporal extension of the promise, which may or may not eventually be kept, is collapsed so that the promise and the fulfillment of that promise become a single, irreversible act. Clara thinks of herself, rightly, as "a person entrapped. In a dream somehow she had committed herself to a life-long imprisonment" (145), echoing Kate Vavasor's image of the ironclad finality of marriage, which allows no movement. Clara can't escape the conviction that it was some other "she," remembered as a dream-self, who thought she loved and made a promise based on that mistake, or that aberration of desire. As the novel proceeds and Clara is asked again and again for "reasons" for her change of heart, she internalizes the imperative of perfect consistency: "She had heard women abused for shallowness and flightiness: she had heard her father renounce them as veering weather-vanes . . . : for her sex's sake, and also to appear an exception to her sex, this reasoning creature desired to be thought consistent" (220). Clara's moral imperatives pull in opposite directions: to be exemplary, yet also exceptional; to be perfectly singular, yet also a perfect general proof. The kind of "consistency" that is asked of Clara (and of women in general in this novel) comes to function as the corollary to Willoughby's bad and coercive uses of tautological conviction. In other words, it requires an unwavering commitment to one's past acts and assertions (I desire you, I want to marry you) that denies the changeability of erotic life. Consistency also presupposes a transparent self-knowledge rather than an acknowledgment that "what I am" may be partially beyond my capacity for meaningful description or prediction. In attempting to account for her indifference toward Willoughby, Clara powerfully disrupts and expands his earlier tautology of self-identity: "I am . . . I wish I were able to tell what I am. I may be inconstant: I do not know myself" (105, ellipsis in original). Slightly later in the novel we get another similarly stuttering attempt at self-definition: Clara begins, "I am a . . . ," before the narrator jumps in, explaining, "But she could not follow his example: even as far as she had gone, her prim little sketch of herself, set beside her real, ugly, earnest feelings, rang of a mincing simplicity, and was a step in falseness. How could she display what she was?" (114, ellipsis in original). Merely to assert that "I am what I am" is for Clara to fall into a "mincing simplicity" that reminds us of Alice Vavasor's guilt at her "girlish facility" in desire, to *seem* to communicate something without actually communicating anything meaningful. This "prim little sketch" only softens or covers over the real, ugly, earnest feelings that complicate any assertion of perfect self-identity.

For Clara, "I am what I am" describes anyone, but no one *really*. And so Clara replaces the bad, closed logic of tautology with an open-ended yearning for certainty: I wish I were able to tell what I am—a worthy goal that one must continually pursue, one that requires intellectual labor, self-questioning, and experience.[39] We hear an echo in the phrase of Newman's way of reckoning with the same difficulty: although I can feel certain that I am what I am and that the self-evident form of this assertion is a secure place from which to begin, the open-ended task remains to fill that empty form with real content, "to ascertain what I am, in order to put it to use." Vernon Whitford, Willoughby's friend and Clara's trusted confidante, argues that Clara is indeed beholden to her promise, since she made it freely, but allows that breaking it might nevertheless be the right thing to do, so long as she can account for that break. He sees the very painful work of pursuing self-knowledge, of learning "what I am," as penitential: "He proposed to help her with advice only. She was to do everything for herself, do and dare everything, decide upon everything. He told her flatly that so would she learn to know her own mind; and flatly that it was her penance. . . . He talked of patience, of self-examination and patience. But all of her—she was all marked *urgent*. This house was a cage, and the world—her brain was a cage, until she could obtain her prospect of freedom. As for the house, she might leave it; yonder was the dawn" (245). The kind of certainty formalized by tautology may not always be as stable as it seems, especially as a strategy for demanding that others assent to one's conviction, and Clara finds in this instability an exit strategy, a way to reconcile the breaking of a promise. But at the same time, this kind of instability can also be understood as a real problem when we want to argue for the self-evidence of sexuality, and we often rely on the force of tautological certainty in order to do so. While erotic certainty or consistency is a trap for Alice Vavasor and Clara Middleton, it is also a necessary resource when we want to refute the idea that sexuality is a matter of debate. Even when I confidently declare that I am what I am, intending to foreclose any possible argument about the matter of my sexuality, I may nevertheless be met with a disagreement that can leave me reeling—a situation of contrasting certainties to which Wittgenstein might respond, "just put up with it."

Annamarie Jagose makes a similar point about the potential instability of erotic certainty when it becomes a tactic of queer visibility in her reading of the crypto- or proto-lesbian Miss Wade, of Dickens's *Little Dorrit* (1855–57) and her problematic place in the history of "female perversity" and in Jagose's own personal history. Jagose argues that if "the indirect raising of the suspicion of homosexuality," which she identifies as the strategy the novel's characters adopt in relation to Miss Wade's sexuality, "might be a more effective means of promulgating that 'knowledge' than an unambiguous nomination, it follows that 'coming out'—the direct self-assertion of one's homosexuality—might not always be as straightforward in effect as in intention." Jagose goes on to relate the story of a friend who, upon coming out to her family in no uncertain terms ("I'm a lesbian"), was met with the bald rebuke, "No, you're not." This kind of denial, Jagose suggests, is based upon the family's sense that the declaration of coming out is "a permission they could refuse, an argument they could win."[40] The power of tautological predication—I am what I am—is perhaps illusory if it can be met with a simple negation, based upon the unreliability or untrustworthiness of sexual self-understanding: you're not really what you claim to be, or you *think* you are what you're really not.

Long after Meredith and Wilde, "I Am What I Am" would become the tautological title of the paean to coming out performed by the drag queen Albin in Jerry Herman and Harvey Fierstein's 1983 musical adaptation of *La Cage Aux Folles*, a song that quickly transcended its specific plot to become an anthem of gay pride festivals. Its strategies (perhaps surprisingly) echo some of the problems that Meredith pursues in his yoking together of tautology and essentialism, and also resonate with Jagose's reading of the potentially unstraightforward act of coming out. But as we've already seen in the introduction how Oscar Wilde's Dorian Gray draws upon the self-evidence of "I am what I am" to put an end to his friend Basil Hallward's desire to debate the morality of queer sexuality and the pleasures of hedonism, perhaps the connection shouldn't be so surprising or so difficult to draw, as "I am what I am" transforms over the course of a century from the stupid egoism of Willoughby to the defensive silencing of Dorian to the vivacious (if still defensive) pride of Albin. I make the leap here from 1879 to 1983 in order to demonstrate how different the coerciveness of "I am what I am" can look depending on the position from which it is spoken, and the strategy that it serves, even as these different strategic uses of erotic certainty draw upon the same problems of essence and self-construction. The delicate balancing of essence and construction, for example, structures the opening lines of the Herman and Fierstein musical, sung by a chorus of drag queens: "We are what we are, and what we are is an illusion," later echoed in Albin's "I am what I am—I am my own special creation."[41] If we accept that various aspects of erotic life—object choice, gender position, the relationship of sexuality to marriage—are moralized or at least morally inflected, both in Victorian culture and in ours, then we have to wonder what form a language of sexual accountability would take, one that might balance the essentialist attitude that grounds a statement like "I am what I am" and the constructionist detachment that can then elaborate, "and what I am is an illusion." Long before the post-Stonewall coming-out story of *La Cage*, in 1921, Edith Ellis wrote in defense of the self-evidence of queer desire and queer identity, " 'I am what I am' should be the true invert's motto; but, added to this, he should say, 'And I refuse to pretend to be what I am not.' "[42] What is at stake, then, in these two different deployments of the all-purpose tautology "I am what I am" as an anchor for queer politics, and for the argumentation that seems to be necessary to each moment of coming out?

Ellis and Herman insist upon both the power and the vulnerability of the circular assertion. In Ellis's case, it is vulnerable to a simple rejoinder, of much the same kind Jagose identifies: you may be what you are, but you mustn't necessarily perform what you are in public. "I am what I am" isn't quite enough, Ellis points out, unless we also make clear that "what I am" must also shape my public life, not only my interiority. In Herman's version, the defense mechanism is built into the ironic wit of drag performance and actually pursues a strategy precisely opposed to Ellis's imaginary argument. Albin and his chorus blur the real and the pretend, insisting upon queerness as an undeniable essence in the same breath that they reveal identity as a matter of creativity and illusion. D. A. Miller, for example, reads *La Cage* as shaped by the context of a gay culture coming to terms with the shattering of its closets. He suggests that the strangeness of the musical's opening line lies in its attempt to combine, in a single turn of phrase, the liberating disclosure of coming out with a nostalgic image of the secrecy of the closet: "To perceive the closet was always also to perceive the multitude of conditions under which closeting was possible. . . . No doubt we like *La Cage* and its meager progeny even less for obliging us to admit, to our confusion, how keenly we miss this sublime vision, though it may have been the only truth that the closet's mendacity ever told."[43] Miller insists, tautologophobically, that the structure of the closet allows, paradoxically, for a freedom of desire and a promiscuity in its signification that is lost once one buys into the singularity and the social legibility expressed by a coming-out declaration that takes the form of "I am what I am." The punctual act of disclosure—which seems to be inherently tautological—constructs a singular, self-centered kind of desire and therefore has the perhaps deleterious effect of foreclosing desire's imaginative promiscuity and multiplicity.

Miller worries that the tautological argument that "I am what I am" may rest upon an essentialism of personal identity that can be tragically narrow, and Ellis and Jagose worry that tautological argument is vulnerable to rejection and less efficacious than we might believe, especially when it comes to making declarations about something as private and opaque as sexual identity. Without its constructionist supplement—the awareness that despite the irrefutability of my identity, that identity is also to some extent fantasmatic and malleable—they suggest that the tautological argument becomes overreaching. "I am what I am" shades into "it is what it is," and soon into a generalized attitude of willful attachment to the status quo. Indeed, essentialism, like tautology, has often been understood as inherently conservative in just this way, especially in the debates over essentialism that arose alongside the development of academic feminist and queer theory through the 1970s and 1980s. But in her now classic defense of what has been called "strategic" essentialism, a term first coined by Gayatri Spivak, Diana Fuss argues that essentialism is not as reactionary as many constructionist arguments would suggest, and I draw upon Fuss's model as I begin to transition from the tautologophobia of Alice Vavasor and Clara Middleton, and the history of queer and feminist ambivalence about the clarity of erotic essentialism, to the decided tautologophilia of Trollope's *The Way We Live Now*. That transition also returns us to Newman, Wittgenstein, and the hermeneutics of surface reading, all of which reclaim tautology as method. Fuss clarifies the distinction between "deploying" or "activating" essentialism versus "falling into" or "lapsing into" essentialism. While the latter implies a political failure, the former emphasizes essentialism's strategic (and potentially temporary) uses, so that "the radicality or conservatism of essentialism depends . . . on *who* is utilizing it, *how* it is deployed, and *where* its effects are concentrated."[44] In asking how erotic essentialism structures the development of character and the complex problems of moral and erotic accountability in Trollope's fiction, and in imaginative writing more generally, we need to attune ourselves to the kinds of self-conscious and cynical relationships to essentialism that Fuss describes.

Disdain is in many ways the expected response to the bad logic of tautology: it's an empty, spurious kind of reasoning that may be fundamentally coercive or constricting as an expression of desire as an unquestionable essence of the self. I've tried to demonstrate, however, that sometimes even as we inhabit the attitude of tautologophobia, we also reveal that that attitude may arise out of a disavowed attraction to the easiness and force of tautology as an assertion of the self-evidence of erotic desire. This is not only tautology anxiety but tautology panic. There is, indeed, something queer about tautology as an end in itself: it refuses a normative mode of logical sequence and therefore logical time, which would proceed forward in the process of deduction rather than spinning in circles. Trollope's Alice Vavasor and Meredith's Clara Middleton are bullied by tautological argument, pushed from the complex wavering that gives them life and space as literary characters to the acceptance of erotic impulse as an inescapable (but also silencing, stilling, killing) conviction. Once argument and debate are settled by the clarity of tautology (diamonds are diamonds, and handsome is handsome), Alice disappears from view, with novel upon novel in the Palliser series simply forgetting her: "Mr Grey had also brought his wife." But despite its use as a technique of patriarchal coercion, tautology seems nevertheless to beckon to us with its transparent irrefutability, its diamond-hard resistance, its beautiful independence: "I am what I am—I am my own special creation." The essence that I bring into view with the tautological assertion of myself may be only a creation, an illusion, but it is one that seems quite often to work, to make audible in language something that is otherwise hidden, insisting, unheeded: "If a man is handsome . . . it stands to reason that he is handsome."

Even Meredith, despite his novel's seeming rejection of tautology as an impoverishing and coercive form, nevertheless maintains his faith in the idea that as readers we must enter a fictional world and simply accept that it is what it is, an idea elaborated by his narrator in the opening paragraph of *The Egoist*: "Credulity is not wooed through the impressionable senses; nor have we recourse to the small circular glow of the watchmaker's eye to raise in bright relief minutest grains of evidence for the routing of incredulity. The Comic Spirit conceives a definite situation for a number of characters, and rejects all accessories in the exclusive pursuit of them and their speech. For, being a spirit, he hunts the spirit in men; vision and ardour constitute his merit: he has not a thought of persuading you to believe in him. Follow and you will see" (3). To conceive a "definite situation" for a specific "number of characters" is to banish the material accessorizing that Meredith associates with much of the realist fiction that precedes him. The reality effect is not, for Meredith, about the accumulation of tactile and perceptual detail but about the imperative power of certainty; it is not about "persuading you to believe" but rather commanding you to follow through the sheer "ardour" of his conviction, much as Trollope aims to transmit his precise meaning to you like an electric current. Once we've entered the world of the Comic Spirit, however, accepting its set of apodictic truths, we must become fully responsible citizens of that world, testing the limitations of what is taken for gospel truth. Well into the novel, Meredith's narrator lays out the reader's somewhat altered responsibilities: "Observers should begin upon the precept, that not all we see is worth hoarding, and that the things we see are to be weighed in the scale with what we know of the situation, before we commit ourselves to a measurement. And they may be accurate observers without being good judges. They do not think so, and their bent is to glean hurriedly and form conclusions as hasty, when their business should be to sift at each step, and question" (193). The hasty conclusion is itself a kind of bad logic, closely akin to the tautology. After all, a hasty conclusion is often one that serves as its own premise, or is at least so shorn of its supporting premises as to stand alone, sufficient and self-evident. Often, Meredith's narrator insists, we believe ourselves to be careful, sensitive observers of the world and of ourselves, when all the while we are making conclusions on sheer instinct, making hasty promises that we can't, in the end, keep. It may be that the "I" who forges through the middle of a novel can look back on the "I" that began it as if remembering a dream, in which I offered a consent or a commitment—a promise—that I couldn't fully understand. But by now I'm beholden to that promise; I must see it through, if only by hoping to be better, more attentive to myself and my judgments, in short a better reader, that I might wish to be able to tell what I am.

Tautologophilia and *The Way We Live Now*

The scattered history of "I am what I am" that I've just presented, which connects Meredith's ideas about coercive self-identity to queer liberation, helps us to see the trouble with tautology. It also helps us to see why I remain attached to the notion of tautology as a strategy of resistance, even after having shown how it can function as part of a strategy of sexual coercion in the Victorian engagement plot. Tautology's coerciveness isn't a negation of its queerness; on the contrary, tautology's way of strong-arming belief and of cordoning off the erotic from the debatable is precisely what makes it so powerful as a mechanism of coming out, of creating erotic certainty even where erotic life might seem most uncertain and most liable to the scoff of puzzlement or, worse, violent rejection. The tautologophilic reading might require us to accept that tautology can have contradictory uses depending on who imposes its certainties upon whom, and that the best we can do is to remain vigilant about tautology's way of slipping from one register into another. It's this slipperiness that can make tautology seem dangerous and meaningless, with its capacity to enforce any certainty and to rebuff the force of doubt. But Trollope's own theory of novelistic clarity, and Meredith's resonant theory of narrative conviction, remind us that there can be a pleasure, too, in this kind of certainty when one feels it deeply, especially when certainty is met with acknowledgment, one battery connecting to another and transmitting that spark of perfect meaning. Even in *The Way We Live Now*, a novel in which erotic certainty becomes a force of critique, that force is often rejected rather than acknowledged within the world of the novel. Yet for the novel's readers, the critique has its effect, asking us to reckon with the irrepressible certainty of desire and the impossibility of fully assimilating such opaque impulses to the instrumental reason of the marriage market.

I'm not the first critic to notice Trollope's abiding interest in states of obstinacy and unswerving conviction, nor the first to identify the deployment of such obstinacy in his fiction as part of an immanent critique of the conventional marriage plot. Indeed, the complexity and variety of Trollope's engagement with the stubbornness of erotic attachment can be measured by the number of critics who have attempted in various ways to account for it and to decipher its ethical, ideological, or narrative purposes.[45] Amanda Anderson, for example, describes "recalcitrant psychology" in Trollope as registering a powerful "limit to the social," but she ultimately insists that such recalcitrance can be reconciled with a liberal model of debate and critique, allowing for an understanding of critique as "an ethos that can be cultivated, rather than simply an estranging practice that threatens traditional ethos."[46] In a reading of Trollope's *Marion Fay* (1881), J. Hillis Miller even zeroes in on tautology as a paraphrase for the recalcitrance of many of Trollope's female characters in their choice of mate: "I love him because I love him" is Miller's own way of putting into words this kind of irrefutable certainty, and it is a turn of phrase that reverberates throughout this chapter. But Miller sees this kind of certainty as fundamentally irrational, unavailable or unassimilable to public modes of reason and persuasion. It represents for him "an inner voice that is the wholly other within the self," an internalization of the voice of ideology, and thus a profound sense of alienation from one's own unexplainable convictions.[47] If I can't "own" my conviction because it seems to be spoken by the voice of another, I cannot effectively use that conviction as the starting point for critique. Like Barthes, Miller sees the assent to tautology as an escape from the demands of rationality—it's more like obeying an inscrutable command that only *seems* to come from within than remaining true to oneself. While I follow Miller, then, in believing that tautology has a connection to a potential critique of the ideology of marriage in Trollope's fiction, I draw that connection in very different ways. Most importantly, by emphasizing that Victorian fiction makes frequent use of tautology and engages with it in varied and often ambivalent ways, rather than seeing tautology only as a pithy paraphrase for a feeling of stubborn conviction, I allow tautology to take on a more multifaceted set of significances than does Miller, and I argue that Victorian novelists (and the characters they create) are far from uniform in their investment in the tautological form of erotic conviction. Indeed, Alice Vavasor and Clara Middleton stand as stark counterpoints to this generalization—they remain suspicious of tautological conviction, and its easiness and clarity, as a model of erotic conviction. Finally, Regenia Gagnier offers a corrective to Anderson's argument (and, more indirectly, to Miller's argument) that I echo and expand upon here: she argues that Anderson's emphasis on rationalism and proceduralism as dominant values in a liberal culture blinds us to the importance of passion and affect in generating critique. As Gagnier puts it, "freedom is not just rational but *passional*, and when frustrated gives rise to physiological conditions of resentment, which govern our actions even when they are life- and self-denying."[48] We might add to Gagnier's final phrase, even when they are dangerously self-*affirming*, even when resentment takes shape as a rebellious assertion of the irrefutability of desire.

Tautology is a marker of unmediated self-identity rather than self-alienation—not the "wholly other within the self" but the *self* within the self, which is nevertheless strangely opaque and difficult to put into words. Opacity, however, doesn't necessarily lead to alienation: that about my own self which is opaque to me and deep and inaccessible within me may nonetheless feel absolutely essential and sure to me, a guiding conviction that I know is profoundly my own, a state of my mind and body that I am unwilling—perhaps unable—to alter. Miller, for example, is only obliquely interested in sexuality as a source of conviction. He zeroes in on "the moment when the unmarried Englishwoman decides, on her own, to give herself or not give herself to this or that man," as if the moment of the marriage proposal or the commencement of courtship by the man is the first time that her desire (or lack of desire) is raised for her as a force, an impulse, a question—and so he recapitulates in some ways the Victorian idea that a woman doesn't really experience desire or attempt to come to terms with its insistence until invited to do so by a marriage proposal.[49] And while this may often be true of Trollope's characters, it is not nearly universal. Part of the recurrent problem in Trollope's fiction is precisely how to make intelligible a rapidly growing acknowledgment of women's erotic certainty as a real ethical and social force rather than a vicious aberration. Miller's reading of *Marion Fay* describes female characters' stubborn convictions in courtship and marriage as an accidental manipulation of the marriage economy, which challenges norms surrounding interclass marriage in particular. For him, the "other within" is something like the psychoanalytic model of conscience or the ego ideal—an internalized version of the divine command—rather than something like the psychoanalytic concept of the drive—the embodied, instinctual energy of libido.[50] For Miller, and indeed for Anderson, the importance of recalcitrance is that it responds to a messy and often incoherent liberal ideology, which values both the smooth operation of social and rational norms *and* the force of individual autonomy and religious models of conscience. The convictions particular to erotic desire, however, represent not only the potential instability of ideology but also an attempt to register possibilities of radical critique. In other words, there might be something parallel to the dominant language or procedure (or the dominant logic) that subjects *it* to critique.

The idea of a "critique of critique" can easily seem overwrought, but it's something close to what I'm pursuing here. I borrow the term from Rebecca Walkowitz, who argues that to mount a "critique of critique" is to extend the scope of our critical attention to include the very categories that seem to make argument possible.[51] I suggest that erotic desire is one of these taken-for-granted categories but also of course that logic as a normative model of argumentative form can be understood along the same lines. In this case, sexuality stands apart from liberal ideals of reasoned exchange and manifests itself in a language of unintelligibility, circularity, and impenetrable hardness—a language that also may seem partially maimed or muted by the requirements of logical accountability that it cannot fully escape. The antisocial nature of tautological conviction is not merely an untapped political resource, gesturing in Miller's version to an unrealized or unrealizable utopia, the "distant horizon of a more perfect democracy to come"; rather, it suggests that some aspects of the self are so singular as to be antithetical to the conventional understandings of concepts like "democracy" or "liberal abstraction" or "public life" or even to the distinction between "now" and "then."[52] They gesture not to a more perfect democracy but to the importance of maintaining a space right here and right now, both in literature and in life, for situated, intimate recognition that doesn't imply recourse to more public or abstract forms of social visibility, or that simply reject those forms as impoverishing or fundamentally oppressive. So often the declaration of coming out, "I am what I am," in its demand for recognition *now*, is met with hedging and with pleas for a saintly liberal patience: the world will come around, the horizon is bright for queer people, "it gets better." Tautology, however, refuses that kind of political pragmatism, and even the happier kind of queer utopianism theorized by José Esteban Muñoz, in which queerness is always a "horizon imbued with potentiality" that in its future-oriented openness "allows us to see and feel beyond the quagmire of the present."[53] Tautology's circularity, its hardness, insists that the future is already here.

The use of tautology as a way to insist upon the ethical significance of desire, even at its most opaque, idiosyncratic, and seemingly self-evident, is quite different, then, from Charlotte Brontë's sensitivity to the imperative to efface oneself or to take an impartial point of view in thinking ethically about desire. Brontë, in other words, represents characters who find ways to work within that contradiction—the contradiction of being both myself and not myself when I try to make erotic desire intelligible—by turning self-negation into a strangely embodied and intimate practice. Trollope, on the other hand, wonders how the very first-person insistence of erotic desire might in fact trump, challenge, or eliminate the third-person perspective of ethical reasoning that is conducted according to the rules of good logic. In both cases, the "solution" to the seeming impossibility of reasoning about erotic desire carries with it the risk (or sometimes the guarantee) of social exclusion, even as it aims to make desire socially intelligible. This is a stubborn paradox common to Brontë's and Trollope's ways of thinking through this problem. Both novelists raise the question: is "dropping out" of social life (when social life is imagined through abstractions like citizenship, good logic, civic participation) a viable mode of critique? This is a question that would reemerge in forceful ways in twentieth-century debates over identity politics, which, like my argument here, often revolved around the crux of "essentialism." It was the ideology of essentialism, and the associated attachment to "difference," that fueled movements such as lesbian separatism and that aimed for forms of intimate belonging founded on a shared essence of identity rather than on more abstract forms of social recognition that would transcend or obscure difference.

That the blunt moral force of sexuality is easily manipulated in the service of patriarchal coercion, however, means that dropping out, insisting upon the essence of the self against the demands of the social, is not always a story of sexual resistance or liberation. All of this is best summed up in Jacques Lacan's famous, and famously difficult, ethical maxim that "the only thing of which one can be guilty is of having given ground relative to [*d'avoir cédé sur*] one's desire."[54] Many critics have pointed out that this maxim can be read as a freeing tribute to erotic pluralism or as a troublingly unreflective commitment to hedonistic satisfaction at all costs, a way of saying "my desire is what it is and so I must not distance myself from it or refuse it; I will obey it unreflectively." This critical reception has been outlined by Slavoj Žižek, who argues that Lacan's maxim is notoriously difficult to square with any of our many well-developed ethical theories, from consequentialism to deontology. The basic function of the maxim, he suggests, is to insist upon moral autonomy, even in our relationship to the law-bound energy of desire. As he puts it, Lacan wants to get us out of "the common misconception that the basic ethical message of psychoanalysis is, precisely, that of relieving me of my responsibility, of putting the blame on the Other."[55] Precisely this slippage of meaning—the embrace of blind hedonism versus the responsibly ethical assumption of erotic autonomy—structures the flexibility of tautology in Victorian fiction, where it can be a form through which an ideology of feminine submissiveness dissembles as sexual liberation, or a form through which to register a critique of the instrumental rationality of moralized sexuality. Most importantly, however, tautology resists symptomatic analysis—the search for repressed causes of desire—by presuming that erotic life is what it is and that it may not be worth interrogating, or indeed that such an interrogation may not even be possible. (Nor may it be morally right.)

Hetta Carbury, the central character in one of the several courtship plots of Trollope's *The Way We Live Now*, provides an apt example of a character who experiences erotic desire as an unquestioned groundwork of the self. Hetta's plot centers on a love triangle. Her older cousin, Roger Carbury, has long courted her and is seen as the sensible match, both by himself and by Hetta's mother, Lady Carbury; Hetta, however, is in love with Roger's friend and protégé, Paul Montague, a dashing but financially unstable prospect. Unlike Alice Vavasor, who sees it as her duty to make a reasonable and socially justifiable choice, Hetta insists that her desire for Paul be accepted as an incontrovertible state of affairs, rather than treated as a proposition that is up for debate. Why does she love Paul? Hetta finds such a question ridiculous. Her refusal to give up on Paul Montague and to explain herself removes desire from the realm of the social or ethical by allowing its signification to be self-generating as well as erotically self-centered. For much of the novel, the narrative withholds any articulate expression of Hetta's desire for Paul. It is simply a fact that Roger and Lady Carbury can take for granted in their clueless attempts to direct Hetta's marital choice. The one miniscule piece of evidence we have that Paul really is a significant obstacle to Hetta's engagement to Roger comes in a minor narratorial aside that closes the second chapter. We have been told that Roger is in love with Hetta, and then the narrator remarks, "He was, however, nearly forty years old, and there was one Paul Montague whom [Hetta] had seen."[56] The emphasis on the erotic is important here—Hetta and Paul barely speak to each other until well into the second volume, at which point her desire for him has already taken hold as an incontrovertible fact. The text's explanation is that Hetta had "seen" Paul, and the "enough-said" of her sexual attraction is put in direct relation to the "enough-said" of Roger's undesirable age. Later, once Paul and Hetta have finally confessed their love to each other, she initiates an exchange in which she explicitly and repeatedly tells Paul, her betrothed, how far inferior he is to Roger, whom she has rejected. She tells Paul that Roger is "as good as gold" and "ever so much better" than Paul, all the while "stroking his [Paul's] hair with her hand and looking into his eyes" (2:149). The erotic trumps the moral, as Hetta goes on to declare, "I suppose we ought to love the best people best; but I don't, Paul" (2:150). Hetta loves with her body, with the hand that strokes and the eye that looks, and she will not apologize for it.

Hetta's desire, then, is deeply unspoken in a certain way, and yet it is spoken *about* at several points in a particularly meaningless version of the language of love. Hetta must use a word like *love*, saturated with social and ethical meaning, in order to cover up the fundamentally erotic basis of her choice: "I love" rather than "I want." Hetta rejects her mother's repeated suggestion that she reconsider Roger by countering, "It is to me horrible that you should propose it to me when you know that I love that other man with my whole heart" (2:385). If we parse the logic of the line of argumentation here, we find that it is circular: "you ought not to press me because you know that I love him; you know that I love him because I said so; I said so because I love him," and so on. *Love* is the assumed conclusion that forms a knot in any attempt to read Hetta's obstinacy. We know not only that Hetta's working definition of love is first of all somehow tautological or self-referential but furthermore, and perhaps more importantly, that it is decidedly different from her mother's socialized conception of falling in love. Although Hetta talks about love, we've already seen that what she seems really to mean is sexual desire. Lady Carbury offers her version of love, more familiar to us as a partially rational and socially intelligible form of attraction, in a rumination on Hetta's stubbornness: "She [Lady Carbury] herself had within the last few weeks refused to join her lot with that of a man she really liked, because her wicked son was so grievous a burden on her shoulders. A woman, she thought, if she were unfortunate enough to be a lady without wealth of her own, must give up everything, her body, her heart,—her very soul if she were that way troubled,—to the procuring of a fitting maintenance for herself. Why should Hetta hope to be more fortunate than others?" (2:383). Lady Carbury acknowledges the weight of "really liking" Mr. Broune, but more importantly, she valorizes love as a social practice that is concerned with the nonfinancial self and with erotic desire in a narrowly limited and conditional way. Love is about "procuring a fitting maintenance" for oneself, and it may in fact mean sacrificing the body itself (including, presumably, the body's desires) in order to achieve its goal. For Hetta, on the other hand, desire is self-centered and self-grounding (as is tautology, assent, or certainty) rather than socially responsible (as is rational debate). The refusal of justification necessitated by an antisocial desire becomes a positive end in itself, or a potent form of recalcitrance, to return to Anderson's powerful terminology, which asserts the presence of the body at the center of questions about love and desire. Once she sets herself in opposition to Lady Carbury, Hetta's rebellion becomes capacious: "She was disposed to do battle with her mother and her cousin in the matter—if only with the object of showing that she would not submit her own feelings to their control. She was savage to the point of rebellion against all authority." "To the point of" becomes the key phrase here if we continue to follow Anderson's idea that recalcitrance registers "a limit to the social." Hetta has indeed registered a limit—brought the massive generalization of "all authority" into view in her local and specific refusal to cede—without really transgressing that limit other than figuratively. There's a paradox here: How can one be "savage *to the point of . . .* "? Doesn't savagery assume the crossing of a limit between the human and the subhuman, the morally upright and the uncivilized, the rational mind and the sexual instinct? Or perhaps, if we follow Wittgenstein's argument about certainty, the regression to the savage, to the merely animal, represents a return to that fundamental "form of life" provided by the certainty of my embodiment, the certainty that this is my body, these my hands, this my sexuality. Unlike Alice Vavasor, for whom the bad logic of tautology represents a feminine evasion of moral responsibility, Hetta Carbury holds tenaciously to tautology as a rejection of a version of moral responsibility that cannot account for the savage force of erotic desire.

Marie Melmotte, the center of another of the novel's marriage plots, presents us with a different version of the same problem: if Hetta seems to resist the authority of socially sanctioned love almost silently, by refusing explanation even in the interiority afforded her by the novel, Marie seems more aware of the physicality and aggressiveness of her rebellious desire. The daughter of the mysterious and morally corrupt banker whose failed Ponzi scheme drives one of the novel's plots, Marie is dissatisfied by her function in the marriage market as a wealthy heiress who must marry into aristocracy to guarantee the social respectability of her nouveau-riche family. She is conscious that her money gives her the power to catch an *attractive* man, and his moral character or suitability as a husband is not especially important to her, let alone a moralized feeling like "love." Early in the novel we get the first implications of Marie's germinal feeling of power in terms that are reworked, repeated, and amplified throughout the novel: "The girl herself, too, began to have an opinion. . . . [S]he had had experience since Lord Nidderdale, with a half laugh, had told her that he might just as well take her for his wife, and was now tempted from time to time to contemplate her own happiness and her own condition" (2:33).[57] She rebels against her family's aspirations by holding fast to her attraction to Felix Carbury, Hetta's debauched brother, who has mercenary intentions in his courtship of Marie. When we see her dancing with Felix at Mme. Melmotte's ball, we understand that sexual desire is the locus of her "temptation" to self-assertion: "To give Felix Carbury what little praise might be his due, it is necessary to say that he did not lack physical activity. He would dance, and ride, and shoot eagerly, with an animation that made him happy for the moment. It was an affair not of thought or calculation, but of physical organization. And Marie Melmotte had been thoroughly happy. She loved dancing with all her heart if she could only dance in a manner pleasant to herself" (2:37). Far from being the mute object of exchange, Marie understands how to exploit the marriage economy to her own ends, for pleasure rather than for status, for the sheer "physical organization" of the body held onto in a dance rather than rational "calculation" of love and courtship.

Marie does at one point doubt that looks can be all. Doesn't she need a reliable husband, kind and dependable? Felix is none of those things, and yet he *is* beautiful—that much is certain. After all, "handsome is handsome," and Marie finds that when she weighs her sexual attraction to Felix in the balance against her feeling of sexual repulsion from Lord Nidderdale (despite his wealth), the answer seems plain: "Sir Felix Carbury was not in all points as nice as she had thought him. Of his beauty there was no doubt; but then she could trust him for no other good quality. Why did he not come to her? Why did he not show some pluck? Why did he not tell her the truth? . . . Lord Nidderdale was, she thought, not at all beautiful. He had a commonplace, rough face, with a turn-up nose, high cheekbones, no especial complexion, sandy-colored whiskers, and bright laughing eyes,—not at all an Adonis such as her imagination had painted" (2:67–68). Marie's single-minded interest in looks once again undermines the social or ethical functions of courtship and marriage. But the difference between Marie and Hetta—and the similarity between Marie and Alice Vavasor—lies in Marie's willingness to vocalize a rationale for her stubborn desire, albeit a rationale that follows the logic of physical force and counterforce rather than the logic of morality. She confesses to Hetta that her desire is a direct reaction against her father's physical abuse: "He beats me sometimes. . . . But I never will yield a bit for that. When he boxes and thumps me I always turn and gnash my teeth at him. Can you wonder that I want to have a friend? Can you be surprised that I should be always thinking of my lover?" (2:167). Sexual desire becomes Marie's way of insisting upon the feelings and impulses of her own body, resisting attempts to cow her through physical intimidation and violence. In *Can You Forgive Her?*, Glencora describes her own fantasy life in similar terms, as a belated program of resistance to the aggressive pressure from her wealthy relations under which she has buckled by abandoning her lover Burgo Fitzgerald to marry Plantagenet Palliser: "They browbeat me and frightened me till I did as I was told;—and now;—what am I now? . . . I tell you that every day and every night,—every hour of every day and of every night,—I am think-ing of the man I love. I have nothing else to think of. . . . I am always talking to Burgo in my thoughts; and he listens to me. I dream that his arm is around me—" (305). While Marie presents her resistance as a proactive strategy (I won't marry him, and my resistance is figured by my insistence that I fantasize about another man), Glencora's situation is marked by erotic privation in which fan-tasy is a tragic half-compensation (I married a man to whom I'm not attracted, so fantasy offers me a surrogate erotic life). In both cases, erotic fantasy allows for a way to maintain the conviction of desire, insisting that desire can be nour-ished and in some sense fulfilled, albeit in a way that Freud would describe as melancholic, in the absence or deprivation of its object. At the same time, erotic fantasy is also a place to which to escape—a pointed refusal of the violent im-pingement of the social world that returns us to the problem of social exclusion and the viability of dropping out of social life altogether.

When her erotic object is denied to her and it becomes apparent that she can-not escape being married off by her father, Marie's mock concession, delivered to her mother, exposes the sexuality at the heart of the exchange in heiresses: "I'll marry Lord Nidderdale, or that horrid Mr. Grendall who is worse than all the others, or his old fool of a father,—or the sweeper at the crossing,—or the black man that waits at table, or anybody else that he chooses to pick up" (2:170). By inserting indiscriminate desire into this economy Marie actually registers sexu-ality as the limit of the purely socioeconomic structure of the marriage market. In other words, her insistence on desire makes the novel's heterosexual marital exchange impossible, since that patriarchal system would then require a wom-an's readiness to desire everyone and anyone chosen on her behalf, or to have that open-ended desire move in highly unpredictable and uncontrollable ways. (Or, alternatively, it would require her to have no desire at all, only indifferent acquiescence.) Just as any proposition can follow from a tautology, the logic of the marriage market can always lead by a similar trick of deduction to miscege-nation. We hear echoes here of Alice Vavasor's insistence to Glencora that "one can't marry all the people one likes" (287). While Trollope often depicts women who fixate with extreme obstinacy on one love object, Marie Melmotte fixates on desire itself as an object and as an essence, a desire imagined as flexible, liquid, and voracious. The relationship between Melmotte's abuse and Marie's rebellion is not one of simple action and reaction; rather, Marie clings to desire and to the irrefutability of tautology because it offers her a way of frustrating her father's power as a trafficker of women—a frustration that parallels his similar impotence as a trafficker in stocks.

If tautology in Victorian fiction is both bad and good, the object of phobic disdain and deep attraction, doesn't the meaning of the term become capacious to the point of uselessness? Can tautology, or the practices of conviction, assent, and certainty that are related to it as a form, ever have a specific significance if it seems to have such a wide range of uses? In setting out to establish Trollope's different uses of tautology, and to compare them to the uses of tautology from Meredith to Newman to *La Cage aux Folles*, I have also intended to indicate one function of this linguistic tic that seems to remain constant: "If P and Q, then P" represents a logical truth, but no matter what real objects its terms represent, the statement can never really say anything new about the world. Kant got it right in this sense. When considered as objects of logical study, tautologies are empty, useless, and contain no new knowledge about reality. But the phrase "handsome is handsome" does seem to describe a particular state of affairs—a particular state of desire—with a power that properly logical language cannot achieve. In other words, tautology is a kind of language through which the body can manifest itself with particular vividness. This vividness is a feature of opaque conviction that Newman associates with the persuasive power of the concrete, sensory impression as compared to that of abstract concepts, mathematical axioms, or ideal truths, and that Wittgenstein associates with animal instinct. And so the ambivalence that surrounds these knots of bad logic echoes the multiple ways in which the body can communicate or refuse to communicate.

Bodies and their desires can seem to hinder social utility by insisting that we obey them unreflectively and impulsively and that we trust the bodies and desires of others in similarly unthinking ways. That unthinkingness, however, seems to be at odds with our concepts of rational social engagement or the intelligibility that would make one person knowable to another. For Alice Vavasor, a character who harbors political ambitions and cares deeply about the ethics of social engagement, the imperative to submit to the circular argumentation of embodied desire can seem positively dangerous. The force of desire, and the force of its bad logic, can be imposed upon one from without as physical force and sexual pressure. It's important, I think, to take Alice's worry seriously, not as an expression of prudishness, but as indicating a real problem as to where we draw the limits between the ethical force of the erotic and the ethical obligations of sociability, the points at which one must begin to question Lacan's dictum never to cede ground relative to one's desire. On the other hand, we might understand bodies and their desires as powerful mechanisms of social refusal when the social seems to promise little in return for accession to its demands. We might in fact go further and claim that understanding the body as a limit point, impervious to certain kinds of social demands and moral duties, can represent a radical rejection of the very idea of civic sociability or public life. It might be a point of view that gestures to intimate rather than abstract understandings of social belonging—opaque idiosyncrasy rather than social accountability—as the novel's proper object of concern when it comes to the representation of in-dividuality and the questioning of the ideology of liberal individualism. Enclos-ing oneself inside a body that desires but refuses to communicate except in the obstinate language of desire is, according to this perspective, an assertion that sexuality has a local, intimate, and personal significance that is not available to public debate.

CHAPTER THREE

George Eliot's Vagueness

"I never before longed so much to know the names of things," George Eliot records in the journal of her vacation to Ilfracombe with her partner George Henry Lewes in 1856.[1] The expedition to the Devonshire coast was an exercise in amateur natural history, and Eliot's journal is filled with the names of species and types—animal, vegetable, and mineral. It isn't until many such names have passed under Eliot's attention that she engages in this moment of self-conscious reflection. What draws her to the opaque contours of the name? What kind of knowledge, or what kind of clarity, does naming allow? "The desire is part of the tendency that is now constantly growing in me," she continues in the journal, "to escape from all vagueness and inaccuracy into the daylight of distinct, vivid ideas. The mere fact of naming an object tends to give definiteness to our conception of it—we then have a sign that at once calls up in our minds the distinctive qualities which mark out for us that particular object from all others" (229). It sounds deeply seductive: the world lit up in the dazzling sunlight of clear ideas, the lines circumscribing each idea so sharp as to gleam, and the human observer whose power of naming admits of no errors and no inconsistencies, who need name only once to carve out a space in her mind for *this* concept, *this* species, *this* set of qualitative features—a world, in short, beautifully and sensitively illuminated by language. Eliot is, of course, indulging in a moment of fantasy, imagining that what she longs for, her constantly intensifying desire for vividness, might be possible—might in fact be as easy as pointing, naming, describing, and listing. Vividness is not, however, easy, and the force of this moment of fantasy in Ilfracombe comes from Eliot's attunement to the difficulty of achieving or maintaining clarity in language. We do not and cannot inhabit a world so perfectly illuminated by language. More often than not, language makes do with its vagueness; it copes with our limited capacity for precision.

Ten years later, in her unpublished essay "Notes on Form in Art," we see
Eliot directly confronting the contradictions inherent in our desire to give our
objects of experience clear, vivid shape. Thinking through the problems of aesthetic form rather than natural history prompts Eliot to wonder about the kinds
of naming and circumscribing beset by vagueness. One may be able to name a
species of plant and distinguish it quite sharply from other species (even if such
naming requires a great deal of empirical research), but when it comes to the
more abstract shapes of aesthetic form, the task becomes differently complex.
"Form," Eliot argues in her first pass at the problem, "as an element of human
experience, must begin with the perception of separateness."[2] No concept of
form is comprehensible, she insists, without a more basic concept of one thing
being different or separate from an adjacent thing, and at this point in the argument we remain close to the model of natural history, in which naming a species
involves separating it from those similar species that might cluster around it in
an evolutionary tree. She restates the point in various ways: "Fundamentally,
form is unlikeness" (432); "every difference is form" (433); and finally, "what is
form but the limit of that difference by which we discriminate one object from
another?" (434). But where, Eliot wonders, does our sense of such difference
come from? How do we perceive things as distinct wholes when they are often
entirely continuous with what surrounds them? If in her Ilfracombe journal Eliot seems dazzled by the power of naming, here she is less confident about the
idea that anything, whether a species or an aesthetic concept, is so easily circumscribed. She insists that "with this fundamental discrimination [of difference] is
born in necessary antithesis the sense of wholeness or unbroken connexion in
space & time: a flash of light is a whole compared with the darkness which precedes & follows it; the taste of sourness is a whole & includes parts or degrees as
it subsides" (433). What begins as an emphatic equation between form and separateness develops into a dialectical model of the manifold ways in which difference and sameness interact in the genesis of form: "And as knowledge continues
to grow by its alternating processes of distinction & combination, seeing smaller
and smaller unlikenesses & grouping or associating these under a common likeness, it arrives at the conception of wholes composed of parts more & more
multiplied and highly differenced, yet more & more absolutely bound together
by various conditions of common likeness or mutual dependence" (433). In this
essay, Eliot pursues not the fantasy of vividness but a way of theorizing form
that would register this paradoxical interdependence of likeness and difference:
the way in which the edges, boundaries, and distinctions that seem to make
form possible and perceptible always appear, upon closer inspection, to waver and to blur. Vagueness hobbles our capacities for perceiving separateness—

the exact point of transition from light to dark, for example, or from sour to sweet.

For Eliot, the philosophical problem of vagueness is also a problem of novelistic representation, especially when it comes to the capacity of language to represent erotic life and its ethical claims with precision. Eliot marks the confluence of erotics and ethics in *The Mill on the Floss* (1860) as the problem of "the seductive guidance of illimitable wants" (325), a phrase that turns the question of the vague boundary to simultaneously erotic and ethical ends. Ethical thinking, it seems to Maggie Tulliver, should be precise, bound to the principles of logic, whereas erotic life tempts us away from precision with its languorous blur, its "illimitable" boundaries. In *Daniel Deronda* (1876), to take another example, it is difficult to tell whether the reader is meant to disapprove of or admire Daniel's frequent sinking into "that solemn passivity which easily comes with the lengthening shadows and mellowing light, when thinking and desiring melt together imperceptibly, and what in other hours may have seemed argument takes the quality of passionate vision."[3] It's in one of these reveries, in which the line that separates reason from desire blurs, that Daniel encounters Mirah Lapidoth as she considers suicide, and saves her—and so we might think that Eliot deploys the "melting together" of these two domains as representing a sympathetic attunement to the world.[4] But Daniel is also anxious about his own aimlessness in life—his inability to focus his energies in ways that would be meaningful or effectual—and in that sense we might understand his habit of vague thinking as a detriment. In *Middlemarch* (1871–72), on the other hand, Will Ladislaw celebrates the vagueness intrinsic to language when he insists that, compared to the precision of painting and sculpture, "Language gives a fuller image, which is all the better for being vague."[5] According to this point of view, vagueness compensates in a satisfying fullness or richness of meaning for what it diminishes in clarity, and it's better for our meanings to be redolent than precise. Eliot's narrator in *Silas Marner* (1861), finally, hesitates as to whether this fullness of language is always a good thing; after all, this quality of language makes it so difficult for us to make our feelings clear to one another in those situations when clarity is most urgent: "I suppose one reason why we are seldom able to comfort our neighbours with our words is that our goodwill gets adulterated, in spite of ourselves, before it can pass our lips. We can send black puddings and pettitoes without giving them a flavour of our own egoism; but language is a stream that is almost sure to smack of a mingled soil."[6] It is often difficult to decide (as this varied set of examples demonstrates) whether Eliot is, like Ladislaw, a straightforward advocate for the evocative power of vagueness, if she only neutrally describes the problem of vagueness in language, or if she shares with Maggie Tulliver and the narrator of *Silas Marner* a sense of the ethical peril of desire and its illimitability, and the equal peril of the mingling of language with the vicissitudes of ego. I insist upon registering all three possibilities, and argue in this chapter that Eliot advocates for vagueness only insofar as it is a real dimension of language—a problem with which we must reckon, and which the novel must be able to capture, if we are to have a full understanding and a full picture of erotic life and its ethical force. The vagueness of language, for Eliot, cannot be pushed aside and must not be merely repressed. We must visit with vagueness, inhabit its blurred forms and understand their meanings, and use its difficulty as an ethical exercise, with the hope that we might return, in the end, to clarity, although perhaps clarity of a different kind than we initially expected or hoped for, a clarity that is only ordinary rather than ideal.

Eliot's engagement with vagueness has two aspects, both of which have to do with the representational capacities and incapacities of language. First, Eliot investigates ordinary language and its often vague form, as opposed to the ideal clarity of logical form, at a moment in intellectual history when, as we've seen, the scope of logic as a science of reason and language was under debate. I've already shown, in the introduction to this book, that Eliot was deeply skeptical of the goal of ideal clarity that prompted the development of symbolic logic. She also engaged quite directly with debates surrounding mathematical logic in her 1856 essay "The Natural History of German Life." That particular "language of the future" aimed for by algebraic logic was, to her, a "melancholy" one, an impoverishment of the sticky attachments of ordinary language. Second, Eliot investigates the power of metaphor and other modes of figuration as a particular practice of literary language, especially in those moments in which she abandons realism in favor of allegory, and in which the imaginative precision of metaphor affords us a unique alternative to a precision that is lost to language itself.[7]

I begin in the next section with the philosophical history of vagueness. While the problem of vagueness as it relates to the binary model of logic has an ancient pedigree, the serious study of vagueness is generally thought to have lain quite dormant until the early twentieth century. I show that vagueness was important to Victorian thinkers too, from Mill to Boole to Eliot herself. I then turn to a reading of *The Mill on the Floss* as a sustained examination of the vague claims of desire and the ways in which they seem to stand opposed, for Maggie Tulliver, to the much more vivid claims of morality. Even in Maggie's pessimism about the vagueness of desire, the novel raises important questions about the structural analogies between erotic life and rational thinking—both of which can be beset by the blur of vagueness. In *Middlemarch*, Eliot attends even more closely to the potential productivity of vagueness as an ethos. Just as in chapter two we saw tautology claimed as method, I read *Middlemarch* in this chapter's final section as Eliot's most fully sustained consideration of vagueness as a way of approaching the world, a form of thought and desire that we must sink into from time to time, even if we also must emerge from it into the dazzling light of clarity, returning with something of the murk of vagueness still clinging to the sharp edges of our thought.

The Suppressed Transitions Which Unite All Contrasts

Ludwig Wittgenstein helps us to see the nature of vagueness as a problem of representation: it only becomes a question when we think carefully about how we picture the world, whether the solid world around us or the abstract world of ethical and aesthetic concepts that we also want to draw with some precision. He asks us to imagine the affinity between "two pictures, one of which consists of colour patches with blurred boundaries and the other of patches similarly shaped and distributed but with sharp boundaries."[8] In such a case, Wittgenstein argues, "the affinity [between these two pictures] is just as undeniable as the difference."[9] He goes on with this thought experiment, trying to find the point at which the undeniable affinity between the blurred and the sharp outline ceases to hold:

> For imagine having to draw a sharp picture "corresponding" to a blurred one. In the latter there is a blurred red rectangle; you replace it with a sharp one. Of course—several such sharply delineated rectangles could be drawn to correspond to the blurred one.—But if the colours in the original shade into one another without a hint of any boundary, won't it become a hopeless task to draw a sharp picture corresponding to the blurred one? Won't you then have to say: "Here I might just as well draw a circle as a rectangle or a heart, for all the colours merge. Anything—and nothing—is right."—And this is the position in which, for example, someone finds himself in ethics or aesthetics when he looks for definitions that correspond to our concepts.[10]

Wittgenstein points out here that some vagueness in language is natural and indeed workable; after all, we need some flexibility in the way that we understand and apply concepts in order to communicate at all. If my concepts are too rigid, and if nothing less than a perfectly sharp overlay of my concept upon yours will satisfy me, then I risk a tragic kind of solipsism in which the world becomes radically unavailable to me, in which nothing can be right, nothing certain.

If I allow vagueness to become too generalized, on the other hand, and lose all sense of boundaries, then I'm equally adrift, groping through a world in which anything—and nothing—is right. It is the idea of the "blurred concept" that eventually leads Wittgenstein to his famous conclusion that language itself "has not the formal unity that I imagined, but is a family of structures more or less akin to one another."[11] This idea of a concept defined by family resemblance is not strictly speaking a logical solution to the problem of vagueness, but Wittgenstein does imagine it as our mechanism for coping with blurred concepts and finding some organizational principle to limit the chaos they seem to promise. "The *preconception* of crystalline purity," Wittgenstein continues, "can only be removed by turning our whole inquiry around. (One might say: the inquiry must be turned around, but on the pivot of our real need.)"[12] We can see in these passages Wittgenstein's insistence upon metaphor as a mechanism of philosophical argument, which contributes to his reputation for a literariness that flies in the face of the analytic tradition and its ideal of logical precision. What would it look like to "pivot" my inquiry into language, as if panning around and changing my point of view, imagining that the pivot around which I rotate is my "real need," something at the center of myself that isn't visible or speakable? We saw in the last chapter that Wittgenstein understands certainty as just this kind of "hinge," the "axis around which a body rotates," and so perhaps what Wittgenstein imagines here is that I might reorient myself, shift my perspective upon language and its uses, even while maintaining a core of certainty about myself and my real needs. But then what real need does our language fulfill, or at least attempt to address, Wittgenstein wonders? How might we see the vagueness of language as born of the messy interconnection of language with something like desire?

Despite the association of the vagueness problem with twentieth-century thinkers such as Wittgenstein and Bertrand Russell, it has ancient origins and continued to be an object of inquiry for philosophers, and for novelists such as Eliot, in Victorian England.[13] Eubulides, a contemporary of Aristotle, is usually credited with the first elaboration of what we call the sorites paradox, from the Greek *soros* meaning "heap," which demonstrates how vagueness inheres in everyday language. The paradox asks us to picture a heap of sand, from which we begin to remove grains one by one. At what point, we're asked, does the heap become a non-heap? We don't doubt that this change must take place at some point, even by the painstaking process of removing grains individually. But it seems absolutely impossible to ascribe the change to the removal of a particular grain. The concept of a heap, in other words, is blurry. It seems to include any number of borderlines cases in which we struggle to assign a truth-value to a simple statement such as "this is a heap." Vagueness poses deep problems, in other words, for logic and epistemology, and as Wittgenstein points out, these problems quickly ramify into fields such as ethics and aesthetics, which seem to rely especially heavily upon our capacity to define intrinsically vague concepts (such as "good" or "beautiful") precisely.

The sorites paradox shows us that binary logic does not work for defining such concepts, since the borderline cases highlighted by the sorites aren't at all amenable to sharp divisions between "true" and "false" or between "this" and "that." This has led some logicians to various versions of "many-valued" logic, whether it's a system that imagines several discrete truth-values between true and false, or a system of "fuzzy" logic that imagines truth as a spectrum. If we decide to stick it out with binary logic, then we're forced to accept that our knowledge about the world has severe limits, that there must be a sharp conceptual boundary between "heap" and "non-heap," specifiable to a single grain of sand, but that it's simply a boundary that we can never intuit. This is the "epistemicist" position. We may also decide that those troublesome borderline cases simply don't have truth-values, and we may stipulate points at which cases become clearly true or false on either side of that indeterminate gap. This is the "supervaluationist" approach.[14] Eliot's Dorothea Brooke, for example, makes the epistemicist plea of ignorance in response to Sir James Chettam's remark that she has the "power of discrimination" that allows her to tell "sense" from "nonsense." Dorothea insists, "On the contrary, I am often unable to decide. But that is from ignorance. The right conclusion is there all the same, though I am unable to see it" (31). Sense and nonsense are different, Dorothea wants to say, and are separated by a line as sharp as any—it's only that it's impossible to bring that line into sharp focus. This may seem like a trivial problem when we're trying to tell a heap from a non-heap, but Dorothea points out that even the line between what has sense and what doesn't is impossible to locate, and she forces us to wonder about all of those crucial ethical questions that might be beset by the fuzz of vagueness. It seems especially worrisome to claim that we cannot know the shape of moral concepts accurately, or that defining those shapes is simply a question of arbitrary agreement. It is important to remember that there are both temporal and spatial dimensions to vagueness: the sorites paradox asks us to consider the difficulty of isolating the moment in time when one thing turns into another by a series of infinitesimal alterations, but it also asks us to consider the insufficiency of our diagrammatic and symbolic methods of representing categories as bounded by sharp lines. Bertrand Russell famously pointed out that vagueness is not an intrinsic property of objects in the world, nor is it an intrinsic property of any given language; rather, vagueness inheres in representation. It arises as a problem only when we consider the relationship between the symbol and the thing that it aims to describe or circumscribe. "Apart from representation, whether cognitive or mechanical," Russell insists, "there can be no such thing as vagueness or precision; things are what they are, and there is an end of it."[15] Vagueness in that sense returns us to the problems of chapter two: it may be tautologically self-evident that "things are what they are," but that doesn't necessarily mean that what they are will be entirely clear to us. That kind of certainty is difficult to sustain when we try to represent what things are to ourselves or to others and realize that in many cases that important "what" begins to blur.

My reading of Eliot, and her ways of dealing with this representational problem, is in many ways in conversation with David Kurnick's work on the relationship in Eliot's fiction "between novelistic eroticism and social understanding," and I follow him in seeing these two domains as intimately related rather than mutually exclusive for Eliot.[16] But while Kurnick focuses on the practice of novel reading as a model for the ways in which detachment and objectivity can themselves be understood as objects of erotic desire, I suggest that in Eliot's fiction erotic desire aims for a kind of miry *depth* of situated ethical knowledge rather than (or perhaps in addition to) the detached, critical view of the narrator or the reader.[17] Franco Moretti, on the other hand, insists upon the quantifiable transition over the course of the Victorian period from "objective" ethical concepts that express judgment, such as "shame" or "virtue," for example, to the dominance of vague adjectives (such as "strong" or "dark") characterized by an "ethico-emotional mix" that aims for "less ethical clarity, but greater emotional strength: less precision, more meaning." Moretti links the "fog" of these Victorian adjectives to the logical problem of vagueness but mistakenly claims that such concepts are *not* logically vague in the same sense as "child" or "heap," "where a certain amount of vagueness is a condition of meaning."[18] My response to Moretti here is twofold. First, I insist that ethical life and affective or erotic life do not stand on opposite ends of a spectrum from clarity to vagueness: rather, ethical concepts, even ones that pretend to clarity, are almost always intrinsically vague and so are not as different from affective or erotic concepts as we might assume. Second, I argue that Victorian writers did not always use vagueness in order to evade precision in naming certain kinds of concepts, as Moretti implies, using the shift from the clarity of "the bourgeois" to the elusive vagueness of "the middle class" as his culminating political example.[19] Eliot provides us with a powerful example of a writer who sees vagueness and clarity as thoroughly interdependent when it comes to ethical thinking and erotic life. The basic question for Eliot is: if it seems dangerous to be guided by what is entirely "illimitable," then when and where do the limits appear that would make erotic desire meaningful rather than merely seductive?

"Every limit is a beginning as well as an ending" (832). This is the narrator of

Middlemarch, opening the novel's final chapter by claiming that a fictional conclusion must be something like a shading off into an implied but shadowy fictional future—an acknowledgment that characters' lives continue somewhere, in the readers' or the author's imagination perhaps, and that our exit from a fictional world is never as sharp or as simple as slamming shut a book. Eliot's narrator shows us a sharp line—a limit—before immediately proceeding to blur it, or to make it vibrate in our field of mental vision through the invocation of a kind of uncertainty principle, much as Eliot does in defining form. And of course, Eliot opens *Daniel Deronda* with an epigraph that picks up where *Middlemarch* leaves off, as ending cycles back to beginning: "Men can do nothing without the make-believe of a beginning. Even Science, the strict measurer, is obliged to start with a make-believe unit, and must fix on a point in the stars' unceasing journey when his sidereal clock shall pretend that time is at Nought."[20] Suddenly, the concept of the limit doesn't seem so easily apprehensible. At the very least it seems thoroughly arbitrary: there's no clear point where the limit necessarily falls; rather, there's a range of possibilities within which we choose, potentially somewhat randomly, where to begin, and where to end. When the narrator of *Middlemarch* describes Dorothea's bewildered experience of Rome, with its many-layered histories crowding in upon her, we get a similar description of "historical knowledge" itself, the elusive distanced perspective which, the narrator tells us, "traces out the suppressed transitions which unite all contrasts" (193). Keen insight and profound knowledge, at least in Eliot's view, promise us not a neatly organized understanding but an often vertiginous sense that there are no real limits, no genuine contrasts—only our words and our forms and our suppressions, which comfort us with the appearance of sharp outlines.

Eliot's understanding of the ancient sorites paradox and the various approaches to it seems to have been deep. In fact, she uses the character of Dorothea's uncle, Mr. Brooke, to mount a clear parody of the Stoic argument that the best way to avoid the trap of the sorites paradox is to refuse to be led down its slippery slope in the first place. "Human reason may carry you a little too far," he warns Dorothea—"over the hedge, in fact. It carried me a good way at one time; but I saw it would not do. I pulled up; I pulled up in time. But not too hard. I have always been in favour of a little theory: we must have Thought, else we shall be landed back in the dark ages" (17). There is a distinct echo here of Cicero's account of an unnamed Stoic philosopher who declared of the sorites paradox, "like a clever charioteer before I get to the end, I shall pull up my horses, and all the more so if this place to which they go is precipitous."[21] For both Cicero and Mr. Brooke, to be carried away by reason, or to cross over the hedge, is to end up outside of the realm of reason altogether. We should have a little bit of thought and theory, Mr. Brooke admits, just enough with which to get by, to make sense, to be civilized, and to be understood. The haunting question posed by his metaphor is, where would I be if I did not pull up in time? What if I drop the reins and allow the "reason" that carries me to gallop on? Even Mr. Brooke understands that finding the limit is often a game of feeling things out. "There are oddities in things," he says: "Life isn't cast in a mould—cut out by rule and line, and that sort of thing" (41).[22] Mr. Brooke tries to avoid vagueness, even though he knows it's in some sense unavoidable. We must work hard to feel out and to maintain "rule and line," even where they don't really exist, even when we confront those "oddities in things" that defy our efforts at precision. His own attempts at clear thinking and speaking, however, tend to fail, spectacularly and comically. The joke is that by blinding ourselves to vagueness altogether, or avoiding the dangerous paths that would lead to its traps, as Mr. Brooke does (and as the Stoics did before him), we might only become more confused. Casaubon is similar, in this sense, to Mr. Brooke, invested as he is in the clear organization of a system of knowledge, the whole of mythology, that may in fact be hopelessly messy. It's probably no accident that Eliot has Mrs. Cadwallader refer to Casaubon in her wry way as "our Lowick Cicero" (53).

Henry James invoked the problem of limits in a different register in his 1873 review of *Middlemarch*, published shortly after the novel's final serial install-ment. "It sets a limit," he writes, "to the development of the old-fashioned English novel." He takes Eliot to task for having become "philosophic" and "obscure," for the novel's "diffuseness," and for her general "loss of simplic-ity," which he suggests "lies buried (in a splendid mausoleum) in *Romola*." He compares the expectations set up by the opening chapters that the novel would be "an organized, moulded, balanced composition, gratifying the reader with a sense of design and construction," with the feeling one has by the novel's conclu-sion that it has been "a mere chain of episodes, broken into accidental lengths and unconscious of the influence of a plan."[23] James's account would have it that Eliot pushes the traditional novel to (or beyond) a clear formal limit by her very skepticism about the viability of limits: the limits, that is, that separate fiction from philosophy, the controlled from the diffuse, the simple from the complex, the composed from the formless, and, of course, the beginning from the end-ing.[24] It's not that *Middlemarch* is without form or moments of direct simplicity, it's that Eliot seems to James recklessly heedless of the outlines that define these categories. She slides in and out of them unpredictably.

Or perhaps, in the end, Eliot is really unconvinced about the efficacy of lim-its, preferring to occupy the fuzzy spaces of uncertainty—the borderline cases, as we call them—that lie between clear categories. Elisha Cohn's reading of *The*

Mill on the Floss helps us to see that Eliot often wants to "linger in the uninte-grated moment—the pause in which desires, memories, thoughts, and actions do not cohere, leaving the boundaries of selfhood porous, and neutralizing in-dividuality in favor of undifferentiation," but while Cohn wants to argue that Eliot's scenes of reverie "endow a state of inefficacy with a mood of warmth or pleasure," I suggest that for Eliot the problem of vagueness is something a bit different. Eliot does associate the vagueness problem with the kinds of states that Cohn describes—porousness, undifferentiation, warmth, pleasure—but not necessarily with the kind of inefficacy or "suspensions of agency" that Cohn is after.[25] John Stuart Mill agreed with Eliot (and Wittgenstein agreed with them both), for example, that some level of vagueness in language is productive and in fact necessary. In *A System of Logic*, Mill argues that "vagueness may ex-ist without practical inconvenience; and cases will appear, in which the ends of language are better promoted by it than complete precision" (46), anticipating Wittgenstein's set of rhetorical questions about vagueness: "Is it even always an advantage to replace a picture that is not sharp by one that is? Isn't one that isn't sharp often just what we need?"[26] Mill offers the example of "human" as a vague concept. Although we might agree to define a human being as a rational animal, we run into trouble when we realize that rationality is "a quality which admits of degrees" and that "it has never been settled what is the lowest degree of that quality which would entitle any creature to be considered a human being" (46). This vagueness is a good thing in Mill's view. It allows us to be open-minded; to consider borderline cases of rationality, such as infant children, with liberal flexibility; to arrive at provisional or working definitions that remain open to change; and to stay in some sense true to the inescapable problem of vagueness while still drawing clear, if temporary, forms on top of it.

Like Wittgenstein, however, Mill is sensitive to the possibility that such ar-guments can easily be taken too far. They might, in other words, give us license to play fast and loose with a whole variety of concepts whose definitions carry enormous ethical weight. It doesn't take much to get from blurry boundaries to no boundaries at all (that is, the states of undifferentiation to which Cohn points our attention in Eliot's work), and so Mill insists that the uncertainty inherent in language "can only be free from mischief when guarded by strict precautions" (46). Mill's precautions are pragmatic, grounded upon the liberal values of reasoned debate and consensus. Rather than pursuing vagueness to its philosophical depths, we can stop its creeping spread by coming to a set of provisional agreements about the uses and definitions of concepts. If sharp boundaries don't always exist in language itself, Mill argues, a person should invent them, "by giving to every general concrete name which he has frequent occasion to predicate, a definite and fixed connotation; in order that it may be known what attributes, when we call an object by that name, we really mean to predicate of the object" (49). When I speak of a "heap of sand" or a "person," I must define my terms: perhaps I insist that when I say "heap" I mean no fewer than five grains, and by "person" I insist that the capacity for abstract thinking is where I draw the line. Ideally, part of the collective project of logic would be to come to a consensus through reasoned debate about what we agree to mean by such words. And yet, as we've seen, vagueness is not merely a problem of unclear social conventions about language, and Mill himself implies as much in his initial assessment of the problem. The model of flexible consensus, while it certainly "works" in the pragmatic sense, amounts to an attitude of denial about the very depth of vagueness as a crisis of logic and epistemology.

Vagueness, in other words, insistently exposes the points at which the ideal language of logic fails to map onto ordinary language, but many logicians, beginning in the Victorian period, have seen this as a boon for logic as a discipline. The response to Mill, in other words, would begin with agreement: ordinary language *is* hopelessly unclear. It makes use of countless concepts that are resistant to sharp circumscription. Logic, however, is decidedly *not* ordinary language, and therein lies its great importance: logic is a mathematically precise ideal language. Even Gottlob Frege, one of the pioneers of modern symbolic logic, admitted that an ideal language missed out on a great deal that ordinary language, with all its vagueness, could best capture. As he puts it in his 1882 essay defending *Conceptual Notation* against its critics, "The shortcomings [of ordinary language] here stressed are caused by a certain softness and instability of language which, on the other hand, constitutes the reason for its many-sided usefulness and potentiality for development. In this respect language can be compared to the hand which, despite its adaptability to the most diverse tasks, is still inadequate. We build ourselves artificial hands—tools for special purposes—which function more exactly than the hand is capable of doing. And how is this exactness possible? Through the very rigidity and inflexibility of parts, the lack of which makes the hand so dexterous."[27] Just as the artificial language of logic is a tool customized for mathematical work, which can admit no vagueness, ordinary language is like the supple hand that can grasp and touch and react in ways that the mechanical hand cannot. In *Conceptual Notation* itself, Frege had used a different metaphor, one that Eliot would have appreciated, when he wrote, "I can make the relation of my 'conceptual notation' to ordinary language clearest if I compare it to the relation of the microscope to the eye."[28] For Frege, as for Wittgenstein, the imaginative resources of metaphor promise clarity when it comes to talking about vagueness.

Like Frege, George Boole was unconvinced that logic must be the only language of philosophical inquiry, and he explicitly allowed that the positive knowledge about thought and its structures that logic affords still leaves out other kinds of knowledge less amenable to mathematical symbolization. It's worthwhile to return to a moment from Boole's *Laws of Thought* that we've already encountered, in which he describes the outer limits of logical insight with a metaphor that itself invokes the idea of vagueness: "As the realms of day and night are not strictly conterminous, but are separated by a crepuscular zone, through which the light of the one fades gradually off into the darkness of the other, so it may be said that every region of positive knowledge lies surrounded by a debateable and speculative territory, over which it in some degree extends its influence and light" (400). The point at which the insights of logic cease to be useful, at which we end up wandering in the darkness despite logic's distant illumination, is itself a kind of vague limit, somewhere at the uncertain edge of that "crepuscular zone" that separates positive knowledge from, for example, ethical or erotic knowledge. In one of *Middlemarch*'s most famous descriptions of the reach and focus of its narrator's "light," we hear an echo of Boole's metaphor as well as Frege's argument for focus and specialization: "I at least have so much to do in unraveling certain human lots, and seeing how they were woven and interwoven, that all the light I can command must be concentrated on this particular web, and not dispersed over that tempting range of relevancies called the universe" (141). Eliot's narrator sets concentration against dispersion, and nothing could seem less vague than the concentration of a spotlight, with its crisp edges keeping that insidiously "tempting range of relevancies" cloaked in darkness and at bay. It seems that there is no "crepuscular zone" here, and yet it's the temptation that's important. Even what's kept in the dark seems in this image to call out to us. We may concentrate our beam of light and draw a clear circle around our objects of interest, but it's only, after all, an arbitrary selection, not a rational or logically necessary one. Desire beckons to us from across that wavering, tenuous edge.

Maggie Tulliver's Illimitable Wants

I've suggested that Eliot's representations of the vagueness of psychic content and its organization, and of individual characters' acts of surrendering to that vagueness, are ethically ambiguous. In turning now to *The Mill on the Floss*, I attempt to flesh out the nature of that ambiguity in this novel that offers us her most extended and focused meditation on desire and its vicissitudes. On the one hand, the confused, languid, eroticized introspection generated by the surrender to vagueness can seem positively reckless for someone as committed as Eliot to an ethics of sympathetic understanding. A commitment to vagueness threatens to turn the mind into an undifferentiated field that might as well be empty, something like a black hole, or the "dark shrouded pool" that comes to mirror for Hetty Sorrel in *Adam Bede* (1859) her own descent into a fuguelike and resigned moral aimlessness: "Her great dark eyes wander blankly over the fields like the eyes of one who is desolate, homeless, unloved."[29] On the other hand, an attunement to the sheer vagueness of one's own reasons, desires, intentions, and feelings often seems to lead to an elision of the very boundaries that fence consciousness in from the outside world, and in this sense might be conducive to the sort of self-forgetfulness and renunciation of egoism that are required of a worldview like Eliot's. When Maggie Tulliver, for instance, first lights upon the idea of religious renunciation, she imagines it as predicated upon a kind of absorption of the self into a wide world: "It flashed through her like the suddenly apprehended solution of a problem, that all the miseries of her young life had come from fixing her heart on her own pleasure, as if that were the central necessity of the universe; and for the first time she saw the possibility of shifting the position from which she looked at the gratification of her own desires—of taking her stand out of herself, and looking at her own life as an insignificant part of a divinely-guided whole" (290). Maggie's epiphany anticipates, of course, that of Wilde's Dorian Gray, who in the scene that I cited at the beginning of this book feels a similarly sudden opening of the mind to the immediacy of desire. It returns us also to Charlotte Brontë's exploration of erotic desire and its difficult relationship to the contradiction of logical or ethical self-negation. Maggie decides to see her desires as centered in the world, or perhaps as part of a "centerless" world in Thomas Nagel's terms, rather than centered in herself, a perspective that can only be made possible by a forceful "shifting" of position, or a conviction that point of view might be dislocated from its rootedness in the self if only one could cease seeing the self as a distinctive form with sharp edges.

Maggie's play with the structure of possession and predication here—her speculation that she should not be the subject or the vessel of her own activity of desiring—in fact develops out of her skeptical curiosity about syntax and logic. In a description of Maggie's autodidactic reading, we're told that she "found the Latin Grammar quite soothing . . . for she delighted in new words. . . . She presently made up her mind to skip the rules in the Syntax—the examples became so absorbing. The mysterious sentences, snatched from an unknown context, . . . gave boundless scope to her imagination" (147). Maggie's interest is in the texture of language and its imaginative suggestiveness rather than in its structures and rules. Even when she embarks upon a more formal education, the distracting experience of pleasure and absorption returns as Maggie tries to study the "masculine wisdom" of Aldrich's *Artis Logicæ Compendium*, a seventeenth-century logic textbook that remained popular throughout the eighteenth and nineteenth centuries: "In the severity of her early resolution, she would take Aldrich out into the fields, and then look off her book towards the sky, where the lark was twinkling, or to the reeds and bushes by the river, from which the waterfowl rustled forth on its anxious, awkward flight—with a startled sense that the relation between Aldrich and this living world was extremely remote for her. The discouragement deepened as the days went on, and the eager heart gained faster and faster on the patient mind" (287). Poised between the eagerness of embodied pleasure and the patience of reasoned self-cultivation, Maggie looks in vain for the mechanism of connection between the elegant and abstract forms of logic and the "anxious," "awkward," and "twinkling" living world. Maggie's father, Mr. Tulliver, repeatedly offers us even more direct expressions of confusion over the strange relation (or surprising nonrelation) between language and the world: "It's puzzling work," he says, "talking is" (10–11). Mr. Tulliver is therefore very cautious in approaching the same vagaries of syntax that leave Maggie cold: "He was not a man to make an abrupt transition. This was a puzzling world, as he often said, and if you drive your wagon in a hurry, you may light on an awkward corner" (15). Rational language, as Maggie comes to understand, isn't well equipped to handle the awkward impasse—one must hope to avoid it, as Mr. Tulliver does, or one must seek out another model for thinking that does justice to one's absorption in a vibrant and complicated world of textures and pleasures, without, of course, tipping so far into irrationality that one can't function in a social world. Indeed, Mr. Tulliver hopes that his son will get along more smoothly than he does in this respect, that he'll learn to "see into things quick, and know what folks mean" (22).

The moral problem at the center of *The Mill on the Floss*—which we might broadly describe as Maggie's painful wavering between ascetic renunciation and the surrender to pleasure—aligns, then, with the difficult relationship between formal reflection and embodied immediacy, or between narrative omniscience and focalization, or between logical reasoning and the sort of absorptive experience that we've identified with vagueness. The novel's opening sentence is already alive with this tension: "A wide plain, where the broadening Floss hurries on between its green banks to the sea, and the loving tide, rushing to meet it, checks its passage with an impetuous embrace" (7). The sentence zigzags, from the "broadening" of the river to its containment between its banks; from the "rushing" of the tide to the check brought about by two opposing movements of water; and finally to the twist in which this check to the river's movement is imagined not as a kind of control or prohibition but as an "impetuous" expression of love—as an "embrace" or a merging rather than a conflict or a clash. We're meant to oppose this loving check to the policing that we see later on in the novel in Tom Tulliver's impulse to control his sister and to force her into submissiveness. We're told that Maggie's "fits of anger . . . towards Tom, who checked her, and met her thought or feeling always by some thwarting difference—would flow out over her affections and conscience like a lava stream" (287). Tom has a severe sensitivity to breaches of limits and boundaries, and his version of the "check" is not to embrace and to merge but to block and to thwart—and so the river flowing between its green banks is transformed into the lava stream that scalds and scars.

We might be reminded here of the scene in *Jane Eyre* in which Rochester warns Jane against the same kind of passive "floating" for which Tom chastises Maggie. For Rochester, as for Tom, one must focus on the obstacles to movement—on the dams and the rocks that block and bound the path of the river—rather than on the freedom and potential shapelessness of movement itself: "Floating on with closed eyes and muffled ears, you neither see the rocks bristling not far off in the bed of the flood, nor hear the breakers boil at their base. But I tell you—and you mark my words—you will come some day to a craggy pass in the channel, where the whole of life's stream will be broken up into whirl and tumult, foam and noise: either you will be dashed to atoms on crag points, or lifted up and borne on by some master-wave into a calmer current—as I am now" (166–67). Rochester makes the metaphor even more explicit than does Eliot's narrator: this is the stream of life itself. Floating, Rochester insists, represents both a willful denial of reality ("closed eyes and muffled ears") and also a moral innocence in which the refusal to make choices or to reflect upon one's choices arises out of the fact that one hasn't yet encountered any truly difficult choices at all. But as in Eliot's narrator's opening description of the Floss, the experience and movement of floating takes on form and shape in this image, insofar as it is defined against the formless "whirl and tumult, foam and noise" that accompanies a moral crisis. The best that one can hope for is to end up in a "calmer current"—in other words, to continue floating along, perhaps now with open eyes and listening ears—rather than be "dashed to atoms" as the self explodes into airy diffusion, or to be disintegrated by the lava stream that floods out over the banks of the obstructed stream of life. Floating along a stream functions as a useful image for Brontë and Eliot of the tenuousness of the formal boundaries that define the self and its experience of movement through everyday life.[30] Riverbanks are notoriously soft, after all, and susceptible to erosion.

Maggie Tulliver's eventual decision to renounce worldly pleasures, under the influence of a momentous reading of Thomas à Kempis's medieval devotional manual *Imitation of Christ*, is something of a reaction to the insistent thwarting that her thoughts and feelings have met with at the hands of her family. As we've seen, Maggie decides that it might be better to have no feelings and no desires of her own rather than be destined to a life in which the pittance of pleasure allowed to her feels achingly and inescapably limited. I've also suggested that this might represent one potential "solution" to the affective experience of vagueness, in which desire always seems to overlap with reason in complex ways, and yet is chastised and blocked by a host of social pressures and norms often identified with logical modes of reasoning and their ostensible clarity and intelligibility. Rather than allow for the vague merging of impulsive erotic feeling and reasoned ethical feeling, which is difficult and painful and requires a concerted effort that seems to get Maggie nowhere, why not eliminate desire and pleasure from the equation altogether? Maggie's self-effacement in the name of a generalized, collective, or third-person pleasure allows her to locate desire and consummation as states not of mind or of body but of the world—a distinct object upon which reasoned ethics can work rather than a vague field that invades and informs reason from within and around its edges.

While Maggie's aspiration to asceticism often seems to be the driving force of *The Mill on the Floss*, it's important to remember that the novel takes seriously the arguments against such an evacuation of the pleasure-seeking self, especially in the debates between Maggie and Philip Wakem in which he tries to persuade her out of her religious severity. "It is mere cowardice," he insists, "to seek safety in negations. No character becomes strong in that way. You will be thrown into the world some day, and then every rational satisfaction of your nature that you deny now, will assault you like a savage appetite" (329). This is a standard enough apologia for responsible self-fulfillment: repress a desire for long enough, and it will transform from a "rational satisfaction" into a "savage appetite"; a total denial of desire requires a total withdrawal from the world, and such a withdrawal is not in fact possible. Better, in other words, to practice, to become "strong" in one's capacity for reasoned desire. And yet Philip's argument falls somewhat short in its concession to the moral dichotomy of reason and impulse—exactly the kind of distinction that leads Maggie to mistrust everything pleasurable, lest it dissolve her capacity for reason and the sort of social belonging and respectability that it promises.

In other words, what if what brings one genuine pleasure *always* feels impulsive, nonlinguistic, irrational? Can there still be a place in such a picture for what we call "reason" or for what Philip calls "rational satisfaction"? It seems to Maggie that the essence of pleasure and erotic desire lies in their chaos and their resistance to organization. It's in this discussion with Philip, after all, that Maggie describes the appealing "simplicity" of her pleasure-denying life. As she considers that her stance might be "unreasonable," we're told that "the severe monotonous warning came again and again—that she was losing the simplicity and clearness of her life by admitting a ground of concealment, and that, by forsaking the simple rule of renunciation, she was throwing herself under the seductive guidance of illimitable wants" (325). Maggie's "simple rule," with its beautiful "clearness," seems to her the only way to ward off the vagueness attendant upon the formless experience of pleasure, desire, and erotic excitement. We see here the two moral dimensions of vagueness that Eliot so often imagines as two sides of the same coin: on the one hand, its dizziness, its confusion, its invocation of a feeling of vertigo or disorientation; on the other hand, its easiness, its floating serenity, its promise of an oceanic absorption of self into world as all kinds of divisions and boundaries lose their forbidding sharpness and offer room for navigation, for feeling it all out.[31]

While Maggie's renunciation shows us one way of displacing or blurring erotic subjectivity by locating desire outside of the self, the immediate feeling of vagueness, in which desire and reason seem for a moment indistinguishable, provides a different model for such an abdication of what we might call "logical" subjectivity, based upon mechanisms of formalization, sorting, naming, reflective self-consciousness, and deliberative reason. We see this other version of self-forgetfulness in the extended episode that forms the climax of Maggie and Stephen Guest's tentative courtship, in which they take a boating trip together that turns into a dreamlike scene of empty-headed surrender. In the chapter titled "Borne Along by the Tide," it appears as if rational thought, rather than erotic desire, is the object of renunciation for Maggie and Stephen alike:

> Some low, subdued, languid exclamation of love came from Stephen from time to time, as he went on rowing idly, half automatically: otherwise, they spoke no word; for what could words have been but an inlet to thought? and thought did not belong to that enchanted haze in which they were enveloped—it belonged to the past and the future that lay outside the haze. Maggie was only dimly conscious of the banks, as they passed them, and dwelt with no recognition on the villages: she knew there were several to be passed before they reached Luckreth, where they always stopped and left the boat. At all times she was too liable to fits of absence, that she was likely enough to let her way-marks pass unnoticed. (464)

Words and thought belong outside of the atmosphere that surrounds Maggie and Stephen, and so it's crucial that this atmosphere is hazy or, in other words, that its boundaries are indeterminate. If this boat becomes what Foucault might call a "crisis heterotopia," defined by its exclusion of the everyday world in order that sexual awakening can be understood to happen nowhere in particular, it is an exclusion difficult to define in space with any precision.[32] Words might be an "inlet" to thought here, which suggests that language might be able to transmit messages across the boundaries of that hazy zone. Time is also blurry here—the present is supposed to stand apart from the past and the future, distinct and thoughtless as against every other time that is saturated with thought. But we know that our mechanisms for organizing temporal experience are notoriously vague, a fact reemphasized by the description of Maggie falling into "fits of absence" and losing track of the waymarks that measure the distance of their journey. In time, as in the floating journey down a river, everything is relative—and so it's easy to lose track of where one is or was, on this side or on that side of the signposts that help to orient us.

Stephen's attempts to persuade Maggie into giving up her resolution against pleasure, and more importantly into breaking her promise to marry Philip Wakem, draw upon the concept of the vague formation of intention that we'll see at work later on in *Middlemarch*. In this case, Stephen takes the idea to its logical extreme, insisting that their tryst has come about through an accidental accumulation of other people's actions or a confusion of necessary causality with deliberative reason. "See, Maggie," he urges, "how everything has come without our seeking—in spite of all our efforts. We never thought of being alone together again: it has all been done by others. See how the tide is carrying us out—away from all those unnatural bonds that we have been trying to make faster round us—and trying in vain" (465). Of course, Stephen's argument is essentially spurious, insofar as it simply reverses the terms of Maggie's grounds for resistance. Rather than expunge desire from the realm of reason, Stephen asks Maggie to expunge the forms of moral reason—particularly the idea of the social "bonds" that are so important to her—from the realm of erotic desire. Maggie is not persuaded by his case for the rejection of duty, and as she begins to come to a panicked awareness of the social implications of her illicit journey with Stephen, her anxiety focuses on the idea that a life with Stephen would entail the loss of her moral direction and of the forms that give life shape and meaning:

> She had rent the ties that had given meaning to duty, and had made herself an outlawed soul, with no guide but the wayward choice of her own passion. And where would that lead her?—where had it led her now? . . . Her life with Stephen could have no sacredness: she must for ever sink and wander vaguely, driven by uncertain impulse; for she had let go the clue of life—that clue which once in

the far-off years her young need had clutched so strongly. She had renounced all delights then, before she knew them, before they had come within her reach. (471)

A life devoted to the frenetic wandering of impulsive drives is, for Maggie, a terrifyingly meaningless life. And even at the height of this extended experiment in surrendering to the pull of erotic desire, we see that Maggie maintains her sense of the mutual exclusivity of impulse and rational intention. Passion feels good, but it guarantees the total dissolution of ethical meaning and of social bonds and duties. At the same time, we see in the final turn of this passage a moment of tentative reconsideration. Maggie remembers the "clue of life" that the simple rule of renunciation had offered to her, but now it is as a distant memory of "far-off years," an object for her "young need." Indeed, when Maggie committed to divest herself of erotic desire and of embodied pleasure, she hadn't in fact known what these experiences were like—they had not yet "come within her reach."

In the chapter of *Romola* (1862–63) entitled "Drifting Away," which reworks in certain ways the central problems of "Borne Along by the Tide," Eliot tries to imagine what it would feel like truly to abscond from moral duties and claims, in the way that Maggie refuses finally to do. Disillusioned after discovering the hypocrisy of her religious mentor Savonarola, Romola decides that "she had done enough; she had striven after the impossible, and was weary of this stifling crowded life. She longed for that repose in mere sensation which she had sometimes dreamed of in the sultry afternoons of her girlhood, when she had fancied herself floating naïad-like in the waters."[33] In order to escape, perhaps into death, but in any case into a state eroticized here as the memory of some "sultry," "floating" feeling, or the naïad's state of "mere sensation," Romola steals a boat, hoists the sail, and allows herself to drift out onto the open sea:

> She was alone now: she had freed herself from all claims, she had freed herself even from that burthen of choice which presses with heavier and heavier weight when claims have loosed their guiding hold.
>
> Had she found anything like the dream of her girlhood? No. Memories hung upon her like the weight of broken wings that could never be lifted. . . . Romola felt orphaned in those wide spaces of sea and sky. She read no message of love for her in that far-off symbolic writing of the heavens, and with a great sob she wished that she might be gliding into death.[34]

The only thing more radically alienating than to repudiate all moral and social claims is to repudiate even the "burthen of choice" that those claims are intended to shape and to guide. In all of Eliot, this scene goes the furthest in imagining the simultaneous bliss and terror of the empty and isolated self. It stands as a particularly powerful counterpoint to the scene of Maggie and Stephen floating down the river, both in its emphasis on social bonds as "guides" that give form and direction to moral intention and in the notion that a dissolution of such bonds in favor of vague wandering might represent an illicit, eroticized fantasy in which pleasure becomes a "guide" to reason.

At the same time, such a fantasy is represented as exceedingly difficult, if not impossible, to realize. Maggie Tulliver does not end up eloping with Stephen Guest. She returns home to be shamed by the community of St. Ogg's, who assume that she has thrown herself at Stephen only to be rejected, since they can't imagine the situation in which she might have claimed the final word. She drowns in a flood. Romola does not drift to her death or divest herself of social ties but washes ashore in a village beset by disease, where she takes on the role of ministering angel to the surviving members of the community, rediscovering the immediacy and simplicity of moral duty and self-sacrifice. Maggie's plot is, in the end, tragic, and it's important to reemphasize here that my argument that Eliot takes vagueness seriously as a mode of thinking erotically does not imply that vagueness necessarily represents for her characters a real or viable route to some kind of sexual liberation.

Indeed, Maggie maintains to the end her insistence that moral forms must trump and exclude the formlessness of her illimitable wants; at the same time, we see in the aftermath of her journey with Stephen a profound and painful regret at the path not taken.[35] But this regret seems also to hint at the possibilities of vagueness: "The thought of Stephen was like a horrible throbbing pain, which yet, as such pains do, seemed to urge all other thoughts into activity. But among her thoughts, what others would say and think of her conduct was hardly present. Love and deep pity and remorseful anguish left no room for that" (479). The throbbing pain of Maggie's feeling for Stephen begins to mingle here with what Maggie understands as moral feelings—with love and with pity and with a remorse that feels like embodied anguish. As she drifts off to sleep that night, she relives the day that has passed, coloring and shading it differently in her memory than in her immediate experience of it:

> Did she lie down in the gloomy bedroom of the old inn that night with her will bent unwaveringly on a path of penitent sacrifice? The great struggles of life are not so easy as that; the great problems of life are not so clear. In the darkness of that night she saw Stephen's face turned towards her in passionate, reproachful misery; she lived through again all the tremulous delights of his presence with her that made existence an easy floating in a stream of joy, instead of a quiet resolved endurance and effort. The love she had renounced came back upon her with a

cruel charm, she felt herself opening her arms to receive it once more; and then it seemed to slip away and fade and vanish, leaving only the dying sound of a deep thrilling voice that said, "Gone—for ever gone." (479–80)

Hindsight allows Maggie to relent somewhat in her narrow pursuit of "penitent sacrifice" and to acknowledge, in the simplest way, that life isn't always "so clear." As Maggie dreams of opening her arms to embrace Stephen's love, we're reminded of course of the "impetuous embrace" of the river as it meets the rush of the tide. Only in this case, the embrace is unreturned and quickly dissolves into the irretrievable past. At least in dreams, Maggie dwells for a moment in the "darkness" where the easy floating of desire and the effort of form and reason come together in a dense intermingling, if only as a way of fully absorbing the irrevocability of her decision: "Gone—for ever gone."

The tragedy of *The Mill on the Floss* lies, finally, in its seeming hopelessness about the possibility of making eros intelligible or vivid as a valid kind of social claim. If Maggie is unable to reconcile "uncertain impulse" with the "claims" and "duties" of her ethical life, it's because her world offers her no formal vocabulary through which to conceive of such a reconciliation. She has, to put it somewhat roughly, no *name* or recognizable category for the kind of thinking or feeling in which these two dimensions of the self might overlap, only a distinct sense that they are separated by a crucial boundary whose dissolution would equal the dissolution of one's very self and one's sense of social belonging. Stanley Cavell follows Eliot in seeing this as a profound problem for our philosophical conception of what kinds of "claims" are understood as vitally social and which are understood as merely personal. He takes the aesthetic claim as his example of a kind of claim that feels "personal" in some sense and yet also seems to call out for sharing, for communication, for the intelligibility of language. He argues that we might compare the idea of "the risk of aesthetic isolation with that of moral or political isolation," and he goes on to describe "the aesthetic claim . . . as a kind of compulsion to share a pleasure, hence as tinged with an anxiety that the claim stands to be rebuked. It is a condition of, or threat to, that relation to things called aesthetic, that something I know and cannot make intelligible stands to be lost to me."[36] While Cavell is interested in aesthetic knowledge, his argument seems readily translatable to the concept of erotic knowledge. In other words, erotic knowledge occupies a similarly liminal position between the idiosyncratic (something that I know and experience and that no other can feel as I do) and the social (something that I want to make known, to share with someone else in a way that is meaningful and intelligible). It also seems to carry with it a similar anxiety about its potential to be "rebuked" or lost if it cannot be made comprehensible—if it cannot, in other words, find a life outside of myself. Maggie Tulliver's desire is indeed something she *knows*, and yet she cannot find a way to put it into the language of ethical forms and of social life. In the end, that knowledge or that dimension of the self "stands to be lost" to her.

The Indefinable Movements of *Middlemarch*

We know that Eliot was very familiar with Mill's *A System of Logic*, with its liberal solution of the problem of vagueness through debate and provisional agreement—and that it left her uninspired. As she wrote to a friend in 1875, "though I have studied his books, especially his Logic and Political Economy, with much benefit, I have no consciousness of their having made any marked epoch in my life."[37] We might imagine, of course, that whatever "epoch" they did make was a vague one rather than a "marked" one, and that the importance of Mill's theory of logic to her conceptualization of human psychology was based upon a fundamental ambivalence toward it rather than an enthusiastic embrace. In any event, it is clear that the narrator of *Middlemarch* shares her proclaimed indifference—even her skepticism—toward Mill's theory, in which vagueness can be resolved by drawing arbitrarily stipulated boundaries. At the same time, without clear concepts and sharp circumscriptions, the representation of psychological life can become difficult. In a description of Fred Vincy's weak-willed return to gambling, for example, Eliot's narrator insists that "Fred did not enter into formal reasons, which are a very artificial, inexact way of representing the tingling returns of old habit, and the caprices of young blood. . . . It is in such indefinable movements that action often begins" (672). This is the ethical equivalent of the paradox of the heap: just as we can't locate the precise tipping point from heap to non-heap, the movement from "tingling" desire to reasoned intention, and from intention to action, is fundamentally "indefinable." Along with Eliot's narrator, we resist the idea that this tipping point is ascribable to any one definable moment, one nameable step in a series of linked premises. But this leads us into trouble, because if the structure of our ethical thinking is vague, the world of reason and desire, and its representation, become a blurry mess. Like Mill, Eliot is careful to guard against vagueness becoming a kind of refuge for the weak-minded, the weak-willed, and the morally careless. If every motive, every stirring of impulse, every movement, seems to add up, bit by bit, grain by grain, until suddenly I've given in to an insidious desire without knowing how, then my ability to absolve myself of moral responsibility becomes radically expansive. Eliot's narrator insists that she truly sees all, that no movement is too miniscule to be registered (if not clearly named and defined) by the precise vision of the novel when it narrows and magnifies, like the microscope that Eliot so often uses as the metaphor for a certain mode of novelistic vision, and that Frege takes as the figure for the mechanically enhanced clarity of logic.

How, indeed, does a novel represent in concrete terms those troublesome borderline cases of psychic life in which erotic impulse and reasoned ethical reflection seem difficult to disentangle? If this is a problem enacted primarily at the level of characterization in *The Mill on the Floss*—Maggie's struggle to represent to herself the ways in which reason can be blurry, or desire crystal clear—then in *Middlemarch* the problem takes on an additional formal dimension, in which the narrator herself often thinks about vagueness as a problem of omniscience and novelistic world building. How can she represent her characters' intentions and desires with precision? How can she clearly circumscribe the world of her novel without slipping beyond the edges of that world into the infinite universe beyond? One solution for these problems of representation is to use metaphor, as Frege and Wittgenstein do in their attempts to define the strange powers and capacities (and weaknesses and incapacities) of vague language, which seems comprehensible only through the metaphoric structure of comparison: ordinary language is the eye as opposed to the microscope, a human hand as opposed to an artificial one, the rough gesture as opposed to the precise mark. In order to represent the indefinability plaguing the interior world of reason and desire, Eliot assembles a family of metaphoric figures that tend curiously to disrupt the novel's realism and veer toward the allegorical form of the psychomachia (a technique for representing the bad logic of desire that we've already seen at work in Brontë). The narrator of *Middlemarch*, after describing Rosamond's complicated attraction to Lydgate, which mixes erotic excitement with a more reflective and strategic interest in the possibility that he is a "man of family," offers an anticipatory response to the skeptical reader:

> If you think it incredible that to imagine Lydgate as a man of family could cause thrills of satisfaction which had anything to do with the sense that she was in love with him, I will ask you to use your power of comparison a little more effectively, and consider whether red cloth and epaulets have never had an influence of that sort. Our passions do not live apart in locked chambers, but, dressed in their small wardrobe of notions, bring their provisions to a common table and mess together, feeding out of the common store according to their appetite. (166)

The narrator tries here to defend the verisimilitude of her representation of Rosamond's motivations: despite our moralizing tendency to distinguish good reasons from bad, or the mere "thrills" of erotic attraction (whether to status or to a man in uniform) from the more deeply reasoned but related response of love,

we must admit that in reality our psychic and erotic lives are far more tumultuous than that. The question then becomes: What is the nature of the "common
table" where our various passions "mess together"? What is the "common store"
out of which they feed?

It is Dorothea Brooke who most stubbornly resists the narrator's picture of
the "common table" and the "common store" in her tendency to separate the
ethical from what she sees as the merely personal. Early in the novel, her ethics
is grounded on a severe impulse to renunciation (common to many of Eliot's
heroines, from Dinah Morris to Maggie Tulliver to Romola), as well as a high
standard of self-knowledge and self-cultivation. She understands the fuzziness
of thinking as a failing that must be corrected by reason or a resolute act of will.
As the narrator puts it in describing her yearning for moral clarity, "For a long
while she had been oppressed by the indefiniteness which hung in her mind,
like a thick summer haze, over all her desire to make her life greatly effective"
(28). And yet, prior to this, the narrator hints at something else in Dorothea,
an openness of vision and feeling that seems oriented toward the very vagueness that she desires to eliminate from her mind. Although she appears to us
as a thorough-going ascetic, the narrator insists that "there was nothing of an
ascetic's expression in her bright full eyes, as she looked before her, not con-
sciously seeing, but absorbing into the intensity of her mood, the solemn glory
of the afternoon with its long swathes of light between the far-off rows of limes,
whose shadows touched each other" (27). Absorbing rather than seeing this
scene, Dorothea's vision encompasses sharp-edged "swathes" of light (this is the
sense of "swathe" as a unit of measurement for a piece of land, or as the sharp
slash of the mower's scythe), as well as the tantalizingly vague image of shadows
beginning to touch, perhaps soon to merge.[38] It is difficult to tell at what point
one shadow ends and the other begins, or to find that zone of deeper blackness
where one overlays the other.

Dorothea, in other words, suppresses what seems to be her natural impulse
toward vagueness. She takes refuge from it in what she understands to be the
highly organized, taxonomizing scholarship of Casaubon: "she was looking forward to higher initiation in ideas, as she was looking forward to marriage, and
blending her dim conceptions of both" (86). Even here, Dorothea's tendency to
the imaginative "blending" of love with wisdom, the erotic with the rational,
is understood by the narrator as a failing, or at least as a kind of "dim" naïveté.
During her honeymoon in Rome, as she grows disillusioned with Casaubon and
his frigid romantic unavailability, she laments in even more pointed terms her
inability to seize upon a "distinctly shapen grievance that she could state even to
herself," since it seems that Casaubon's failure to excite her must merely be a re-

sult of "her own spiritual poverty" (192). Without the active mentorship in reason that she had expected from Casaubon, she again feels unable to know and to shape her own mind: "by a sad contradiction Dorothea's ideas and resolves seemed like melting ice floating and lost in the warm flood of which they had been but another form. She was humiliated to find herself a mere victim of feeling, as if she could know nothing except through that medium" (198). Here, the image of the common table at which the passions feed out of a common store is refigured as a body of water filled with quickly melting floes of ice. But in this revised metaphor, instead of separate passions emerging from locked chambers and coming to feast together, we have a change of state. Indistinct eros and the finished shape of reason have the same molecular structure, which only has to change the frequency and heat of its vibrations in order to take on new appearances and new functions. We can't help but hear in this metaphor the echo of Lucy Snowe's "brittle speech," which "shivers" to pieces and then "dissolves" like ice in her attempts to make her feelings for M. Paul clear.

The culmination of Dorothea's vagueness plot returns us to the problem of limits when, late in the novel, Dorothea discovers Ladislaw and Rosamond in what she mistakenly believes to be a moment of illicit intimacy. She sees them together "in the terrible illumination of a certainty which filled up all outlines," admitting no vague undecidability (775). But this bright certainty leads to emotional tumult: "She had seen something so far below her belief, that her emotions rushed back from it and made an excited throng without an object" (776). These are not the passions seated together at a common table but a chaotic mob of emotions searching for a clear concept to which they might attach themselves. Dorothea tries to find an "object" around which to organize her emotional energy, but that object has now become hopelessly general. When her sister Celia asks what's vexing her, she replies, "Oh, all the troubles of all people on the face of the earth" (776), turning the vague "indefinable movements" of emotion toward an equally indefinable generality (672). Later, Dorothea hides herself in a locked room and sinks down, broken, into the "throng" of her emotions:

> The limit of resistance was reached, and she had sunk back helpless within the clutch of inescapable anguish. . . . [S]he locked her door, and turning away from it towards the vacant room she pressed her hands hard on the top of her head, and moaned out—
>
> "Oh, I did love him!"
>
> Then came the hour in which the waves of suffering shook her too thoroughly to leave any power of thought. (786)

Even as Dorothea crosses the "limit of resistance" by which she has tried unsuccessfully to contain and circumscribe her emotions (or, indeed, to organize them by sublimating them) and sinks back into anguish, announcing her love as the clarity of hindsight washes over her, her last, literal gesture of repression is to press her hands down upon her head, to try to maintain a physical limit in the place of the psychic limit that has dissolved into painful indistinctness. And then come the "waves"—in French, of course, *les vagues*—of suffering that presage a kind of rebirth for Dorothea as she rises the next morning: "she had awaked to a new condition: she felt as if her soul had been liberated from its terrible conflict; she was no longer wrestling with her grief, but could sit down with it as a lasting companion and make it a sharer in her thoughts. For now the thoughts came thickly" (787).[39] The imagined animosity between Casaubon's moral claim to Dorothea's loyalty and her own feelings for Ladislaw transforms into an image of sharing, a companionship of self with self, thought with thought—and the thoughts swarm "thickly" in this shared psychic space, impossible to corral.

Dorothea, long a pursuer of the "distinctly shapen" idea, arrives at a different conception of psychic organization and, indeed, of the kind of accountability that we can expect of ourselves where the moral claims of erotic desire are concerned. This is a mode of accountability that must be clear about vagueness and its real impact upon our thinking, desiring, and speaking, measuring the impact of "indefinability" by trying to clarify the relation between vague categories through metaphor: as friends eating at a common table, as ice melting into water, as the violent throng that settles into friendly companionship. Form is, after all, about difference for Eliot, and metaphor is fundamentally a study of difference and similarity as they interact in unpredictable ways. The question of vagueness, then, is a question of form and formlessness and what lies between them. How do thoughts and desires take form from what Eliot imagines again and again as an infinitesimal unit of form, not least in Lydgate's search for the "primitive tissue" that underlies all organic structures or Casaubon's search for the master key of mythological structures (148)? Lydgate's scientific ambition is later subtly refigured as a more expansive pursuit of the mysterious turning points of psychic experience: "he wanted to pierce the obscurity of those minute processes which prepare human misery and joy, those invisible thoroughfares which are the first lurking-places of anguish, mania, and crime, that delicate poise and transition which determine the growth of happy or unhappy consciousness" (165). It seems that our only way to access the "minute processes" or principles organizing the "delicate poise and transition" of thought and desire is to look closely at the finished forms that these infinitesimal gradations produce.

What remnants of that origin cling to their edges, making their shapes blurry, difficult to behold steadily in our field of inner vision? Freud takes up these same questions in his concept of the intensely pleasurable "oceanic feeling" of infancy, "a feeling of an indissoluble bond, of being one with the external world as a whole," and in the related concept of the polymorphous perversity that distributes erotic pleasure indiscriminately over the entire surface of the body.[40] But these powerful metaphors nonetheless figure vagueness as a developmental stage to be outgrown in the shaping and circumscribing of our erotic selves and in the naming of our erotic investments, a process that Freud compares to the building of "dams" that over time "restrict the flow" of pleasure toward normative stimuli and erogenous zones.[41] In the end, Freud offers us little sense that vagueness might be not an incipient threat of psychic disintegration but a place in which to dwell or to return to periodically, as an object of reasoned reflection or a real mechanism of psychic and erotic organization.

Freud comes close to taking vagueness seriously in his attempt to come to a psychoanalytic explanation for the "oceanic feeling" and the conditions under which we might reexperience it in adulthood, once the defensive line between self and world has been so clearly drawn. He begins by reminding us about the continuity of the ego with the unconscious: "the ego is continued inwards, without any sharp delimitation, into an unconscious mental entity which we designate as the id and for which it serves as a kind of façade."[42] But despite such inward continuity (the lack of a precise limit between conscious and unconscious self), the line between the ego and the outside world is unmistakable. The only exception occurs at "the height of being in love," when "the boundary between ego and object threatens to melt away."[43] Although an easy alignment of Eliot with Freud is tempting here, I want instead to emphasize the way in which Freud, like Mill, represses what is most difficult about the problem of vague boundaries, that is, the sheer muddle that it represents, the irreducibility and the inescapability of the vague field between clear concepts. The indeterminate zone between unconscious and ego is in Freudian theory reduced to a kind of waiting room with its own definition and boundaries, the transit point called the preconscious, which lies between two carefully delineated realms, one of libidinal drives and the other of reasoned formalism. The preconscious is at best a point or a field through which messages are relayed from id to ego and back again, but it has no substance or texture of its own. The dissolution of the line between self and other, on the other hand, if indeed it ever makes good on its *threat* of melting away in love, is imagined as a utopian disappearance of all boundaries or, in other words, as an ecstatic return of the oceanic feeling.

Leo Bersani's response to this tendency of Freudian psychoanalysis to rarefy and pathologize our states and feelings of formlessness returns us to the question of the outer limits of a novelistic world, those limits that Eliot found so hauntingly impossible to draw. ("Every limit is a beginning as well as an ending.") In "Sociality and Sexuality," Bersani revisits the psychoanalytic question of the origin of relationality, an origin that is in some sense impossible to represent, he suggests, because such a representation would require that we imagine the scene of nonrelation, of sheer undifferentiation, that would have to precede it. Because we can't comfort ourselves by telling fully the story of how relationality begins, we are beset by the anxiety that what has taken form might just as easily have failed to take form out of that bogeyman fantasy of nothingness. Art, Bersani argues, is the means by which we come closest to understanding the tenuousness of form and the inaccessibility of its origins, because it allows us to imagine situations in which formal relations dissolve: "the coming-to-be of relationality, which is our birth into being, can only be retroactively enacted, and it is enacted largely as a rubbing out of formal relations. Perhaps traditional associations of art with form-giving or form-revealing activities are at least partly a denial of such formal disappearance in art."[44] What begins, in other words, must end; what takes shape must be rubbed out, or at least smudged. Bersani is, like Freud, thinking about the relations between self and world, rather than primarily about the reflective relationship of self to self or, indeed, of novelist to fictional character.

My argument so far has been that we might read Eliot not only as a novelist of ethical clarity or "sharpness" but also as an artist who registers the sheer difficulty of the kind of self-understanding required to give erotic life a meaningful shape, to speak about erotic feeling as a "lasting companion" to reason, a "sharer in thoughts." In Eliot, thoughts come thickly, and ideas and desires often change from solid to liquid and back again—before we know it. We must reckon with vagueness, and in doing so risk becoming stuck in its mire, because not to do so would represent a dangerous superficiality in ethical thinking, a refusal to acknowledge the real ethical force of erotic life, and a gullible overinvestment in the arbitrary lines that we so often use to organize our psychic lives and our rational concepts. Indeed, when Lydgate tries to "pierce the obscurity" of the mind, to burrow down to the place where all form disintegrates, he finds himself cast adrift despite his careful scientific method, and feels "that agreeable afterglow of excitement when thought lapses from examination of a specific object into a suffusive sense of its connections with all the rest of our existence—seems, as it were, to throw itself on its back after vigorous swimming and float with the repose of unexhausted strength" (165). Eliot's description enacts the kind of suffusion it describes, as "thought" and thought's "specific object" can each be understood as the antecedent of the unclear pronoun "its": "a suffusive sense of *its* connections." If we're meant to imagine *thought's* connections, then we might see this as something like Freud's oceanic feeling, in which the psyche feels so vibrantly connected to the external world as to lose its defensive outlines and its spatial bearings. On the other hand, we can easily understand this pronoun as referring to "the specific object" of thought—in Lydgate's case, the mysterious process by which thoughts and desires take form out of obscurity, or the infinitesimal transition from desire to desire, thought to thought. But the more we try to bring such a process or mechanism or structuring principle into focus, the more it seems that form and obscurity, taxonomy and tumult, are so intimately connected as to be inseparable—so densely admixed that they are suffused by their very interconnections.

The image of Lydgate's mind thrown on its back and floating suggests one example of what an ethos of vagueness might look like: a lived commitment or aspiration to the kind of epistemic disorientation that comes with submerging oneself in the dark places between, behind, or before clear forms. Amanda Anderson has argued that theorists too often invoke "ethos" as a way of describing situated commitments and practices while nonetheless attempting to avoid the normativity associated with liberal and rationalist models of ethics: "ethos," she insists, allows these theorists to have their cake and eat it, too, rejecting what they understand as the coerciveness of norms while still describing aspects of life that seem inherently normative.[45] In characterizing vagueness as an "ethos," I risk seeming to idealize (or suggesting that Eliot idealizes) states of confusion and ethical debilitation as a kind of utopian liberation from norms of rationality. But the problem of vagueness is internal to systems of language and rationality and, therefore, to the practice of making normative claims at all, a practice Eliot undoubtedly values. And so while vagueness is not an ideal for Eliot, it is nonetheless an important point of orientation in our ethical lives, something that one must experience and acknowledge in order to understand it and make use of it, but also something that would make ethical life untenable if it became a permanent condition of hazy confusion. If vagueness is real, Eliot suggests, and if we cannot get away from it either as a property of language or as a property of feeling, desire, and thought, then we must learn how to use it or how to see it as strengthening, rather than disintegrating, our ethical lives.

Lydgate's suffusive connections might also suggest the idea of vagueness as a "mood" or a "background" that enables and underlies structured thought. Rita Felski and Susan Fraiman, for example, have argued for "mood" as a concept that might complicate the theory of affect, particularly insofar as the generality and aimlessness of mood "circumvents the clunky categories often imposed on experience: subjective versus objective, feeling versus thinking, latent versus manifest. The field of affect studies," they point out, "is sometimes taken to task for reinforcing such dichotomies, creating a picture of affect as a zone of ineffable and primordial experience that is subsequently squeezed into the rationalist straitjacket of language."[46] Far from Mill's solution of pragmatic efficiency or Boole's escape to the ideal (and ideally lucid) language of symbolic logic, Eliot's psychological realism commits her to a reckoning with our all-too-human confusions of desire and reason, of erotic impulse and reasoned intention. Rather than considering vagueness as a philosophical problem to be neatly solved, Eliot's fiction asks: What is the experience of vagueness? What does it *feel* like to take the borderline case as an object of examination, as a guide to action, or simply as an inescapable state of psychic existence? When Dorothea, for example, struggles to sort out her complicated feelings upon reading the letter in which Casaubon proposes marriage, her best course of action seems to be not a steeling of the reasoning mind for communication with God, but the warm and pleasurable emptying of the mind: "She could not pray under the rush of solemn emotion in which thoughts became vague and images floated uncertainly, she could but cast herself, with a childlike sense of reclining in the lap of a divine consciousness which sustained her own" (44). One possible response to the onslaught of psychic vagueness is to give up on the sense of a bounded, agential self, and in doing so to "cast" oneself free. In this case, the experience of thoughts and images and desires haphazardly blending and overlapping extends outward to a sense that consciousness itself blends with some wider "divine" consciousness.

Of course, such a response doesn't get Dorothea very far and seems emblematic at this juncture of her "childlike" longing for an imperious but nurturing authority to whom she might entrust her moral guidance. Later on in the novel, as Dorothea navigates married life, the narrator offers us a famous description of the process of learning to separate one's own identity from that of others:

> We are all of us born in moral stupidity, taking the world as an udder to feed our supreme selves: Dorothea had early begun to emerge from that stupidity, but yet it had been easier to her to imagine how she would devote herself to Mr Casaubon, and become wise and strong in his strength and wisdom, than to conceive with that distinctness which is no longer reflection but feeling—an idea wrought back to the directness of sense, like the solidity of objects—that he had an equivalent centre of self, whence the lights and shadows must always fall with a certain difference. (211)

The problem here is the distinction of the "easiness" of subsuming one's own identity to another's versus the difficult effort of feeling with "distinctness" the difference between oneself and another.[47] The strangeness of the passage is in its unexpected reversal of the roles of "reflection" and "feeling." How, we're forced to ask, does a profoundly metaphysical problem such as our capacity to imagine and to know other selves come to be an object of "the directness of sense, like the solidity of objects"? It seems that the kind of distinctness that Eliot's narrator is after is not one of abstract, conceptual lines and boundaries but instead the sort of undeniable feeling of distinctness that comes from pressing up against another with one's very body. The project of feeling out limits and forms and lines can't be a logical project at all, it seems. Rather, it must be a project of a body groping in the darkness, just beginning to emerge from "moral stupidity" and looking outside of oneself for the limits so solid, so directly *there*, that they can't dissolve into vagueness. Lydgate's experience, on the other hand, is a kind of involution of thought, in which the elements of consciousness appear so densely interconnected as to seem infinitely deep and infinitely expansive.

In either case, what I've been calling Eliot's vision of vagueness as "ethos" or "mood" is linked to images of floating, swimming, reclining, passively receiving: in short, to images of deeply pleasurable surrender and oceanic feelings. Whether this is understood as an ethically good or bad kind of pleasure in the world of Eliot's novels is so far unclear, or at least the possible outcomes of such states are various enough that they can seem ethically neutral or contingent. In other words, while "ethos" provides us with a broad sense of the kinds of commitments and goals that would lead one to sink into the comfort (or the disorientation) of vagueness, it also might encompass a set of norms about how and when to deploy the seductive haziness of vagueness as a mode of reflective self-understanding and moral reasoning. The sense that all is interconnected, that no true lines can be drawn, and that no valid taxonomies exist, can lead to an exhausted disavowal—an emptying out of the self, or as we saw in the case of *Romola,* a dissolution of social and ethical connections. This sense can also lead to a kind of giddy lightheadedness in which vagueness becomes eroticized as a source of pleasure. This mode of vagueness is often described by Eliot in terms of absorption and involution, as in the image already discussed of Dorothea "absorbing into the intensity of her mood" the sensation of a beautiful afternoon, or Maggie Tulliver's compulsion toward the maximum fullness and depth of pleasure. "I was never satisfied with a *little* of anything," she tells Philip Wakem: "That is why it is better for me to do without earthly happiness altogether. . . . I never felt that I had enough music—I wanted more instruments playing together—I wanted voices to be fuller and deeper" (328). As we can see from Maggie's account, the two reactions to vagueness that I've been describing can easily combine—the pleasure of the excessive fullness of the erotic self can be counteracted by a moralizing tendency toward total renunciation. Since the kind of maximum pleasure that Maggie so painfully and desperately desires is impossible, better to do without pleasure altogether, to stop the drive toward pleasure at its source and thereby to foreclose disappointment.

Critics have understood Eliot's interest in representing the dense interconnectedness and overlapping of psychic life, and her skepticism toward easy classification, in various other ways. I want to pause here before concluding to take stock of how our understanding of Eliot has tended to circle around versions of vagueness as primarily a scientific or aesthetic problem, without being fully able to account for its force as a problem of language and logic. In the 1980s, Gillian Beer (in *Darwin's Plots*) and Sally Shuttleworth (in *George Eliot and Nineteenth-Century Science*) pointed to Eliot's interests in evolutionary theory and the Victorian movement toward a model of organic form in biology, psychology, and social theory as contextual explanations for her ambitiousness in representing infinitesimal shades of psychological detail, formal complexity, and social interdependence.[48] More recently, Nicholas Dames has argued for a powerful link between Eliot's theory of the long novel form and Wagner's theory of long musical form, both of which work to achieve a combination of "elongated temporal length and insistent complexity" or, in an even more suggestive formulation for our purposes, "demanding and exhausting forms" of "unbroken complexity."[49] Jed Esty reads *The Mill on the Floss* as a Victorian origin point for his story of the modernist bildungsroman, partly for the way in which Eliot positions "the mediating, reconciling chronotope of the nation" as the seemingly impossible "overlapping" of local space and imperial global space.[50] Evolution, organic theory, musical form, and the relationship between local, national, and global spaces all provide Eliot with useful analogues for the theorization of forms that are fundamentally continuous, overlapping, or interpenetrating in space and time but also are overwhelmingly complex in that continuousness—made up of indistinguishable elements that are thickly layered and overlapping.

Indeed, Catherine Gallagher has taken the very concept of the category or the "type" in its supposed opposition to the instance or the particular as a crucial problem for Eliot's strategies of characterization. Gallagher suggests that in Eliot's work, fictional individuals take general types as their referents, even while realist novels always "conjured as their own 'background' an empirical cultural understanding that the type is only a mental abstraction from more real concrete individuals in the world." The novel form is therefore "structured like a triptych, in which ontologically distinct categories of 'the particular' appear on either side of a category of 'the general,' creating a centrality for the middle category not normally sustainable under the empirical assumptions that contrast the ideality of the type with the substantiality of the experientially available individual." According to Gallagher's model, the "general" characterizes the zone of overlap between distinctive versions of particularity, one fictional and the other real, rather than merely standing in opposition to a monolithic concept of particularity. Gallagher goes on to argue that we have overemphasized Eliot's *ethical* conception of particularity, which is the basis of her theory of sympathy and which inspires the caricature of her stern Victorian moralism; instead, "Eliot's ethics are preceded and animated by an *erotics* of particularization" generated by the reader's identification with fictional characters who yearn to pass to the other side of the zone of "generality," to become embodied and concretely real.[51]

We might imagine Gallagher's "triptych" form of novelistic characterization—and, indeed, Esty's overlapping chronotopes—as Venn diagrams. And yet even John Venn himself, the Victorian logician who popularized this distinctive diagrammatic way of representing overlapping categories, understood that such a representation, with its sharp solid lines, conceals the vagueness intrinsic to the very concept of "overlap." He suggests using dotted lines in the overlap segment of the diagram or, in the case of diagrams that include many categories, filling different areas with different saturations of color, from shades of grey to the black of maximum density of overlap. Finally, he points out that we might use other shapes that have a better capacity than circles for representing vague boundaries.[52] Venn goes on to argue that a rigid insistence upon the exactness of logical diagramming as a mathematically precise representation—in which the sizes of individual compartments would "match up," for example, with the relative extensions of various categories—actually confuses the qualitative aspects of logical set theory with its more quantitative mathematical aspects: "The compartments yielded by our diagrams must be regarded solely in the light of being bounded by such and such contours, as lying inside or outside such and such lines. We must abstract entirely from all consideration of their relative magnitude, as we do of their actual shape, and trace no more connection between these facts and the logical extension of the terms which they represent than we do between this logical extension and the size and shape of the letter symbols, *A* and *B* and *C*."[53] In other words, diagrams act as visual aids that offer us easily apprehensible boundaries, contours, and shapes by which to understand the relationships between various concepts or classes; and yet, as Venn points out, these shapes are in another sense mere phantasms, arbitrarily situated in space, something like the many shapes that we might choose to draw within the blurry edges of Wittgenstein's rectangle. As Eliot puts it in relation to aesthetic form, "Boundary or outline & visual appearance are modes of form which in music and poetry can only have a metaphorical presence" ("Notes" 433). The shapes of a Venn diagram are in fact used as *variables* in just the same way that we use other symbols as simplified stand-ins for a dizzyingly complex range of possibilities. They represent, as Venn says, a qualitative kind of experience rather than a quantitative mapping of logical language onto empirical reality.

In this sense, Venn's model of logical representation is at least partly analogous to Eliot's model of fictional representation, in which the qualitative experience of the zone of overlap is much more important than the rational project of drawing exact boundaries or, perhaps more precisely, in which the drawing of boundaries is constantly exposed in all its arbitrariness. This aid to understanding might comfort us, Eliot tells us in many ways, but it is temporary and superficial and will never exempt us from a reckoning with vagueness. The painfulness and the confusion of apprehending what Dames might call the "unbroken complexity" that vagueness captures is counterbalanced by the ethical productivity of such apprehension. The vagueness inherent in the continuity of lived experience can serve as a strategic cover, as we've already seen, in which small decisions add up as if by magic to moral failure, but vagueness also accurately represents the difficulty and swampy thickness of ethical thinking as against the clear outlines that are at best pragmatic aids to efficient or casuistic moral classification.

And so finally, vagueness in Eliot takes shape as a question both of space (the problem of imagining a spatialized organization to psychic life in which different kinds of knowledge and feeling are separated into distinct categories) and of time (the problem of dividing one's life, one's reasons, one's desires, one's language, into discrete and apprehensible segments). As Will Ladislaw insists to Dorothea, "To be a poet is to have a soul . . . in which knowledge passes instantaneously into feeling, and feeling flashes back as a new organ of knowledge. One may have that condition by fits only" (223). Perhaps, then, to be a novelist is to have a soul in which knowledge passes slowly and laboriously into feeling, and feeling flows or diffuses itself—just as slowly and laboriously—back again. Ladislaw is, of course, oblivious to the problem of vagueness in his description of poetic sensibility; to him the transformation of knowledge into feeling and back again is an instantaneous flash. Now you see it, now you don't. And yet when feeling "flashes back as a new organ of knowledge," it seems it must be bringing something with it, interfusing itself with knowledge in a way that raises all of the problems of vagueness which have by now become familiar to us. What is the maximum amount of feeling that can be imparted to knowledge before we cease to call it knowledge and insist that it's something else entirely? Does feeling in this case overwhelm knowledge, so that we have a simple transition of one to the other? Or do we need another name for what happens when these two kinds of experience become thoroughly mixed?

If the philosophical interest in vagueness is, at its root, a challenge to the idea that our language can be represented by the formal system of logic, Eliot's interest is in discovering what other forms we might imagine as guiding our rational, ethical, and erotic lives, especially insofar as these various modes of knowing and thinking merge together. I've argued that figurative language provides one such model, one that helps Eliot to clarify the concept of vagueness, and one useful to philosophers struggling to be precise about what we might gain and lose when we toggle between ordinary language and logical formalism. What does logic look like beyond form or at its vague edges? As we have seen, "logic" was undergoing a redefinition in nineteenth-century England, from a concrete science of ordinary language and ordinary reasoning to a mathematical science of the objective relations between truth-functional propositions, relations that are self-evident and are thus not contingent upon particular psychological states. Aligning logical form with mathematical form, Frege writes, "Neither logic nor mathematics has the task of investigating minds and the contents of consciousness whose bearer is a single person. Perhaps their task could be represented rather as the investigation of the mind, of the mind not of minds."[54] With this shift away from the particular mind and toward the ideal mind, away from the vagueness of ordinary language and toward the purity of an artificial language, the realist novel takes on a new significance as an arena for the investigation of individual or private psychology as we represent it to ourselves and others. But what if the structures of language that provide this representation are, no matter what we do, fuzzy instead of clear? Theorists of "fuzzy" logic have taken this question very seriously but tend to do so at a high level of mathematical abstraction. Eliot, however, tries to show us what such a fuzzy structure looks and feels like, what it enables and disables in our everyday experience of the world—what we might gain by sinking into and possibly emerging out of vagueness, and "what stands to be lost," as Cavell would put it, to sharpness.

CHAPTER FOUR

Henry James's Generality

The plot of Henry James's *The Awkward Age* (1899) revolves around the circulation of erotic desire and erotic knowledge: who knows what about the sexual schemes and attractions and dalliances that structure the novel? This is a particular problem in the case of Nanda Brookenham, whose potential marriage to Gustavus Vanderbank—a marriage to be bankrolled by the withdrawn and genteel Mr. Longdon, the erstwhile lover of Nanda's grandmother—provides much of the narrative momentum of the novel. Nanda is balanced between a model of erotic knowingness (the outré Tishy Grendon) and a model of erotic ignorance (the sheltered and naïve "Little Aggie," who after her marriage reveals herself to be not so prudish after all), and so it makes sense that Nanda's own uncertain knowledge, her ability or inability to decode the workings of the plots and dealings of which she is the central object, preoccupies almost every other character in the novel. "She knows everything, everything," says Vanderbank at one point to his friend Mitchy, who responds with an incantatory echo that only intensifies Vanderbank's opacity: "Everything, everything."[1] Vanderbank quickly qualifies: "But of course she can't help it. . . . Everything, literally everything, in London, in the world she lives in, is in the air she breathes—so that the longer *she's* in it the more she'll know" (221, original emphasis). The paradox that Nanda knows everything and yet might still find that there's "more" to know—or that she contains everything (as knowledge) but at the same time everything exists outside of her, as the world, or as the very air that sustains her—aligns with the paradox of the word itself, "everything," which is balanced on the line that separates the infinite from the countable. The quintessentially ambiguous Jamesian syntax only intensifies our uncertainty about the spatial limits or, indeed, the formal properties of the "everything" under discussion: Is Vanderbank saying that everything *in London* is in the air that Nanda breathes?

Everything in Nanda's particular and limited "world"? Or is everything itself—a much more indefinite or infinitely expansive everything—in London? Does the city, and Nanda's place within it, somehow hold within itself everything at all? Drag culture has often ironized this paradoxical usage of "everything" as a slangy shorthand for a kind of overwhelming glamour: "Judy Garland? She's *everything*." This item of praise, both voracious and pointed, implies an infinite fabulousness that must also maintain, in the very act of impersonation, a relationship to the particular material reality of clothes, voice, hair, and makeup—to the idiosyncrasy of style that elicits desire or identification in the first place. To say that Nanda knows everything or that the air she breathes is or contains everything is to perform a similar feint. Nanda's knowledge is both of her world and radically beyond it, is both contained by her and always threatens to disperse or dilute her particularity, to flatten her out in every direction.

The word "everything," in other words, seems to point to a limited number of things—all the things that exist in the world or in the universe or in a novel or a character as potential objects of knowledge. At the same time, in its everyday usage, it's often meant to evoke a sheer sense of infinity. If an unmodified "all" seems clean and simple in its inclusiveness, then "everything" still maintains an attachment, at least etymologically, to materiality or countability. There can only be so many discrete things, after all, for me to touch and to count, and yet there are enough of them out there that to try to hold in mind the idea of "every" thing can prompt a kind of exhausted resignation: they may as well be infinite for all I can know of them. Of course, encountered in a different aesthetic mode, we might also confront "everything" with the fever-pitch intensity of awe that we call the sublime. As the *Oxford English Dictionary* elegantly puts it in one of its rare entries to have remained unaltered since 1894, "The distributive sense etymologically belonging to the word is often absent, its force being merely collective; hence it is the current substitute for *all*."[2] "Everything" slips from the fastidious project of accumulation and distribution, of a counting out that seems never to end (we might think here of Mrs. Gereth's hoard of art objects in *The Spoils of Poynton*), into the "merely collective" flattening and attenuation (another favorite word of James) by which everything becomes indistinguishable from, or in effect interchangeable with, everything else.[3] It's not the *things*, after all, that tend to matter once "everything" is invoked, but the rhetorical force, the hazardous overreaching, of *everything* as an idea, or as a placeholder for a kind of incapacity of expression. "What is it?" "Oh," one might wearily respond under the weight of what seems an unbearable burden, "it's simply everything." We often forget that "everything" is a pronoun because it tends to have a profoundly unclear antecedent, difficult to point to and identify—or maybe that antecedent is always meant to be irrecoverable, painfully lost to us or to our language, somewhere out there, or everywhere.

This chapter argues that generality, a problem of logic distilled with incredible concision in the pronoun "everything," functions in James's fiction as a surprisingly labile concept through which to think about form (the form of language and the form of the novel) and its difficult relationship to the erotic life that seems most resistant to formalization. The irreverent, irresponsible, and sometimes inaccurate or unintelligible uses of "everything" in James function, in other words, as a potent kind of bad logic by which erotic desire becomes both wildly expansive and infinitely diminished, diluted, or attenuated. After all, if it's everything, it's also, in some sense, nothing at all. To attempt to speak about everything always involves us in a kind of trickery of reason, which takes advantage of the mathematical forms of modern logic that are so much more at home with the infinite than are our ordinary ways of thinking and reasoning with one another. And so the problem of generality returns us to the concept of logical space that we encountered in thinking about contradiction (a form that marks the limits of logical space) and tautology (a form that leaves logical space completely open). If it's possible to be absolutely general in our language—to take "everything" as a meaningful object of reason or attachment—then the limits of logical space seem no longer to exist, an idea that we might find alternately liberating, vertiginous, or simply numbing. We tend to think of erotic life, on the other hand, as bound up with particularity, directionality, or pointedness—the sharpness and embodied specificity of a pang—rather than with the generality and the refusal of particularity that "everything" seems to signify: the wet blanket it would seem to throw over a set of specifiable erotic cathexes. Even Freudian polymorphous perversity shares its limits with the limits of the body, and as we found in chapter three, Freudian psychoanalysis tends to see this kind of vague diffusion of pleasure as something to leave behind. This problem was the impetus for Foucault's most important insight about Freudian psychoanalysis—that its claims to clearer or deeper insight into the erotic self might be only another use of knowledge as power, which controls more than it liberates. My argument here aims to elide the tense opposition between the psychoanalytic and Foucauldian readings of the relationship between language and sexuality by pushing aside the question of insight and the question of the repressive hypothesis. What I'm after in following "everything" in James's fiction and in his theory of the novel is a different kind of "knowledge" about the erotic, one that's invested primarily in form rather than content. For Eliot and James, this formalism is why logic provides such a productive counterpoint in thinking about erotic desire: logic is a science of form indifferent on some level to content, or a formal philosophy of first principles that determines the possible shapes of our thinking without forcing us into a moral judgment about what that thinking contains. And yet the fact that logic is, above all, a normative philosophy of *right* reasoning suggests that even its form, taken as a space that must find its limits or edges somewhere, must already carry with it an ethical significance. Of course, James's interest in "everything" does not represent a coded discourse of sexual liberation. "Everything" in James is by no means a shorthand for "everything goes," precisely because it doesn't carry with it a predictable ethical evaluation about the content or the objects of erotic desire, which "everything" does so much to make indefinite and diffuse.

I begin in what follows by thinking in greater detail about how James understands "everything" as an object of erotic knowledge and as a crucial principle or problem of novelistic form, and I set that understanding against philosophical traditions of thinking about "everything" in logical terms. I then move on to an analysis of *The Portrait of a Lady* (1880–81), in which James figures Isabel Archer's self-exemption from the logical space of "everything" as a mode of erotic skepticism. "Everything" as a mechanism of negation or exclusion works quite differently in *The Golden Bowl* (1904). To talk about "everything *but*" one particular thing (often the specificity of the body or the self and the idiosyncrasy of erotic desire) in that novel is seemingly to negate particularity in favor of a diluted and evasive generality, often read in the history of James criticism as representative of an attitude of sexual repression. But for James it also provides an occasion to think through what he sees as the hazards of circumscription or at least the varied ethical complications that arise when one tries to get specific about erotic life. I move on in my reading of *The Golden Bowl* to an examination of the paradoxical concept of super-addition by which James's narrators and characters often refer to what exists outside of everything but in an intimate relation to it—often behind it, or beneath it, or reflecting it as in a mirror.[4] One might read these usages of "everything" as another version of exclusion or repression; after all, when we push something outside of the bounds of everything, we seem necessarily to make it unavailable, particularly on a logical theory of language that relies upon the set, class, or category as a crucial formal concept, of which "everything" provides the all-encompassing first principle. But I'll argue that James's interest in the possibility of "everything *and*" represents an interest in establishing a position from which to turn "everything" into an object of sympathy, identification, or perhaps fantasy, rather than an object of skeptical aversion. This is a position, in other words, from which to investigate the formal contours of everything, the possibilities it offers, and the kinds of knowledge it enables in addition to the kinds it disables. It's in these moments that James turns from an erotics of particularity or idiosyncrasy to the challenging notion of an erotics of generality.

The Most Promising Quantity

In his *New York Edition* preface to *The Ambassadors*, James offers one of his many reflections on the process of building a plot out of a small idea, a process he describes here as an easy following of "inductive steps" that led him from the idea of Lambert Strether's "position" in a specific, instantly conjured scene to the larger plot into which that scene would fit: "I accounted for everything," James tells us, "and 'everything' had by this time become the most promising quantity."[5] In looking back on his own fiction, James tends to be obsessed by the idea of a moment, an image, or a concept that produces ramifications and entailments, ballooning outward, potentially out of control. This is one of the few instances in which he seems content to allow that ballooning to proceed unimpeded, infinitely, to encompass *everything*, that "most promising quantity." The thrill of a potential relation to everything clearly represents for James a triumph of logic, a system in which the connectivity of entailment generates an unending series of linked ideas, apparently without any active effort on the part of the author. In his preface to *The Awkward Age*, on the other hand, he is at pains to defend the novel's highly circumscribed scope—its stubborn interest in representing the idiom of a strange, unrepresentative social group. "The circle surrounding Mrs. Brookenham, in my pages," he writes, "is of course nothing if not a particular, even a 'peculiar' one—and its rather vain effort (the vanity, the real inexpertness, being precisely a part of my tale) is toward the courage of that condition" (8). "Everything" is in some sense the antonym of "nothing," and yet, as I've suggested, they're often closely aligned for James, who suggests here that a failure of particularity in his treatment would, in fact, make it a treatment of nothing. Mrs. Brookenham's set is "nothing if not" particular, or perhaps it would have much the same rhetorical effect to say that if they're not particular, they're everything. The "circle surrounding" Mrs. Brookenham is analogous to the circle that circumscribes the novel itself, preventing its form from becoming too vague around the edges, and containing it as a discrete whole or composition.

This is much the same formal problem that we've seen Eliot grapple with, and James's way of describing it is strikingly similar here. He invokes, as Eliot does, the problem of shape, line, sharpness, and containment, or in other words our Venn-inspired way of understanding ideas and their relationships to one another diagrammatically: "though the relations of a human figure or a social occurrence are what makes such objects interesting, they also make them, to the same tune, difficult to isolate, to surround with the sharp black line, to frame in the square, the circle, the charming oval, that helps any arrangement of objects to become a picture" (*Awkward Age*, 5). James offers us a wavering shape, which shifts in one sentence from an indeterminate borderline to a square, to a circle, to an oval, and the lack of conjunctions makes the relationship of these shapes doubly opaque.[6] It's difficult to tell whether we should imagine these shapes as simultaneous and overlapping, as fundamentally interchangeable shapes subsumed under the metaphor of the ordinary "frame" of a picture, or as a set of alternatives, each of which carries its own formal implications. While on the level of novelistic form Eliot worries about beginnings and endings—those moments of entrance into and exit from a novelistic world, or the moments of formal genesis and dissolution as they occur in time—James worries about the out-of-control expansion of what he calls here the "little idea" that serves as the seed of the story in the author's imagination, the "proposed scale" of which story was intended to be "the limit of a small square canvas" (4). In this case, the drawing of the "charming oval" represents an achievement of aesthetic appeal and a kind of rite of magic—the drawing of the charmed circle—by which to defend against the threat of total attenuation, of the particular story overflowing its proper bounds or branching out into infinite connections—into everything.

In the case of *The Awkward Age*, James tells us that his experimental method of containment was his emulation of dramatic form in the decision to write a novel almost exclusively in dialogue. Even the few scenes of third-person narration in this novel pointedly eschew any hint of insight into characters' interiority, focusing instead on description of setting, clothing, and (sometimes) facial expression. If the English novel tends to be "a perfect paradise of the loose end," as James argues, then "the play consents to the logic of but one way, mathematically right, and with the loose end as a gross impertinence on its surface, and as grave a dishonour, as the dangle of a snippet of silk or wool on the right side of a tapestry. We are shut up wholly to cross-relations all within the action itself; no part of which is related to anything but some other part—save of course by the relation of the total to life" (14). Here we have a total reversal of the version of logic that James elaborates in the preface to *The Ambassadors*, where it is a self-directing mechanism that allows the author to lie back and bask in the wonderfully open-ended expansiveness of connection that develops out of a single scene. Now logic is a tool of mathematical precision that cuts a narrow path and is the absolute enemy of the loose end.

In the final afterthought of this passage—"save of course by the relation of the total to life"—James's plan seems to crumble: neither the novel nor the play can be formally airtight, sewn up at the edges with the kind of sharp finish for which James seems to yearn. Novels and plays have audiences, and both purport to represent an actual world, and these relations of the aesthetic to the actual are, of course, formally constitutive. The very openness to the outside that James calls loose constitutes in some sense the guarantee of wholeness and circumscription that he desires. Joseph Conrad, writing in 1904, before the magnum opus of the *New York Edition*, goes so far as to identify the conspicuous lack of a collected edition of James's work with something in his fiction itself that resists circumscription: "in the body of Mr. Henry James's work there is no suggestion of finality. . . . It is impossible to think of Mr. Henry James becoming 'complete' otherwise than by the brutality of our common fate whose finality is meaningless—in the sense of its logic being of a material order, the logic of a falling stone."[7] The material weight of the stone, or indeed of the book as an object, which seems to Conrad the only possible anchor of finality, is in itself meaningless. But as we've seen, the meaninglessness of completion that Conrad is after in fact might merely be exchanged for the meaninglessness of an oeuvre that's so open-ended as to be everything. As the narrator of *The Sacred Fount* puts it in describing his attempted escape from the relentlessly formalizing, rationalizing, systematizing drive of his own imagination, "I should leave behind me my tangled theory, no loose thread of which need I ever again pick up, in no stray mesh of which need my foot again trip. . . . Only I must break off sharp, must escape all reminders by forswearing all returns."[8] James circles back here to the terror of the loose end and its capacity to be picked up and attached onto everything in view, and to the careful craft of closure, which requires not a languorous complexity or ambiguity but a ruthless break and a confident escape into whatever lies beyond the novel's infinite capacity of expansion.

All of this is to say that we might understand James's interest in the potentially hazardous infinitude of the erotic, and similarly of novelistic form itself, as a further development or torqueing of George Eliot's interest in vagueness as a problem of logic, form, ethics, and, finally, erotics. For Eliot, the forms of desire and reason alike—their shaping, separation, and circumscription—tend to suppress an underlying field of vague interpenetration, a field that might be ethically productive as a place to revisit, or pleasurable as a place to lie back and float along with erotic impulse. We can't deny vagueness as a problem of ordinary language, and yet, for Eliot, to admit it is also to risk admitting too much of it. To commit oneself to the recognition of vagueness as a state of mind, an ethical mood, or a kind of erotic pleasure is also to commit oneself to exercising a precarious control over the extent to which vague boundaries bleed into each other, or over our ability to return each time from the murk of vagueness to the clarity of form. Close attention to vagueness, coupled with a desire for form and clarity, is a matter not of an infinite expansiveness but of an infinitesimal focus on, for example, grains of sand or finely drawn, delicate limits.

James's novelistic uses of vagueness, on the other hand, sometimes seem to pursue as their object the flattened field of undifferentiation or attenuation that precedes or underlies the forms of separateness and limitedness that Eliot works so diligently to theorize—those forms that she represents so often just as they begin to come into view as sharp lines and shapely contours.[9] Eliot insists that form is nearly synonymous with our capacity to perceive separateness and that this perception exists for us only in a kind of dialectical tension with the smooth continuity implied by vague boundaries. But James again and again refuses the resolutions promised by this dialectical model, asking us to imagine how the nebulous "everything" that would seem to terrorize Eliot might itself be a kind of form, a thing that one might talk about meaningfully and take as an object of reasoned consideration. As I've already indicated, James by no means celebrates "everything" as a shorthand for liberation, erotic freedom, or infinite knowledge; in fact, tracking "everything" in the prefaces reveals the essential in-consistency of James's theorization of his own novelistic practice. Or perhaps it's unfair, after all, to assume that the prefaces should present a consistent theory—what works for one novel, in other words, might not work for another. If an ex-periment in *The Ambassadors* with the formal device of focalization seems ame-nable to infinite expansiveness and the inductive logic of what James describes as "groping knowledge" (xxxix), it might nonetheless be true that an experiment in *The Awkward Age* with the formal features of drama necessitates a rejection of that expansiveness in favor of a narrow world, mathematically logical, in which "everything" is more of a mystical incantation than an object of representation. "Everything, everything," we hear Mitchy chant.

The question in philosophy that maps onto James's shifting understanding of "everything" is a question on which the Continental and Anglo-American tradi-tions are thoroughly divided, and James's uses of "everything" as a device of for-malization are interesting in precisely the way that they shift between these two modes: does "everything" refer to a mathematical set or invoke a metaphysical problem? For the symbolic logicians of nineteenth- and early-twentieth-century Britain, "everything" is primarily a mathematical concept—it's a way of describ-ing the set that includes all things that exist and, therefore, all smaller sets as well. In other words, it's an enabling background concept or first principle for a basic set theory, since we must be able to imagine the set that includes ev-erything in order to begin to divide everything into narrower categories. John Venn, for example, refers to "everything which the universe contains" as the referent of the number "1" in the binary algebra invented by George Boole and carried on by Venn, and simply "nothing" as the referent of "0." The mathematical notation for "everything except x," or more simply "not-x," would be "$1 - x$."[10] Everything and nothing are binary concepts of existence for a symbolic logician such as Venn or his forerunner Boole—everything that exists, or some things, or nothing; yes, maybe, or no. In 1901, however, set theory became much more complicated with Bertrand Russell's discovery of what came to be known as "Russell's paradox." Russell noticed that problems arise when we consider that some sets are members of themselves—the set of all sets, for example. The paradox is generated when we imagine a set of all sets that are not members of themselves. If this set is not a member of itself, then it simultaneously *is* a member of itself; and if this set is a member of itself, it necessarily *isn't* a member of itself.[11] We might see James's interest in "everything" as connected to an interest in this mind-bending paradox, but in fact the set of "everything" runs up against a different kind of logical weirdness, not directly related to Russell's paradox, since the set of everything decidedly *must* include all sets including itself. The problem generated here might be one of infinite regress: if everything contains itself, then what contains everything? This is not a logical paradox, but it does perhaps contribute to the vertigo of trying to bring everything into view. As I explain further later in this chapter, contemporary study of the problem of generality tends to bracket this problem altogether by understanding "everything" to refer to a "domain of inquiry" rather than a mathematical or logical set.[12]

Bertrand Russell's work on the problem of linguistic reference provides us with a different kind of contribution to our understanding of how "everything" might be understood as a set. In his 1905 essay "On Denoting," Russell takes up what had become by this time a serious problem for logic: how to deal with phrases that had, as Gottlob Frege had first described it, sense without reference, or as Russell translates it, "meaning" without "denotation."[13] These are phrases that appear to denote nonexistent or fictional objects—"The present King of France," for example, which Frege argues can still *make sense* to us as a phrase even if its referent is null. (Frege's own example is the fictional entity "Odysseus.")[14] But Russell points out that Frege's theory runs into problems if we think carefully into the logical relationship of meaning to denotation: the meaning of a phrase, Russell argues, seems as if it must *denote* its denotation, since its meaning is so bound up in its bare denoting function, in the absence of an actual object to which to point, and we've only created another layer between ourselves and the problem of empty reference. "The difficulty which confronts us," he says, "is that we cannot succeed in *both* preserving the connexion between meaning and denotation *and* preventing them from being one and the same; also that the meaning cannot be got at except by means of denoting phrases" (486). But perhaps more importantly, even denoting phrases that do refer to real objects maintain their capacity to do so in the absence of any direct knowledge of the object denoted—those objects that might as well be fictional given how remote they are from our intimate understanding. As Russell explains, "'the center of mass of the Solar System at the beginning of the twentieth century' is highly complex in *meaning*, but its *denotation* is a certain point, which is simple" (483). How do phrases that don't have any concrete meaning to me because they are so foreign to my everyday experience—such as "the center of mass of the Solar System,"—exist in propositions that *do* have meaning to me? "Nothing," "something," and "everything" are in Russell's view "the most primitive of denoting phrases," with "everything" singled out as the "ultimate and indefinable" denoting phrase by means of which all others are defined. Their special status arises from the fact that it is most obvious in the case of these phrases that they are "not assumed to have any meaning in isolation, but a meaning is assigned to *every* proposition in which they occur" (480, original emphasis). Russell points our attention to the paradoxical emptiness at the heart, or perhaps in the background, of denoting phrases, which appear to point to singular and material things while in logical terms they must point only to categories modeled after those slippery pronouns: nothing, something, everything. In the same journal forty-five years later, P. F. Strawson would criticize Russell for failing properly to distinguish the meaning of a term itself, such as "everything," from the meaning elaborated in any individual "utterance" and its potentially changing "use," a subtle modification of Russell's idea which would allow denoting phrases to have a meaning informed by performance, a meaning which could shift as the world shifts.[15] Strawson's response to Russell can be understood as an early example of the mid-twentieth-century shift away from the relentless mathematicization of symbolic logic toward what would be called ordinary language philosophy, with its sensitivities to the social life of language. In short, tracing the history of "everything" in British logic might give us a kind of miniaturized version of the history of the discipline, its innovations and controversies.

For Hegel, on the other hand, and the Continental tradition that would follow him in the philosophy of language, "everything" is not a particularly important term. Hegel is primarily interested in logic not as a mathematics but as the science of the forms of thought that enable rational consciousness at all. Logic in the Continental tradition is a first philosophy of the form of language, without the heavily normative focus on "right reasoning" that tends to preoccupy the British tradition. Instead of "everything," Hegel is after the infinite and, more specifically, what he calls the genuine or true infinity as opposed to "bad infinity" (sometimes translated as "spurious" infinity). Hegel argues that the bad infinite aligns with our everyday way of thinking of infinity as a never-ending series or collection of finite things, or to put it more simply, as the opposite or negation of the finite. If we imagine infinitude and finitude as opposites, Hegel insists, we miss the point. We imagine an infinitude that is never complete, always expanding and always limited externally by the finite things that continue to be added on to it, always needing to add one *more* thing, and then another, to its series in order simply to *keep going* to infinity. In James's *What Maisie Knew* (1897), the governess Mrs. Wix invokes just this kind of infinitude when she imagines that her ward Maisie "was distinctly on the road to know Everything," before this "road" is then refigured as "a long, tense cord, twitched by a nervous hand, on which the valued pearls of intelligence were to be neatly strung."[16] This kind of beading, stringing things (one pearl neatly after another) toward the destination of everything, is what Hegel describes a "*finitized* infinite," in a paradoxical turn of phrase that echoes the tension within the word "everything." Hegel's emblem of "true" infinity is the circle, which has no beginning and no end and therefore represents infinity as a whole concept or totality that contains the finite within itself as "moments" or "internal differentiations." In other words, Hegel's true infinity represents the core of his mystical brand of transcendence. It is "the true being" and "the elevation above restriction," and "at the mention of the infinite, soul and spirit *light up*, for in the infinite the spirit *is* at home, and not only abstractly; rather, it rises to itself; to the light of its thinking, its universality, its freedom." For Hegel, the finite contains within itself the will to the infinite as a kind of energy of potentiality: the infinite is its "affirmative determination, its vocation, what it truly is in itself."[17]

Henry James's uses of "everything" as a device of formalization are interesting in precisely the way that they shift between the two modes I've outlined, and particularly because the work in logic and epistemology that James would have been more intimately familiar with, that of his friend Charles Sanders Peirce especially, draws so heavily upon both of these traditions. If we look to an essay such as "Logic as Semiotic," we see Peirce appealing to the idea of "mathematical reasoning" and to the principles of set theory in formulating his idea of logic as a "doctrine of signs," while in the movement from traditional logic to the idea of the semiotic, his attention to the sociality of meaning, constructed by a relationship between a sign, an object, and a subjective "interpretant," anticipates somewhat the later shift in England toward ordinary language philosophy. If we look, on the other hand, to "The Law of Mind," we find a thoroughly Hegelian concept of consciousness as an irreducible "continuity" or what Peirce terms "synechism," rather than as a series of fully differentiated impressions.[18]

In the contemporary study of logic, the problems I've been tracing fall under the rubric of "absolute generality," a concept of logical quantification over which philosophers are divided. Agustín Rayo and Gabriel Uzquiano, in their introduction to a 2006 anthology devoted to treatments of the problem of absolute generality, point to the issue I've just been tracing: that this problem has both metaphysical and logical-epistemological implications. On the one hand, we must ask, quite simply, a question about whether the domain that includes everything *exists* in the first place: "Is there an all-inclusive domain of discourse?" On the other hand, even if we understand such a domain to exist, we must go on to ask whether we can know it or understand it, whether it is "available to us as a domain of inquiry."[19] In a tantalizing footnote to these questions, Rayo and Uzquiano point out that it's possible to answer "yes" to the latter question (yes, an absolutely general domain is available to our inquiry), even while answering "no" to the former (no, this domain does not actually exist). As they put it, in the philosophical and mathematical use of quantifying language, "It might be claimed . . . that since there are no linguistic or contextual mechanisms restricting the relevant quantifiers, the all-inclusive domain would be available to us as a domain of inquiry, if only it existed. Were the world to cooperate, absolute generality would be achievable."[20] The vision presented in the conditional of this final sentence hovers between the utopian and the dystopian. Would such a world be one we'd want to live in? It seems to suggest a world that cooperates with *me*, but it does so in a strange way, by becoming infinite, or by making its infinite extension into an object, a "domain," that fills the meaningless and empty concept that I've been gesturing at, "everything," with a broad, frustrated sweep of my arm. This is a world that is made pliable to the ambitions of my language and to my desire to make that language cover and embrace everything at all. Rayo and Uzquiano offer one important qualification, however, that seems to deflate these desires for an ordinary, individual relationship to everything: "Whether or not we achieve absolute generality in philosophical inquiry," they argue, "most philosophers would agree that ordinary inquiry is rarely, if ever, absolutely general. Even if the quantifiers involved in an ordinary assertion are not explicitly restricted, we generally take the assertion's domain of discourse to be implicitly restricted by context."[21] When characters in James say "everything," according to this view, we can't actually take them to mean *everything*, and in some sense this caveat is absolutely correct. James often exploits the wavering focus of generality when it is deployed in ordinary language and taken as an object of erotic attachment: everything seems to bring a dizzying absolute generality into view even while it constantly shrinks down to the point of banality, to *this* or *that* limited, personal kind of everything. Nanda Brookenham always knows everything, everything, and yet perhaps it's only everything in London, perhaps everything in the air she breathes, or perhaps not quite everything at all. Suffice it to say that James's shifting understandings of "everything" might be understood as analogous to, if not by any means perfectly aligned with, these competing philosophical approaches to the concept, and in turning to James's interest in the ethics and erotics of skepticism, we begin to see the ways in which "everything" can represent in his fiction both a limited, normative world of things and logical rules, and also the metaphysical infinitude promised by a consciousness that luxuriates in introspection.

Everything *But* . . .

James criticism offers us no shortage of ways to talk about the concept of exclusion as sexual repression in his work: the ellipses and indirections, in other words, by which James's queerness is excluded from his texts. Much of this tradition of reading sexuality in James begins from Eve Kosofsky Sedgwick's influential argument that, in "The Beast in the Jungle," "an embodied male homosexual thematics" is present only as "a thematics of absence, and specifically of the absence of speech."[22] Sedgwick is, of course, not arguing that James "excludes" sexuality from his work in any consistent way; on the contrary, she poses his complex ironizing of secrecy, his ways of making its absent meanings proliferate, against the discourse of the closet which would equate secrecy and silence with a monadic, seamless homosexual content. Her reading of James has produced a wealth of critical debate over the extent to which James was or was not beset by a self-loathing terror of his own sexuality. Hugh Stevens, for example, has argued that, while James persists in a "refusal to name the sexual," we might understand this evasiveness as merely a rejection of essentialism or sexual identity politics; that is, we might think of repression in James as a rich source of "pleasure, humour," even "narrative itself," a model that is proto-constructionist in its play with sexual signification.[23] Michèle Mendelssohn, on the other hand, by approaching this problem from the angle of biographical and cultural-materialist criticism, has recently called into question the myth of James's internalized homophobia by calling into question the equally persistent myth of his homophobic rejection of Oscar Wilde and aestheticism.[24] If these critics disagree about many things, particularly about the biographical reading of James's experience of his own sexuality, they tend to agree that the dynamics of sexual repression and avowal are crucial to an understanding of James's fiction and that these dynamics tend to elaborate into a related dynamics of vagueness and specificity. The negative or the silent is vague or pleasurably ironic, and, on Sedgwick's reading, a thematics of absence in James allows for a powerful uncertainty of erotic meaning that resists the culture's desire to make that absent meaning into a coherent idea of homosexuality. The positive or the avowed (or in the case of homophobia, violently ascribed) sexual "truth" is confining, coercive, clear-cut, and singular.

Sedgwick's later work on James somewhat revises her position, or at least pursues Jamesian eroticism through a very different set of psychoanalytic and linguistic terms, replacing silence and secrecy with shame and performativity. Sedgwick suggests that for James, and for queerness in general, shame may in fact be precisely that which individuates—that which structures identity rather than threatening its coherence—and takes as her evidence the "specificity" and "explicitness" of the "particular erotics" (in Sedgwick's reading the complex anal erotics) of the prefaces. Rather than understanding the "forms taken by shame" as forms of exclusion, in which " 'toxic' parts of a group or individual identity . . . can be excised," Sedgwick argues that these forms are "instead integral to and residual in the processes by which identity itself is formed. They are available for the work of metamorphosis, reframing, refiguration, *trans*figuration, affective and symbolic loading and deformation, but perhaps all too potent for the work of purgation and deontological closure."[25] If Sedgwick's initial point about James in *Epistemology of the Closet* was that the closet itself was more open to the multiplicity of sexual meaning or the polymorphousness of queer desire than had traditionally been allowed, then in *Touching Feeling* she adds to this reading by insisting upon shame as an affect uniquely attuned to the dialectical relationship between specificity and indefiniteness, or between exposure and hiddenness. Sedgwick insists that, for James, shame first of all circumscribes and defines sexual pleasure, attaching it for better or for worse to specific bodily zones (and this is a familiar enough psychoanalytic story about shame and desire). But she goes on to insist that the specificity of shame might also provide the impetus for a kind of infinite project of meaning-making, the potentially endless moments of metaphorization and proliferation that Sedgwick describes, which crucially *resist* closure: rather than closing off or making absent its objects, shame in fact makes them "available" for manipulation. Sedgwick's emphasis on "reframing" and "deformation" is, of course, crucial for our purposes: she offers us an echo of the flexible, shape-shifting narrative frame that James imagines in the preface to *The Awkward Age*, and she insists that, for James, the particularities of erotic life are not mere circumscriptions. What seems to be purposefully left out of the logical quantification of "every" thing, every desire, in other words, might not be an abjection—at least not *only* an abjection—but might after all represent a perspective of its own. It's true that this perspective—a quasi-omniscient point of view that seems to have a privileged relationship to "everything" by virtue of standing outside of it—is often in James's fiction cast as an immature or naïve will to freedom, which ends with the willful character being chastened into an acceptance of the limitations of one's knowledge. The refusal of "everything," or the attempt to exclude oneself from its parameters, is an important problem for the Jamesian plot of *bildung* and, I argue, particularly for its dimension of erotic self-knowledge.

Early on in *The Portrait of a Lady*, for example, Isabel Archer's ideas and thoughts, whether about ethics or politics or erotic desire, are no better than "a tangle of vague outlines which had never been corrected by the judgement of people speaking with authority," and they seem confused precisely because they refuse those foundational logical practices of discrimination that would narrow "everything" into discrete classes and objects.[26] At one point during a discussion of the idea of revolution, Isabel's uncle Mr. Touchett says to her, "I forget whether you're on the side of the old or the side of the new. I've heard you take such opposite views." Isabel responds by simply refusing the distinctions that Mr. Touchett has drawn: "I'm on the side of both. I guess I'm a little on the side of everything" (126). Her refusal to choose is in another sense a positive choice to distribute herself in every direction—to be "a little on the side of everything," it seems, is to dissolve oneself into pieces, with all the freedom and all the terror that such an infinite self-dispersal would imply. The narrator of the novel goes so far as to represent this refusal as an embarrassment—a sort of touchy subject—which leads to his own refusal, or perhaps incapacity, of specificity in favor of generality: "Her errors and delusions were frequently such as a biographer interested in preserving the dignity of his subject must shrink from specifying" (104). Isabel's erroneous practices of generality are so simply *stupid* in the narrator's eyes that they threaten to make her dangerously unsympathetic or unbelievable; they're so off the mark that they seem actually vulgar, and so, surprisingly, the narrator decides to "shrink" out of sight at this moment and to become general himself—to leave it to our imaginations to play over a kind of infinite and indefinite field of potential stupidities rather than mark Isabel out with any too-specific offense against reason. If the narrator tends to be ashamed of Isabel or nervous about her likeability, she rejects that stance: "She had a fixed determination," we're told, "to regard the world as a place of brightness, of free expansion, of irresistible action: she held it must be detestable to be afraid or ashamed" (104). To rein in her thoughts—or to ask them to submit to a normative form—would be to limit their expansion, to set up resistances and phobias where Isabel wants none. If, in logic as set theory, "everything" only *appears* to indicate infinity and actually refers to the whole contents of a carefully defined space, everything available to *these* forms of thought, everything that I might be able to know and to reason about in *this* context, then Isabel wants to make available to herself much more freedom of movement than that. It's this fantasy that sustains her and that in James's treatment threatens to debilitate her as well.

The shamefulness that the narrator attaches to Isabel's over-certainty about the expansiveness and free movement of her knowledge also begins to hint at its relation to the more specific problem of erotic knowledge, the source of several major dilemmas in the first half of this novel. Isabel is faced with a series of suitors and must decide whom she desires and why. Perhaps just as importantly, she must account to herself and to others for her conspicuous failures of desire in the face of attractive men such as Caspar Goodwood and Lord Warburton. These failures are inexplicable—they simply *are*—and yet Isabel and the narrator take very different tacks in nonetheless attempting to account for each one. The best that Isabel can do in explaining to herself her indifference to Goodwood's good looks is to say that "he was not romantically, he was rather obscurely, handsome; but his physiognomy had an air of requesting your attention" (90), or, to put it even more baldly, "she sometimes thought that he would be rather nicer if he looked, for instance, a little differently" (170). Goodwood is, on some basic level, not Isabel's type, he doesn't turn her on, or as Isabel thinks in a somewhat more Platonic mode, "he had never corresponded to her idea of a delightful person" (171). Erotic knowledge seems to Isabel self-evident, and yet this is something slightly different from the tautological refusals of depth that we get in Trollope. Despite Isabel's conviction that she can't desire Goodwood—can't simply because she doesn't—her feeling of being in the wrong about it leads her into a careful investigation of the nature of erotic desire. What's the difference after all, Isabel seems to wonder, between having your attention requested and having your desire stimulated? The refusal of Goodwood's erotic advances finally forces Isabel into a choice, if only passively—the kind of choice she won't make between the old and the new.[27] Solicited bodily, Isabel feels herself unable simply to disappear in every direction or to choose to be "a little on the side of everything"—one desires or one doesn't. One discovers resistances there, in those convictions of desire, along with freedoms; there may be inexplicable dislikes and indifferences, the remnants of choices one didn't know one had made.

The terror of erotic choice is only intensified by the time Gilbert Osmond proposes to Isabel—at which point choice represents for her a kind of exposure that she is reluctant to hazard. Her first feeling in thinking about the proposal, after the drama of Goodwood and Warburton, is "the dread of having, in this case too, to choose and decide": "What made her dread great was precisely the force which, as it would seem, ought to have banished all dread—the sense of something within herself, deep down, that she supposed to be inspired and trustful passion. It was there like a large sum stored in a bank—which there was a terror in having to begin to spend. If she touched it, it would all come out" (360). Isabel's fear here seems to be a fear of sexuality itself, and this has been a popular critical diagnosis of Isabel's romantic choices and rejections.[28] I think this somehow misses the mark or at least oversimplifies the kind of "dread" that Isabel is trying to describe here. The fear is not of desire itself but is rather born out of a willful alienation from desire as that which forces one to choose, which seems to beckon from the "real world" that Isabel rejects, beholden as that world is to the norms and beliefs and laws that would limit one's utter freedom. What terrorizes Isabel is the sense that one can't simply dip one's toe into the water to test its temperature—can't in other words seem to enter into a tentative, "free," experimental relationship with one's erotic desires. (She's right to be terrorized by this restriction.) Rather, to come into contact with one's desiring self seems to Isabel to mean absolute exposure, plunging in head first: "If she touched it, it would all come out." James represents the circulation of erotic energy as simultaneously exciting and terrifying—both a necessary practice in acceding to social belonging and a potentially horrifying dissipation of oneself, by which one is spent and emptied if one doesn't know how to direct or control that outpouring of resources financial and erotic.

We might, then, read Isabel's avoidance of choice, particularly erotic choice, as a kind of skepticism, in which she turns away from the real world of everything and everyone that exists—away from the logical idea of the world of sets— in favor of a Hegelian fantasy of the limitless consciousness in which anything is possible and everything allowed, in which one's savings grow and grow without ever having to be spent. Virginia Woolf, in *To the Lighthouse* (1927), would later describe a similar situation for the painter Lily Briscoe, who is terrified to make the first mark on a blank canvas: "Where to begin?—that was the question; at what point to make the first mark? One line placed on the canvas committed her to innumerable risks, to frequent and irrevocable decisions." For Lily, as for Isabel Archer, choice itself is terrifying—and particularly the first choice, which would begin to shape the openness of "everything," the limitless possibility of the blank canvas, into merely *something*, a path already taken. Woolf's Lily later connects the blank canvas and the terror of the first mark with the struggle to begin speaking: "She wanted to say not one thing, but everything. Little words that broke up the thought and dismembered it said nothing." It's easy to moralize and to consider Isabel and Lily naïve in their unyielding attachment to the freedom of everything, to the possibility that one might be and remain on the side of everything, might say everything rather than the nothing that comes of "little words" and the particular things they name. These are, after all, novels of development, and it would make sense that characters who begin with starry-eyed aspirations to absolute freedom end up chastised, accepting the limited, imperfect, "dismembered" world in which they must live. This is the case for Isabel—James does not allow her to stay on the side of everything—and of course, Lily Briscoe does mark that canvas, even complete it with the final brushstroke that ends Woolf's novel. And yet I argue that we can and should take the desire for everything seriously—despite being a desire that these novels ultimately designate as impossible for their protagonists, it is a desire that elaborates its own system of (bad) logic. Being outside of or beyond everything sometimes means seeing everything clearly for once. It's the feeling that comes upon Woolf's Mrs. Ramsay when she, for a moment, steps out of herself, asking, "But what have I done with my life?" as she ladles out soup for a dinner party: "She had a sense of being past everything, through everything, out of everything, as she helped the soup, as if there was an eddy—there—and one could be in it, or one could be out of it, and she was out of it. . . . [S]he felt, more and more strongly, outside that eddy; or as if a shade had fallen, and, robbed of colour, she saw things truly." The choice to leave everything behind, to see it over *there* suddenly diminished to one mere eddy in a very big stream, is for Mrs. Ramsay to perform a kind of reverse free-indirect style, to speak in her own voice while also occupying the colorless but true vision of omniscience.[29]

Isabel, Lily, Mrs. Ramsay: all insist upon a skepticism as to the necessity of one's remaining stuck in this particular eddy, the "everything" over which our logic would allow us to quantify. This is bad logic manifesting as a refusal to believe in the reality (or at least the necessary significance or centrality) of the world in which logic holds—a conviction that those rules may bind everyone and everything, but not *me*. Reflecting on her refusal of Lord Warburton's proposal, Isabel realizes that what repels her is his way of seeming to solicit her on behalf of a system, "the system in which he rather invidiously lived and moved" (156). The adverb "invidiously" takes on the full range of its ambiguous meaning in this phrase. It could mean that Isabel sees Warburton as trapped in a system that he resents; it could mean that his easy movement in the system makes Isabel herself grudging or jealous of him; it could, in a related way, mean that his belonging in this system simply offends her, or that the distinction between his system and hers, designed to incite strong feelings in her, to force her to choose, is merely arbitrary. For Isabel, after all, all distinctions seem invidious. One thing is certain, however: Warburton is *in* his system, whatever it comprises, and Isabel is out of it. "A certain instinct," the narrator tells us, "not imperious, but persuasive, told her to resist—murmured to her that virtually she had a system and an orbit of her own. It told her other things besides—things which both contradicted and confirmed each other" (156). The instinct that murmurs to Isabel might be "certain" both in the sense of indefiniteness and of decidedness: this is *a* certain instinct, difficult to tell which one exactly, but also a *certain* instinct, confident in its pronouncements about Isabel's being exempted from the rules of reason itself. Instead of everything, she has "other things besides" which have the mystical power to simultaneously contradict and confirm. This "system and orbit of her own" might, in other words, place her both outside a system of good logic, in the other place where everything contradicts everything else, and inside that strange black hole of tautology, in which everything is confirmed, everything left open. (More on tautology later.)

Ralph Touchett gets to the heart of the matter when he explicitly invokes logic in asking Isabel to account for her decision to reject Warburton's proposal. "What had you in mind," he asks her, "when you refused Lord Warburton? . . . What was the logic—the view of your situation—that dictated so remarkable an act?" (202). Ralph makes logic into an epiphenomenon of a kind of narrative point of view. If each of us has a particular view of our situation, then that view forms and directs the specific "logic" within which one reasons. For every view, a different logic. Isabel responds by implicitly rejecting the terms of Ralph's line of questioning: "I didn't wish to marry him—if that's logic"; to which Ralph finally rejoins, "No, that's not logic—and I knew that before. It's really nothing, you know. What was it you *said* to yourself? You certainly said more than that" (202). According to Ralph's reading, Isabel's insistence upon standing outside of everything, creating a system and orbit of her own, does not allow her to elaborate an independent "everything" inside consciousness—it's "really nothing" in the end. Logic doesn't have to be complicated, he seems to insist, or mathematical, at least when it comes to the kind of moral reasoning or accountability that interests him here. It's only a kind of talking to oneself about oneself. Merely feeling something, such as a desire or a repulsion, is not logic, but deciding to say something, anything, to oneself about that feeling, desire, or repulsion—that's logic. We would probably call it a philosophy of ordinary language: a philosophical and indeed narrative inquiry based upon the question that we have already encountered, of "*what we should say when,* and so why and what we should mean by it."[30] What matters is that, at least in Ralph's view, logic doesn't try to encompass "everything," nor does it necessarily work solely in sets and categories of objects. Its structure is analogous, rather, to that of the narrative point of view that must try to account for its own formal limitations and peculiarities.[31] Before this exchange, Isabel has admitted to herself that there might be something bad in her logic. It isn't that she doesn't like Warburton, she reflects, it's that "she liked him too much to marry him, that was the truth;

something assured her that there was a fallacy somewhere in the glowing logic of the proposition—as *he* saw it—even though she mightn't put her very finest finger-point on it. . . . [S]he was wondering if she were not a cold, hard, priggish person" (164–65). Isabel seems to anticipate Ralph here in taking a pragmatist's view of logic; there's a fallacy as Warburton sees it, but for Isabel, the error is hopelessly indefinite. Is it, she wonders, that the mistake is so hard to point to because there's nothing there after all, only coldness and hardness where it seems there should be desire?

Of course, the tragedy of this novel is that, once finally forced to choose (and again, we must insist that this coercion toward the single object of desire is tragic because unjust, no matter what the outcome), Isabel seems immediately to have made the wrong choice or to have given herself over to the wrong kind of desire in accepting Osmond. This is the point at which it becomes clear where "everything" fits in James's intertwining of plots of erotic and moral development. While Isabel thinks that her position of exclusion—the impossible place outside of everything that she believes she can carve out for herself—is a guarantee of freedom and the expansion of the mind, it somehow ends up imprisoning her:

> The desire for unlimited expansion had been succeeded in her soul by the sense that life was vacant without some private duty that might gather one's energies to a point. . . . What had become of all her ardours, her aspirations, her theories, her high estimate of her independence and her incipient conviction that she should never marry? These things had been absorbed in a more primitive need—a need the answer to which brushed away numberless questions, yet gratified infinite desires. It simplified the situation at a stroke, it came down from above like the light of the stars, and it needed no explanation. There was explanation enough in the fact that he was her lover, her own, and that she should be able to be of use to him. She could surrender to him with a kind of humility, she could marry him with a kind of pride; she was not only taking, she was giving. (403)

In hindsight it seems that what had paralyzed Isabel in the face of erotic choice was not an incapacity of desire but rather the pleasure of promiscuous, imaginative desire, a pleasure that doesn't need to attach to a real object and that Isabel hesitates to relinquish. Once invested in Osmond ("if she touched it, it would all come out"), desire tethers Isabel not only to the real world in which "everything" surrounds and smothers her but to one small corner of it, one person in it who over time seems less and less remarkable than he once did. Her energies are now gathered "to a point," and Isabel has given up the pleasure of questioning in exchange for the "infinite" pleasure of gratification. She has given up unlimited expansion in exchange for a simplification by which desire follows a straight-forwardly economic, binary system: ownership and usefulness, give and take.

While Isabel's regret is at first only half-acknowledged, it later comes to over-whelm her as the magnitude of her loss in marrying Osmond at last becomes clear to her. James's tragic conception in *The Portrait of a Lady* of the attitude of exemption from "everything"—the sheer illusion of freedom that it repre-sents for him here, an illusion bound to come crashing down—is an important benchmark of comparison for the ways in which he reworks this same problem in later novels. Isabel, as she understands more and more about Osmond's re-pellent personality, realizes that the infinite freedom she had hoped for was, all along, its very opposite:

> She had taken all the first steps in purest confidence, and then she had suddenly found the infinite vista of a multiplied life to be a dark, narrow alley with a dead wall at the end. Instead of leading to the high places of happiness, from which the world would seem to lie below one, so that one could look down with a sense of exaltation and advantage, and judge and choose and pity, it led rather downward and earthward, into realms of restriction and depression where the sound of other lives, easier and freer, was heard as from above, and where it served to deepen the feeling of failure. (474)

It's in trying to translate solipsism into desire that Isabel finds her infinite vista suddenly shrinking to a dark, narrow alley that leads to a dead end. Most im-portantly, instead of the "exaltation and advantage" of a position something like that of an omniscient narrator, who oversees everything and doles out judgment and preference and pity, Isabel finds only the "restriction and depression" of be-ing tied to the world of things, the world of every thing, with its stubborn limi-tations. And yet, by the end of the novel, with Isabel once again fully conscious of the burden of choice in her final confrontation with Caspar Goodwood's seemingly tireless patience, the narrator offers us a revised image of the "infinite vista," now made brutally worldly and disorienting: "The world, in truth, had never seemed so large; it seemed to open out, all round her, to take the form of a mighty sea, where she floated in fathomless waters" (634). But then the image is turned outside in, with a philosophical flourish: "This however, of course, was but a subjective fact, as the metaphysicians say; the confusion, the noise of waters, all the rest of it, were in her own swimming head" (635). If Isabel has earlier felt that "introspection was, after all, an exercise in the open air" from which one might return "with a lapful of roses," the novel ends with an image of introspection gone awry—with introspection, in other words, as a kind of aimless philosophical skepticism, divested of the forms that language and intimacy together might provide, or as a terrifying floating in an infinite space that knows no bounds.

"What's language at all but a convention?" Isabel asks at one point in the novel, defending her interest in Madame Merle; "she has the good taste not to pretend, like some people I've met, to express herself by original signs" (244). If Warburton moves within a system "invidiously," then Madame Merle does so with great gusto: "Isabel found it difficult to think of her in any detachment or privacy; she existed only in her relations, direct or indirect, with her fellow mortals" (244). One of the most famous passages in the novel is Madame Merle's bravura claim that "there's no such thing as an isolated man or woman; we're each of us made up of some cluster of appurtenances. What shall we call our 'self'? Where does it begin? Where does it end? It overflows into everyone that belongs to us—and then it flows back again" (253). This is almost the opposite of Isabel's philosophy of skeptical exemption from the world and its forms, and the related idea that in introspection one can generate a world unto oneself, even more expansive and open than the actual world. Her response to Madame Merle is telling in the way it finally specifies the form of Isabel's exemption of herself from "everything": "Nothing that belongs to me is any measure of me," she says; "everything's on the contrary a limit, a barrier, and a perfectly arbitrary one" (253). "Everything" is deployed in a strange way in this sentence, but we're now in a better position to understand its conspicuous equivocality. In other words, we can now read "everything" as a vague gesture toward a vague collection of all the things that belong to Isabel, or that might belong to her, but we can also read it as an abstract concept that describes a mode or field of logical thought. It might not be that *things* are separate from Isabel, outside of the contours and limits that define her subjectivity rather than a mere extension or "measure" of that subjectivity. It might be, instead, that the logical space allowed by "everything" is experienced by Isabel as paradoxically limiting and constraining. Everything's a limit, on the other side of which Isabel prefers to wait and to watch. Everything's a barrier or a dam, erected in the process of making choices or of blocking off one avenue of erotic possibility in favor of another. Everything's arbitrary—defined by a set of rules, divided by principles of classification and laws of sound reasoning, that seem difficult to grasp, convoluted, invidious.

Everything *And* . . .

In *The Portrait of a Lady*, the specific, the embodied, and the circumscribed point of view tends to be a trap, a prison, or a narrow and painful limitation.

In James's late novels, on the other hand, the "specific" is often an elusive object of desire in its own right, a particular something that seems difficult to put into words, even taboo or disallowed, as characters talk *around* the thing in question, wandering in the kind of pained, weary indefiniteness that James's late style so perfectly evokes.[32] Maggie Verver, one of the central characters of *The Golden Bowl*, feels this powerfully when, after her marriage to Prince Amerigo and her father Adam Verver's marriage to her friend Charlotte Stant, she and her father finally have a moment alone together, a moment that would seem the perfect opportunity for Maggie to discuss with him what she thinks of as the "particular difference" that his marriage has made in their lives:

> It [the act of sitting down alone together in the park] made her feel but the more sharply how the specific, in almost any direction, was utterly forbidden her—how the use of it would be, for all the world, like undoing the leash of a dog eager to follow up a scent. It would come out, the specific, where the dog would come out; would run to earth somehow the truth—for she was believing herself in relation to the truth!—at which she mustn't so much as indirectly point. Such at any rate was the fashion in which her passionate prudence played over possibilities of danger, reading symptoms and betrayals into everything she looked at and yet having to make it evident even while she recognized them that she didn't wince. (382)

This scene already begins with a strange overlapping of the specific with the indefinite, in that classically Jamesian use of "it" from which one has to trace back for several pages in search of the vague antecedent that ends up being the somewhat unremarkable event of sitting down on a bench during a walk in the park. Maggie's relation is, similarly and paradoxically, both to *the* truth and undoubtedly to *a* truth—some specific truth that's denied to her. She's free to range over everything but *that*, the specific fact, the particular difference, at which the best she can do is indirectly point. That vague indirection quickly spirals out of control: suddenly, it seems that everything she looks at might be a symptom or betrayal of the specific thing she's after, and so it loses, again and again, its claim to specificity. And yet each time she thinks she's lighted on something specific, the important thing is not to show it, not to "wince" in a way that would reveal that specificity's bodily effect upon her as a kind of localized, stabbing pain. The truth—in its transcendent, nonspecific sense—is at risk of being "run to earth" by the specific; to point too directly to the specific is to risk making the pursuit of truth nothing better than a dog sniffing in the dirt.

The metaphysical complexity and abstraction of the questions raised here about truth as a concept and its dependence upon (or antagonism to) the specificities of the material world—the sniffing dog and the wincing body—can easily lead us away from what's actually meant to be at stake for Maggie in following this winding philosophical road. It's crucial that "the specific" here represents a fact about erotic life in this novel that is so concerned with the erotic "arrangements" that might stabilize what threatens to be a disruptive or antisocial energy of desire and jealousy. Maggie's marriage to Amerigo leaves her father cast adrift after the loss of their intensely close relationship, and so she arranges his marriage to Charlotte Stant, her friend and the past love interest of Amerigo himself, the woman who threatens to break up Maggie's own marriage. The equilibrium of this group of four becomes so tenuous as to be thrown off balance by the lightest touch. ("If I touch it, it will all come out.") The problem is that by putting one's "finest finger-point" on erotic knowledge, one seems to destabilize it or to deaden it, to run it into the dirt or to deny its essential unknowability. To see it only obliquely, only out of the corner of one's eye, seems at least a halfway solution, a way of acknowledging the specificity of the erotic without coming to know what that specificity consists of or what exactly it means.

If Isabel Archer aims to elaborate a self-sufficient infinitude of consciousness outside of the limiting category of "everything," then in this version of the story, it's erotic knowledge in all its intractable, unintelligible particularity that seems to be hauntingly missing, excluded from the logic of "everything": "the specific, in almost every direction, was utterly forbidden her." What remains to be seen is what kind of latent possibility that conspicuous "almost" signifies. In which direction might the specific take shape, or does it only take shape through the complex practice of *in*direction that Maggie elaborates? If the specificity of the erotic often seems to James's characters frustratingly unavailable, so that they feel constantly adrift in a relation to everything that always precludes an apprehension of something, *any*thing, then they also elaborate two important ways of thinking about desire and its specificity that I've classified together under the attitude of "everything *and*." First, the specific is imagined as a kind of inaccessible zero-point of perspective that exists alongside or in addition to everything rather than within it: this is what is happening in Maggie's reflection that the specific is denied to her "in *almost* every direction." The second form that this logic of super-addition takes (upon which I'll elaborate later) is an understanding of embodied erotic contact as a way of "letting everything go." The erotic embrace is imagined by James as, on the one hand, a bracketing of "everything" in favor of the narrowness and specificity of intimacy and, on the other hand, a potentially coercive and tragically constrained mode of erotic life.

What, then, do I mean by this almost Heideggerian formulation of a consciousness existing "alongside" everything? I read what may seem to be an attitude of exclusion or repression—much the same self-exclusion that appears so tragic in *The Portrait of a Lady*—as actually more complicated than the dichotomy of erotic freedom versus erotic denial allows, particularly in James's late fiction. In a later conversation with her father, for example, Maggie explains that she could never be jealous of Amerigo; something about the precise character of their relationship and the pitch of her feeling for him makes it impossible. "You *could* be [jealous]—otherwise?" her father asks. Maggie responds by explaining how her attachment to Amerigo prompts a complex orientation toward everything:

> "Oh, how can I talk," she asked, "of 'otherwise'? It *isn't*, luckily for me, otherwise. If everything were different"—she further presented her thought—"of course everything *would* be." And then again as if that were but half: "My idea is this, that when you only love a little you're not naturally jealous. . . . But when you love in a deeper and intenser way, then you're in the very same proportion jealous. . . . When however you love in the most abysmal and unutterable way of all— why then you're beyond everything, and nothing can pull you down." (506, original emphasis)

When Mr. Verver asks Maggie if she loves Amerigo in that "abysmal and unutterable" way, she responds that she didn't quite mean to imply that, but "I do *feel* however beyond everything—and as a consequence of that, I dare say, . . . seem often not to know quite *where* I am" (506, original emphasis). It's an extremity of love—both as deep as an abyss and entirely unspeakable or unintelligible— that puts Maggie in this strange position "beyond everything." And yet unlike Isabel Archer, for whom everything needs to be put at a distance, bracketed or forgotten or looked down upon with self-aggrandizing pity, Maggie's position, similarly "beyond" everything, leaves her nonetheless determined by its shape and its pressures. Only if everything were otherwise would everything be otherwise—but on the contrary, Maggie insists, everything is what it actually is, and so even in feeling herself beyond it, lost, and disoriented, she nonetheless feels bound to its preconditions. Even in trying to make herself clear to her father, Maggie aims for totality, pushing herself beyond the truth that seems at best "but half" of what she's after.

If Maggie's concerns about erotic feeling and erotic truth already differ in important ways from those of Isabel Archer, then the plot of Amerigo's ongoing affair with Charlotte Stant offers us a further elaboration of what it means to take "everything" as an object of identification, possession, or exchange. When Amerigo finally lights upon the "happy principle" by which to govern his illicit relationship, he describes it to himself in terms of its capacity to objectify "everything" as something that might be given up or passed around:

> This principle was simply to be, with the girl, always simple, and with the very last simplicity. That would cover everything. It had covered then and there certainly his immediate submission to the sight of what was clearest. This was really that what she asked was little compared to what she gave. What she gave touched him, as she faced him, for it was the full tune of her renouncing. She really renounced—renounced everything, and without even insisting now on what it had all been for her. Her only insistence was her insistence on the small matter of their keeping their appointment to themselves. That, in exchange for "everything," everything she gave up, *was* verily but a trifle. (106, original emphasis)

Simply to be simple, with simplicity—that will certainly cover everything. For now, we should note that the intensity of the tautology here has the effect of allowing for everything or, perhaps more accurately, being prepared for the arrival of every possible thing. We will return to tautology's relationship to openness in the concluding section. What's more important for our present purposes is the way in which the "everything" that Charlotte renounces—or in fact *exchanges* for Amerigo's discretion about their secret meeting—shuttles back and forth between the sense of particularity and the sense of indefiniteness. Amerigo imagines that Charlotte renounces "everything," certainly, but we're also given the sense that "everything" might be an indirection that allows her to refuse to name or to "insist" upon "what it had all been for her." If what it had all been was love, desire, erotic attachment, then that specific set of feelings is perhaps covered up or denied by "everything," or perhaps those feelings are, for her, "everything." Things only become more fraught as her renunciation of "everything" is qualified or limited, defined as "everything she gave up." But haven't we just been told that "everything she gave up" *was*, in fact, "everything"? If so, how do the two become distinguishable, one scare-quoted and standing alone, and one extended into a somewhat more definitive noun phrase? Whatever the object of this exchange is, it gets stuck in a kind of immobilizing fug of indefinite denotation as Bertrand Russell might describe it, somewhere between "everything" and "something." As it gets passed back and forth, turned this way and then that, "covered" and then "renounced" and then "exchanged," its form seems to change, from vague to sharp-edged and from wide to narrow.

If Amerigo's principle is sure to cover everything, then what does everything cover? When, in an erotic exchange, everything is at issue, or at least everything that one has to give, what is it that we're trying to talk about? It's a problem of reference, or "denotation" in Russell's terms, except that logic seems inca-pacitated when it comes to denoting the particularities of desire. As Amerigo and Charlotte while away the time alone together on the eve of his wedding to Maggie, Charlotte invokes just this problem of logic and what it covers or "refer-ences."

> "Would it be," Charlotte asked, "your idea to offer me something?"
> "Well, why not?—as a small ricordo?"
> "But a ricordo of what?"
> "Why of 'this'—as you yourself say. Of this little hunt."
> "Oh I say it—but hasn't my whole point been that I don't ask you to. There-fore," she demanded—but smiling at him now—"where's the logic?"
> "Oh the logic—!" he laughed.
> "But logic's everything. That at least is how I feel it. A ricordo from you—from you to me—is a ricordo of nothing. It has no reference." (116)

Charlotte demands that reference be mediated by logic, which seems in one sense simple enough. Russell would heartily agree. And yet what she's concerned with is not a linguistic problem of reference but a problem of recording—the memorialization of an erotic secret that in being kept secret must evade refer-ence altogether. The "logic" that covers everything for Charlotte, much like the "principle" that covers everything for Amerigo, has nothing to do with the laws of thought as we usually understand them. Rather, it has to do with the logi-cal laws of concealment and revelation—or in Amerigo's case, "simplicity" and obscurity—that circulate around the question of linguistic reference, a question made particularly complex in the case of erotic desire and its messy proliferation of ethical meanings.

At the very least, however, Charlotte finds logic a useful metaphor here for the sort of rule-bound stabilization of meaning that seems threatened by Ameri-go's too-overt revelation of the open secret of his desire. Logic *must* cover ev-erything, or at least everything that we want to bring out into the open. That which we want to conceal or wish to leave suspended as to meaning—that which has no reference, at least as far as we are concerned—must remain silent and unrecorded. We hear an echo here of Wittgenstein's famous ethical injunc-tion against going beyond the limits of logic: "What we cannot speak about we must pass over in silence."[33] Or we might also think of the moment in *The Spoils of Poynton* when Fleda Vetch finally admits her love for Owen Gereth with a rep-etitious wailing—"I cared, I cared, I cared!"—before immediately swearing him to a pact of silence: "But you mustn't, you must never, never ask! It isn't for us to talk about. . . . Don't speak of it, don't speak!" Fleda then tries to return herself from the frantic unintelligibility of desire to the world of language and meaning: "It was easy indeed not to speak when the difficulty was to find words. . . . She stilled herself in the effort to come round to the real and the thinkable."[34] In Charlotte's case, logic (which is everything) provides a crucial limit alongside which to suspend oneself in refusing to account for, to "refer" to, desire. This is, in fact, a refusal to orient oneself in terms of reference at all, as Charlotte hints that her relationship with Amerigo and their mutual desire are—must be—incompatible with reference. If a ricordo from Amerigo to Charlotte is "a ricordo of nothing," then where they are, what they're doing, whatever is exchanged between them, must also be nothing—but a nothing that maintains an intimate proximity to everything.

In linking Charlotte's invocation of logic as everything to the open secret (which for her must stand alongside everything, must be an object of acknowledgment, but must not be an object of logical reference), I'm invoking a rich history of critical readings of the open secret as a literary concept. D. A. Miller has argued that the realist novel relies on characters' performance of a kind of open secrecy that convinces us of their deep, private interiority even while that interiority is actually something of an epiphenomenon of narrative omniscience and the disciplinary power of social norms.[35] Eve Kosofsky Sedgwick makes the open secret the primary epistemological underpinning of the cultural discourse of the closet, by which a complex dynamics of secrecy and revelation become definitive of sexuality, at least on the level of its cultural representation, rather than a careful attention to the sheer multiplicity of sexual desires, attachments, turn-ons, and behaviors that might shape any individual's sexual life.[36] More recently, Anne-Lise François has proposed a counterargument to these Foucauldian readings, which focuses on "the ways in which the open secret as a gesture of self-canceling revelation permits a release from the ethical imperative to *act* upon knowledge."[37] In other words, rather than being a form born of social discipline or effected by repression, the open secret for François represents a potentially viable form of minimal affirmation or "nonemphatic revelation," a reading that might allow us to understand "never-acted-upon passions and uncounted experiences not as *nos* disguising incipient, concealed, or denied affirmatives but rather as aimless, innocent, minimal, all but negative, contented affirmations."[38] This reading of the open secret, then, allows us to escape the repression-avowal binary that still so often structures readings of sexuality in James's fiction. More importantly, François suggests a subtle way of differentiating between denial or negation, and something more like the "alongside" attitude that I've been after here. If the affirmations that François describes are "all but negative," then we might say something similar about Charlotte's seeming refusal of logical reference when it comes to erotic desire. We might say, in other words, that her affirmation of desire takes a form other than the expression of a logical truth—other than a reference to, or a "ricordo of," something existing in the world of everything—and instead affirms almost "nothing."

Later on in the novel, we see Amerigo seem to come around to Charlotte's way of thinking about their relationship and its tenuous position in relation to logic, and to everything. During a vacation to Fawns, Adam Verver's rented country estate, at which the novel's entire cast of characters is present, Amerigo finds himself suddenly stunned by Charlotte's straightforwardness in referring to herself and himself publicly as a pair: "we've settled, Amerigo and I," she says to Fanny Assingham, "to stay over till after luncheon." It's Charlotte's "nonemphatic revelation," to return to François's terminology, which brings into focus for Amerigo "the idea with which, behind and beneath everything, he was restlessly occupied":

> She had answered Mrs Assingham quite adequately; she hadn't spoiled it by a reason a scrap larger than the smallest that would serve, and she had, above all, thrown off, for his stretched but covered attention, an image that flashed like a mirror played at the face of the sun. The measure of *everything*, to all his sense at these moments, was in it—the measure especially of the thought that had been growing with him a positive obsession and that began to throb as never yet under this brush of her having, by perfect parity of imagination, the match for it. His whole consciousness had by this time begun almost to ache with a truth of an exquisite order, at the glow of which she too had so unmistakably then been warming herself—the truth that the occasion constituted by the last few days couldn't possibly, save by some poverty of their own, refuse them some still other and still greater beauty. It had already told them, with an hourly voice, that it had a meaning—a meaning that their associated sense was to drain even as thirsty lips, after the plough through the sands and the sight, afar, of the palm-cluster, might drink in at last the promised well in the desert. (283, original emphasis)

If Amerigo has been laboring away, trying to decipher the idea that preoccupies him, "behind and beneath everything," then Charlotte's nonchalance suddenly reorients him, provides him with a particular image that gives him back "everything," takes its "measure," as if by a reflection in a mirror—an overwhelmingly bright reflection, as if of the sun itself. But as we've seen again and again, "everything" appears only intermittently here, as we shuttle back and forth between its flashes of blinding solar light and the more muted particularities of Amerigo's desires. The measure of everything is in the image that Charlotte provides, and yet this is soon narrowed; it takes the measure *especially* of "the thought" over which he has obsessed, which "throbs" under Charlotte's sympathetic pressure, the "brush" of the matching thought in her. What's revealed in this wavering set of images is "a truth of an exquisite order," which seems to promise them more and more, always holding in store "some still other and greater beauty," promising them over and over again that it will deliver in full its meaning, which they suck and slurp and drain like desert wanderers who have happened upon water, or possibly only a mirage. There is an echo here of Maggie's own desperate and perhaps delusional attachment to a truth that seems necessarily to elude her grasp, at which she can only indirectly point. ("For she was believing herself in relation to the truth!") Of course, this passage, and my reading of it, make "everything" seem in this case nothing better than a ghostly reflection, a fantasy conjured by a thirst for meaning or a stunning flash that only blinds us. We get, at best, its afterimage glowing on our eyelids. And this isn't wrong. Precisely what Amerigo realizes in this moment, and what Charlotte seems to capture in her understanding of desire's incompatibility with reference, is that to hover alongside everything is painful, disorienting, blinding, literally dumbfounding. In much the same way that Eliot seems to understand descents into the mire of vagueness as potentially dangerous, even if ethically illuminating and necessary, James's repeated descriptions of characters coming into a kind of intimate communion with "everything" balance vertiginous terror with the power of ethical and erotic epiphany. Amerigo's "stretched but covered attention" is primed, it seems, for the sort of expansively open point of view required of this kind of epiphany, which hurts, aches, and throbs as much as it satisfies.

It's also important, of course, that Amerigo's tarrying with the specificity of his desire happens "behind and beneath everything" rather than, for example, in front of and above it. Behind and beneath are positions associated with repression (putting a feeling or a desire behind a barrier, or burying it beneath consciousness in the unconscious mind), but they're also positions associated with hidden supports and foundations (the work being done behind the scenes or the foundation sitting beneath an edifice). Kaja Silverman has offered us what is still perhaps the most thorough reading of James's interest in the position or orientation of "behind," but her analysis remains attached to a model of sexual repression without considering the varied meanings that "behind" might carry aside from or in addition to what she casts as a kind of tortured relationship to anal eroticism, particularly in its association here with "beneath." For Silverman, James's fondness for describing his authorial perspective as "behind" the world of the text has to do with a " 'sodomitical identification' with 'the father,' an identification which permits the fantasizing subject to look through that figure's eyes and to participate in his sexuality by going 'behind' him."[39] Silverman is attempting to get at the paradox by which James minimizes his presence as author and at the same time uses that position to appropriate the kind of sexualized potency that he associates with the father—he uses the father as a kind of proxy for the wielding of narrative authority and also as a cover. But when we dial down from the level of omniscient narration to the level of character, we get a very different understanding of "behind" and indeed "beneath." For Amerigo, being behind and beneath everything means a kind of withdrawal from the world of the novel in which he moves, a "restless" preoccupation that stretches his capacity for attention to a painful tautness or a vapid thinness. Charlotte's minimal acknowledgment of their mutual attachment finally draws him out of his "behind and beneath" position into a more active, sympathetic, flashing vision of "everything."

So far I've focused on the idea of being alongside everything in *The Golden Bowl* as a matter of position, perspective, reference, or orientation, but the novel includes an important pair of images of erotic intimacy between Amerigo and Maggie that gesture to an alternative understanding of the "everything *and*" position that I've been tracing. This is what I described earlier as the practice of "letting everything go" in the literal, embodied particularity of the embrace. In the first of these scenes, Amerigo's embrace of Maggie is described as a power play, as an act of physical domination and coercion, as Amerigo attempts to make Maggie give up her obsessive attention to his relationship with Charlotte:

> She gave up, let her idea go, let everything go; her one consciousness was that he was taking her again into his arms. It was not till afterwards that she discriminated as to this; felt how the act operated with him *instead* of the words he hadn't uttered—operated in his view as probably better than any words, as always better in fact at any time than anything. Her acceptance of it, her response to it, inevitable, foredoomed, came back to her later on as a virtual assent to the assumption he had thus made that there was really nothing such a demonstration didn't anticipate and didn't dispose of. (345, original emphasis)

Amerigo, as usual, discovers a way to "cover everything," this time with an uncanny mixture of affectionate solicitude and physical coercion. The embrace, Maggie realizes only after the fact, is "always better . . . at any time than anything," in a turn of phrase that closely echoes Amerigo's tautological principle: simply to be with Charlotte always simple, with simplicity. But what's most important here is that in being embraced, Maggie's response, "inevitable" and "foredoomed," is to let her idea go, and in doing so, to let everything go. In letting everything go, she gives herself over to the thought that Amerigo is actually ready for everything, prepared to dispose of anything and everything she might seize upon as evidence of his infidelity. The novel's final scene is almost a reenactment for which this earlier scene prepares the ground. Now that Maggie has shuttled Charlotte off to the United States, her marriage has been secured against the threat that she has been so jealously aware of—but it has also meant for Maggie the loss of her father, who accompanies his wife across the Atlantic. The novel concludes with a mixed sense of Maggie's privation and her erotic security. She poses a question to Amerigo as if to try to close the books on Charlotte—"Isn't she too splendid?" (579)—before adding the ambiguous qualification, "That's our help, you see" (580). Amerigo responds with the embrace that concludes the novel: "close to her, her face kept before him, his hands holding her shoulders, his whole act enclosing her, he presently echoed: ' "See"? I see nothing but *you*.' And the truth of it had with this force after a moment so strangely lighted his eyes that as for pity and dread of them she buried her own in his breast" (580, original emphasis). The novel ends, in other words, with Maggie positioned as the real negation of "everything" in Amerigo's eyes—"I see nothing but *you*"—and yet this positioning continues to seem a terrible burden, heightened by the invocation of those quintessential tragic emotions, "pity and dread." Maggie hides her eyes from the strange light in Amerigo's eyes, which in their laser focus have finally denied everything in favor of a specific desire for a specific person who can be enclosed in his arms. There's a kind of pained closure to this novel, which seems in the figure of the tight embrace and the eyes buried in dread to present an image of coupled, marital love with which to draw the curtain down and also an image of that circumscribed, monogamous love as intrinsically constricting, negating, terrifying—a beautiful truth run to the ground like a dog sniffing in the dirt.[40]

Wide Open Spaces; or, Everything Is Everything

The problem of "everything" is for James a problem of openness and closure, of the diffusion of thought and desire versus the focusing of thought and desire on specific objects. If everything were otherwise, Maggie Verver reflects, it would be otherwise—but it isn't. Everything is everything, and that opens up a space for us within which to find our way. This is the entirety of what Wittgenstein describes as "logical space": "The facts in logical space," as he puts it, "are the world."[41] In thinking through Trollope's understanding of tautology, we had recourse to Wittgenstein's insistence that with tautology, logical space remains open: no possibility has been foreclosed, since any other proposition can follow consistently from a tautology. But logical space might not reach as far as we'd like it to. Even as it appears to be everything, to cover everything, it might come to feel restrictive. Its edges might seem to foreclose too many possibilities already. The idea of figuring logic as a "space" in the first place carries with it several ramifications about how to find the edges of that space (a question with which Eliot is concerned) and also about whether one's body or one's particular self can survive in that space or whether to occupy it requires a difficult practice of self-negation (a question with which Brontë is concerned). Finally, we might say that James is most concerned with how to orient oneself in that space, or how to orient oneself toward it from a position outside its limits.

Sara Ahmed has argued for a philosophical reconsideration of the "orientation" in "sexual orientation," and if her concerns lead her naturally to phenomenology, then my concerns lead to the more metaphoric concepts of "space" and "orientation" that logic invokes through its practices of reference, entailment, and delimitation. If Ahmed, in other words, wants to think about "the sexualization of space" and "the spatiality of sexual desire," I'm suggesting that James tries to represent the erotics of our logical and sexual orientations in the metaphoric space of language.[42] Ahmed points out that, in phenomenology, the appearance of objects to consciousness relies on the bracketing of what is relegated to the background; as we've seen, logic often asks us to perform similar operations of bracketing, narrowing, or putting to one side. But as Ahmed clarifies, "We remain reliant on what we put in brackets; indeed, the activity of bracketing may sustain the fantasy that 'what we put aside' can be transcended in the first place. The act of 'putting aside' might also confirm the fantasy of a subject who is transcendent, who places himself above the contingent world of social matter."[43] We hear an echo here of Hegel's fantasy of the spirit's ultimate potential, its fullest self-affirmation, which would be to transcend itself and become infinite. We're always, however, in the world of "everything," even when we try to put it, or parts of it, in brackets, and this very well might be true for James also; after all, it's difficult to speak very intelligibly about our relationship to "everything," and we often come out of such an enterprise seeming to have circled around and around a concept that never quite jells. Part of the aim of Ahmed's queer critique of phenomenology is to recuperate disorientation—to maintain its painfulness, its terror, its vertigo, while also acknowledging that even if disorientation represents a loss, it also directs us toward new ways of knowing and desiring, toward the difficult practice of reorientation.[44] Both Eliot and James in their different ways, of course, struggle to come to terms with the affective experience of disorientation, but they have a common conviction that the source of this disorientation lies in the rich defectiveness of language. Vagueness and the indeterminate denotation of "everything" represent impasses internal to logical models of linguistic meaning, argument, and reference, but they are impasses, Eliot and James suggest, that we'd do better not to break through or cover up. Their dizzying effects might be just what we sometimes need.

Stanley Cavell's essay "The World as Things" considers just such dizzying questions of how we constitute, and how we might rearrange, the very form of our attachment to the world. The essay opens with an epigraph from *The Spoils of Poynton*, in which Fleda Vetch tries to come to terms with her friend Mrs. Gereth's "strange, almost maniacal disposition to thrust in everywhere the question of 'things,' to read all behaviour in the light of some fancied relation to them. 'Things' were of course the sum of the world; only for Mrs. Gereth, the sum of the world was rare French furniture and oriental china."[45] In this essay Cavell is interested, clearly, in taking literally that dangling "thing" at the end of "everything." What would it mean, Cavell wonders, if we took seriously and philosophically the concept of collecting? What if we understood our selves and our worlds as collections of things or moments, whether accidentally accumulated, meticulously curated, or jealously hoarded? Such a philosophical enterprise, which is often borne out most fully, Cavell suggests, in the intricate quotidian detail of aesthetic realism, might allow us to pose a range of questions about how we "orient" ourselves in the world according to a particular set of attachments and how that orientation might be, as Ahmed would say, "contingent." "Why do we put things together as we do?" Cavell asks: "Why do we put ourselves together with just these things to make a world? What choices have we said farewell to? To put things together differently, so that they quicken the heart, would demand their recollecting."[46] Such questions ask us to hearken back with a kind of nostalgia to the wide-openness of logical space, before any potential "choices" have been closed to us. This is the space held open in tautology (or indeed in silence, before anyone has spoken), and which narrows further and further as propositions and entailments cut their paths, shaping "everything" into the particular world that accretes around us. Once "everything" has a definite form, it becomes more and more difficult to move through it.

To finally renounce "everything" means in novelistic terms something like "closure," the pain of ending one story, finding the limit of that fictional world, and looking ahead with disoriented anxiety toward the beginning of a new one. We've seen that Eliot felt that pain keenly. The obsessive narrator of James's *The Sacred Fount* feels it keenly too. His story revolves around his attempt, over a weekend at a country house with many visitors, to detect the secrets of various erotic liaisons by tracking their visible signs, mostly through a quasi-supernatural theory by which one lover always vampirically drains the other of some potent energy such as youth or intelligence. At one point, talking to his friend Ford

Obert, the narrator tries to trace back to the moment from which "everything" began for him. "What do you mean," Obert asks, "by everything?" The narrator responds, "Well, this failure of detachment" (127). Once attached to everything, it's difficult to detach oneself—one after all feels a kind of responsibility to the world in which we're mired, a responsibility perhaps to make complete sense of it and moreover to make sense of our particular way of being attached to it, erotically drawn to particular points within its field, and repelled from others.[47] "You've extraordinary notions," Obert says to the narrator, "of responsibility" (127). To give up on that responsibility, to succeed at detachment (and perhaps reattachment, or reorientation, elsewhere) is, for James, the great challenge of novelistic form and also the great challenge of reasoning about erotic desire. How do we talk about the way in which desire expands and contracts, from a diffusive attachment to "everything" to the focused, potentially obsessive attachment to "something" or "someone" in particular? Once circumscribed, once directed in a particular way, how might we choose to disorient ourselves? What pains, and what new pleasures, might that entail?

Queer Fiction and the Law

"Law" has haunted these pages. Of course, *law* has two meanings: the law that is imposed as a prohibition versus the law that describes an axiomatic truth. Things must be this way, lest you be punished; or, things must be this way because they simply must, because some things must simply be true. The latter is the version usually understood to be appropriate to logic insofar as it begins from the formal mathematical axioms of noncontradiction and self-identity that are the subject of the first two chapters of this book. When George Boole published *An Investigation of the Laws of Thought*, the title itself presupposed the law of logic as something independent of human morality or jurisprudence, those messier and more unpredictable (because more subjective and more social) forms. Boole's laws of thought are objects of investigation, not disciplinary injunction. This is the way our thought is structured, says the modern logician, not the way it *should* ideally be structured. And yet, as we've seen, when logic is positioned as one particularly powerful interface between the individual and the social—the set of forms through which I may be clear, or through which I may account intelligibly for my orientation toward the world, my erotic attachment to *him* rather than to *him*, and the ethical deliberations that guide my movement through life—it can often be experienced as constricting. In its formal soundness, it excludes too much that I nonetheless want to think and talk about and that I want, moreover, to be entirely clear about. What is my recourse and where is my escape when I seem to be denied any mechanism by which to think and speak about those depths that don't want to stay buried?

Our concern in this study has been with the connection in Victorian thought between logic and ethics, and in turn between ethics and erotic desire, but it hasn't been primarily with the law in the juridical sense—the very real and very painful laws that regulated and criminalized particular sexual acts and identities in the Victorian period. But the question persists, particularly as we conclude with Henry James, a gay novelist whose fiction has felt so closeted to so many readers. Just as law has haunted these pages, so has queerness hovered around the edges and in the interstices of my argument, which, in its reading of Victorian novels and those novels' representations of characters and narrators thinking and speaking about erotic life, has been largely restricted to the heterosexual plot of courtship and marriage. Despite the queer energies that so often circulate in Victorian novels, as in Jane Eyre's eroticized attachment to Helen Burns (to take only one particularly relevant example), such energies rarely achieve the kind of articulacy reserved for the plot of heterosexual desire, in which erotic life becomes an object of careful and reasoned reflection and communication rather than an indeterminate energy that lurks in the places where it has been elided. Even a decade after James's last novel and almost twenty years after the Oscar Wilde trials, as E. M. Forster composed *Maurice*, his one "gay novel," in 1914, the legal danger of publication seemed intense enough to Forster that he circulated the manuscript only among close friends and insisted that it only be published after his death. In his "Terminal Note" to *Maurice*, Forster intensifies the question I've been pursuing: what good is bad logic when it comes to the real legal claims of sexual life and the power to make intelligible sexualities that have been forcibly and violently silenced? If I've focused in my selection of evidence upon more intimate kinds of claims—claims to simple acknowledgment or recognition or meaningfulness—then Forster, and queer people of this period more generally, needed necessarily to stake more serious claims and make more serious cases for the "good logic" of queer desire.

Written in 1960, Forster's note is in part an angry reaction to Parliament's lengthy delay in implementing the recommendations of the Wolfenden Report of 1957, which had come to the conclusion that gay sex should be decriminalized. The report led to a decade of protracted debate over its clear and sensible conclusion, which finally ended in the decriminalization of almost all gay sex acts (except, importantly, sodomy) by the Sexual Offences Act of 1967. In 1960, Forster was simultaneously optimistic and morose about the possibility of this kind of legal recognition: he had dedicated *Maurice* upon its completion in 1914 "to a Happier Year," and yet, even forty-six years later, he assumed that that happier year was still distant, a utopian epoch that could only come after his own death. It was the happiness and optimism of the novel's ending that Forster worried would get him into legal trouble, with Maurice and Alec in love and having a real, pleasurable sex life, even fleeing to the "greenwood" that provides the novel with its own utopian metaphor: "If it ended unhappily, with a lad dangling from a noose or with a suicide pact, all would be well, for there is no pornography or seduction of minors. But the lovers get away unpunished and consequently recommend crime. Mr Borenius [the overbearing church rector of the novel] is too incompetent to catch them, and the only penalty society exacts is an exile they gladly embrace."[1] Gay sexuality, in other words, can be made intelligible in literature only in all its badness, as the object of cruel and unusual social punishments, and only in the sterilized form that would protect it from being understood as pornographic. The only thing for it, at least in the world of a novel, is to escape to the greenwood, the utopia of sexual freedom that can at least be elaborated in fiction, which has its own laws, more flexible than those of reality. As Forster puts it, "A happy ending was imperative. . . . I was determined that in fiction anyway two men should fall in love and remain in it for the ever and ever that fiction allows, and in this sense Maurice and Alec still roam the greenwood" (218). There's a tragedy, in the end, to this fictional utopian exile, which remains suspended in time as a kind of permanent condition—these lovers *still* roam the greenwood, even in 1960, even as the Stonewall riots rage in 1969, even as Forster dies in 1970, even as the United States Supreme Court rules in favor of the constitutional protection of same-sex marriage rights in 2015, and long beyond.

It seems that for Forster, at least part of the problem is the fundamental ir-reconcilability of sexuality and the law, since the decriminalization of gay life seems to require the possibility or the desirability of making rational arguments on its behalf—of accounting for it, in other words, in the kind of good logic that works in legal cases. Better to hit the road, Forster thinks, than to be forced to plead a case for our sex lives and by doing so to divest sex of its frisson, its electric shock. The opening of the "Terminal Note," for example, recounts Forster's own sexual awakening and the immediate inspiration for the composition of *Maurice* as taking place on a visit to the home of Edward Carpenter and George Merrill, and it imagines the interaction of the erotic and the intellectual as a form of creative epiphany that is nevertheless opaque, punctual, and inscrutable. Forster remembers how on his third visit to their home, "the spark was kindled" as the couple "combined to make a profound impression on me and to touch a cre-ative spring. George Merrill also touched my backside—gently and just above the buttocks." The "spark" of creative intellect and the "spark" of sexual arousal are indistinguishable in Forster's account, and this leads him to a rumination on the impossibility of accounting intelligibly for the excitement of desire: "The sensation was unusual and I still remember it, as I remember the position of a long vanished tooth. It was as much psychological as physical. It seemed to go straight through the small of my back into my ideas, without involving my thoughts." The arousal of the erotic touch doesn't involve thought, nor does it wait upon ideas—its sensation passes "straight through" the body's exterior and enters into the immaterial realm of ideas in what Forster imagines as a kind of spiritual fertilization. "If it really did this," he continues, "it would have acted in strict accordance with Carpenter's yogified mysticism, and would prove that at that precise moment I had conceived" (217). While Forster wants to elaborate a connection between arousal and intellect, it's not the rational or logical picture of intellect giving eros a meaningful form but rather a picture of eros penetrating reason and fusing with it; it's a picture in which Forster casts himself as the woman penetrated and impregnated by the simultaneously psychic and embodied "sensation" of sexual desire. Forster echoes the erotic epiphany of Dorian Gray, touched by the words of Lord Henry Wotton, except that in this moment, the mind stirs in response to the sexual excitement of a touch, rather than the body thrumming in response to a series of beautifully articulated words. In this scene, a sexual charge passes into the body and then into the creative mind, not as an elusive and empty object around which reason circles but as a seed planted in the very ground of reason. Sex bypasses the slow orderliness of reason on the way to more fertile pastures for the germination of erotic ideas, putting down roots in the realm of creativity rather than the realm of logic.

Of course, none of this provides a legal argument, does it? In the late nineteenth century, debates over the scope of logic had entered into questions about the nature of law. Is law a logical enterprise, or is its shaping based on mechanisms more ordinary than the purity of logical deduction would allow? Perhaps logic is thoroughly beside the point, or only a small part of the point, when it comes to the workings and the evolution of the law. As Oliver Wendell Holmes famously writes in opening his book *The Common Law* (1881), "The life of the law has not been logic: it has been experience. The felt necessities of the time, the prevalent moral and political theories, intuitions of public policy, avowed or unconscious, even the prejudices which judges share with their fellow men, have had a good deal more than the syllogism in determining the rules by which men should be governed."[2] Holmes's appeal to the embodied reality of experience as opposed to the mere formalism of logical argument remains unhelpful, however, if what one seeks is legal recognition of a kind of sexual experience that dare not speak its name and so remains cut off from the civic, shared experience Holmes has in mind. Wilde finds his way circuitously toward just this kind of argument in the reflections of Dorian Gray, who comes to believe that to found any system upon the supposed wisdom of "experience" can only be a grave error:

> As it was, we always misunderstood ourselves, and rarely understood others. Experience was of no ethical value. It was merely the name men gave to their mis-

takes. Moralists had, as a rule, regarded it as a mode of warning, had claimed for
it a certain ethical efficacy in the formation of character, had praised it as something that taught us what to follow and showed us what to avoid. But there was
no motive power in experience. It was as little of an active cause as conscience
itself. All that it really demonstrated was that our future would be the same as our
past, and that the sin we had done once, and with loathing, we would do many
times, and with joy.[3]

Mere experience is bound, Dorian concludes, to become a tautological loop that
in its tendency toward repetitiveness (the return again and again to predictable
sources of satisfaction) turns even self-loathing into a kind of masturbatory,
masochistic pleasure. Experience lacks what Dorian calls "motive power," or the
structure of the active, forward-moving sentence—it is a passive construction,
an indifferent container for all that we do and for every way in which we succeed and err, and so it lacks teeth. As a concept, it can't get us going, nor can it
provide us with a strong enough model for understanding the sudden change,
the left turn, the experiment, the sharp and pointed pleasure of erotic epiphany
and the potentially antisocial insistence of sexual desire—the vicissitudes, in
short, of the singular erotic self, which seem to shape our lives so much more
meaningfully and forcefully than mere "experience."

The language of Forster's "Terminal Note" may be typical of the bad-logical
modes of reasoning about desire that have occupied us over the course of the
preceding chapters—his effort to imagine the role of the intellect in making
visible and intelligible the force of sexuality—but in the end, while the "badness" of his creative reasoning without reasons might be meaningful in all sorts
of profound ways, these are not the kinds of sound logical arguments that win
us legal rights. They may, however, be the kind of intimate appeals that would
shape a smaller, more limited version of what Holmes describes as our collective
civic "experience" or what Wilde might persuade us to think of under the rubric
of Dorian Gray's "experimental method" of living (52)—just as Wittgenstein
has pointed our attention to the "civic status of a contradiction" or as Roland
Barthes has registered the possibility that tautology is a radically dead, antisocial
form of language, a use of language to escape experience rather than to mold
it. In 1921, Edith Ellis would argue for the sociability of sex by insisting that
sexual desire operates according to discoverable laws much like those of physics
or mathematics or symbolic logic; for her, criminal laws controlling sexuality
are provisional "swaddling bands" for a culture that deems itself unprepared for
the ideal, axiomatic truth of sexuality. But Ellis advances from her conviction
that "sex is not a mania" but rather "a mysticism," and even an "inevitable logi-

cal conclusion," to a premise that we would balk at—that we can derive from the laws of sexual desire an understanding of the laws of eugenics. "Through a new education of sex," she argues, "through scientific knowledge and human understanding of the laws of love, of life, and of affinity, and also through sane experiments as a result of this knowledge, we may gradually arrive at the point where we may dare to pass eugenic laws, founded on an understanding of spiritual laws."[4] It seems to be but a short step from discovering the scientific law of sexual affinity to the ominous idea of "experiments," however "sane," in genetic engineering—not to mention, of course, the heteronormative assumption that defines the mystic law of sex primarily in terms of its reproductive ends. Forster might finally argue that it's all for the best that logic, bad or good, only participates weakly in the development of the law, or at least that it takes a careful balancing act to weigh the embodied pleasures of sex against the security of legal recognition and the civic bonds of collective "experience." These, he argues, are different things, and they require different kinds of thinking and speaking, different languages and different claims to truth. And he wouldn't, of course, be alone in thinking that the pressures of the law and its apparatuses of rational argument can only miss the point when it comes to our erotic lives and sexual identities.

I end on this note, with Forster and the queer fiction of the early twentieth century, in order to pose some open questions about the relationship between bad logic and the law, or, perhaps more accurately, the relationship between the bad logic of the Victorian novel and the complex twentieth-century historical development of sexual identity politics, insofar as that development necessarily involves problems of legal argument and legal recognition. None of this is to make the clearly false claim that the legal regulation of sexuality only began to be challenged or debated in the twentieth century, and indeed this would have been a different book if logic and legal argument, or logic and legal rights, had been my focus all along. Rather, my aim is to conclude by speculating about one potential afterlife of bad logic as it finds its way into the early, tentative moments of queer activism in the English realist novel. What good are the kinds of claims that bad logic makes? If that good is necessarily narrow, "personal," intimate, and ordinary, then is it really, after all, important? Forster's refusal of the pressures of good logic—he'd prefer to leave it all behind, or to wait it out with his novel in a drawer, rather than capitulate to such a demand—shows us that the force of bad logic might persist even in those situations where it might seem most reckless or even quietist to remain attached to intimacy instead of pursuing more public kinds of recognition. While we might expect, in other words, that a burgeoning antihomophobic activism would lead Forster toward publically sanctioned forms of good logic, we see him instead forging ahead with the novelistic tradition of bad logic that I've been analyzing in the preceding chapters, escaping to the greenwood of fiction, where intimacy is enough, away from the real world and its unreasonable expectation that we must be fully reasonable about desire in order to avoid the punishment of the law. As Lauren Berlant and Michael Warner have argued, intimacy is always "publicly mediated," and to claim otherwise is only to reinforce the power of a "heterosexual culture" that would "block the building of nonnormative or explicit public sexual cultures" by diminishing sex as something "merely personal."[5] I think Forster would agree. But what if bad logic, then, participates in reproducing precisely this heterosexual culture, insisting that sex remain only teasingly visible, muted in its public intelligibility by the badness of its forms, and therefore unable to make sex more than merely personal, merely intimate. This problem resonates in the tragedy of Stephen Gordon, the protagonist of Radclyffe Hall's *The Well of Loneliness* (1928), who struggles to embrace the vibrant lesbian subculture into which she is reluctantly initiated, and who ends the novel alone, haunted by an army of queer ghosts, "unbidden guests" who press upon her and warn her: "You dare not disown us!"[6] Finally, we're told,

> They possessed her. Her barren womb became fruitful—it ached with its fearful and sterile burden. It ached with the fierce yet helpless children who would clamour in vain for their right to salvation. . . .
>
> And now there was only one voice, one demand; her own voice into which those millions had entered. A voice like the awful, deep rolling of thunder; a demand like the gathering together of great waters. A terrifying voice that made her ears throb, that made her brain throb, that shook her very entrails, until she must struggle and all but fall beneath this appalling burden of sound that strangled her in its will to be uttered.
>
> "God," she gasped, "we believe; we have told You we believe . . . We have not denied You, then rise up and defend us. Acknowledge us, oh God, before the whole world. Give us also the right to our existence!"[7]

Hall's novel ends with a solitary woman possessed and impregnated by the choral voice of millions, and yet despite Stephen's assumption of plural pronouns, this is far from a public mediation of sex. Stephen is haunted, engorged, invaded bodily by this queer collective after being accused of indifference, but the appeal, and her pain, is personal and intimate—an affair of the shaking entrails, the throbbing brain that remains bound within the horizon of the body, the "sterile burden" that refuses to be born into the world. It's a voice, after all, that possesses her, but we might easily read this plural voice as, really, her very own ("her own voice unto which those millions had entered"), yet a voice that she insists must come from without. We might read the "sound that strangled her in its will to be uttered" as the urgent, trembling, nauseating impulse simply to speak her own desire, a desire intelligible to her only by analogy to the desires of the band of outsiders whose imprecations batter her. Finally, she speaks, but not in public and not with the force of logical clarity, except perhaps in the syllogistic symmetry of her quid pro quo. Instead, she prays, and the prayer takes the form of an angry imperative: defend us, acknowledge us, before the whole world. Stephen passes the buck. It's her omniscient God who must make queer desire public; a private prayer is the best that one person possessed by the voices of millions can do to make her desire minimally visible, intelligible perhaps only to herself.

Forster and Hall help us to see that the relationship between public and intimate mediations of sexuality need not be that of the either/or proposition. There is space for more than one kind of erotic truth, and for more than one kind of acknowledgment—and for each kind of truth, for each mode of acknowledgment, a different kind of claim. The challenge is to remind ourselves that these different vocabularies and different formalizations of erotic life are only, after all, different, rather than at odds. They might, together, speak loudly and clearly. Whether one hears me or not, whether one acknowledges the self-evidence of my claim—indeed, whether or not I can entirely understand it myself—I am what I am.

Introduction • To Give a Form to Formless Things

1. Wilde, *The Picture of Dorian Gray*, 19–20. Further citations appear parenthetically within the text.

2. Sedgwick, *Epistemology of the Closet*, 137.

3. James, *The Golden Bowl*, 68.

4. As Audrey Jaffe points out, this novel engages in an "eroticization of identity . . . in which Dorian's wish to change places with his picture reveals identity itself, here allegorized as culture's visible form, to be one of the modern subject's most sought-after objects of desire" (*Scenes of Sympathy*, 164). While Jaffe is interested in the "identity" of "identity politics" or "sexual identity" rather than that of logical self-identity, the concepts are nevertheless resonant.

5. Bain, *Mental and Moral Science*, 185.

6. Wittgenstein, *Tractatus*, 41.

7. Wilde, *De Profundis*, 101. Jonathan Loesberg has recently taken this epigram as the starting point for a model of queer formalism inspired by Wilde: "if reality is non-contradictory," Loesberg argues, "paying attention to paradox amounts simply to turning one's head willfully in the other direction," away from reality and toward language. "From this perspective," he continues, "an interpretive indulgence in paradox is a species of perversity. One might say there is something queer about it" ("Wildean Interpretation," 9).

8. Quine, *From a Logical Point of View*, vii.

9. Nagel, *The View from Nowhere*, 3.

10. Eliot, *The Mill on the Floss*, 325.

11. Rayo and Uzquiano, "Introduction," 1–2.

12. Sedgwick, *Epistemology of the Closet*, 164.

13. James, *The Wings of the Dove*, 89, original emphasis.

14. Friedman, "Negative Eroticism," 623. Friedman's reading follows but to some extent resists, as do I, William A. Cohen's argument that "Wilde's career forms the horizon for a specifically literary practice of rendering sex unspeakable," his encoding of sexual meanings in his work and his consequent refusal to make these meanings explicit when they led to scandal representing a kind of historical crisis in the relationship between literature and sexuality (*Sex Scandal*, 192). I'm more sympathetic to Friedman's approach, as I think of Wilde's commitment to bad logic as a creative way of accommodating language to the ethical dimensions of sexuality while also recognizing the formal limitations intrinsic to language as a mechanism of reason and intelligibility.

15. Mao and Walkowitz, "Introduction: Modernisms Bad and New," 4; Puckett, *Bad Form*; Ngai, *Ugly Feelings*, 3. For the negative turn in queer studies, see Bersani, "Is the Rectum a Grave?" and *Homos*; Cvetkovich, *An Archive of Feelings*; Edelman, *No Future*; Love, *Feeling Backward*; and Halberstam, *The Queer Art of Failure*.

16. Wittgenstein, *Philosophical Investigations*, §108.

17. Butler, *Gender Trouble*, 24. In drawing a connection between Wittgenstein and the poststructuralist tradition, I am inspired by Terry Eagleton's insistence upon the connections between Wittgenstein's theory of language and Derrida's theory of deconstruction in "Wittgenstein's Friends."

18. Austin, *How to Do Things with Words*; Cavell, *Philosophy the Day after Tomorrow*, 183.

19. Bain, *Mental and Moral Science*, 68, 240, 107.

20. Havelock Ellis, *Studies in the Psychology of Sex*, 1:91, 90.

21. Freud, *Introductory Lectures*, 373.

22. Cohn, *Still Life*, 29.

23. Jarvis, *Exquisite Masochism*, viii.

24. Bersani, "Sociality and Sexuality," 644.

25. A skeptic may object that literary language, because of its aesthetic formalization, is not the same thing at all as the "ordinary language" investigated by this philosophical tradition. For a persuasive rejoinder to this claim, identified in this case with the tradition of Russian Formalism and the New Criticism, see Perloff, *Wittgenstein's Ladder*, 51–82. I follow Perloff's rejection of the idea "that the ordinary must be defined in relation to its opposite, the extraordinary, or indeed in relation to anything outside it. Wittgenstein's *ordinary* is best understood as quite simply *that which is*, the language we do *actually* use when we communicate with one another. In this sense, the ordinary need not be literal, denotative, propositional, neutral, referential. . . . On the contrary, our actual language may well be connotative, metaphoric, fantastic" (57, original emphasis). For an earlier rebuttal of the distinction between literary and ordinary language, but one more marginally engaged with the field of ordinary language philosophy, see Fish, "How Ordinary Is Ordinary Language?"

26. Bauer et al., "Introduction," v.

27. Cavell, *The Claim of Reason*, 20.

28. Lacan, "The Instance of the Letter," 164–65.

29. Levine, *Forms*, 6, 9.

30. For an expansive recent overview of this period in the history of logic, see Gabbay and Woods, eds., *British Logic in the Nineteenth Century*. For a more detailed account from the point of view of the history of mathematics, see Cohen, "Reason and Belief in Victorian Mathematics." Cohen also points the way to a host of questions beyond the scope of this book that might be illuminated by an attention to the development of mathematical logic in the Victorian period. In particular, he notes that almost all of the leading figures in this movement were disillusioned by Anglicanism and moved toward "more ecumenical expressions of spirituality," and that their social views tended disproportionately toward "liberalism, cosmopolitan internationalism, and pacifism" (142). Cohen expands his argument about the history of Victorian mathematics and mathematical logic, its lines of influence, and its connection to Christian faith in *Equations from God*. British logicians of the nineteenth century, including William Hamilton, Augustus De Morgan, and George Boole, were also familiar with the important tradition of Indian logic. See Ganeri, "Introduction: Indian Logic and the

Colonization of Reason." This fact suggests many ways in which the history of British logic is entangled with the history of the colonial occupation of India.

31. For a different but related recent reading of the realist novel as enacting or unfolding a theory of language—in this case a theory of reference—see Bartlett, *Object Lessons*. Dora Zhang has recently called attention to the ways in which even modernist novelists, so deeply concerned with the representation of immediate psychological experience, struggle to describe the utterly indescribable feelings and sensations that make up so much of this experience. She also sees such literary concerns (in this case having to do with techniques of psychological description) as being connected to problems in the philosophy of language. See Zhang, "Naming the Indescribable." Megan Quigley's *Modernist Fiction and Vagueness*, to which I return in chapter three, makes a different kind of case for the interaction between the logical problems of fuzzy meanings and the literary problems of the modernist period. I hope that my study might provide one potential prehistory, however indirect, for Zhang's and Quigley's accounts. For other important recent studies of the relationship between logic, ordinary language philosophy, and twentieth-century fiction, which draw upon a different philosophical context than I do but help to offer a fuller story about logic and literature, see LeMahieu, *Fictions of Fact and Value*, and LeMahieu and Zumhagen-Yekplé, eds., *Wittgenstein and Modernism*.

32. For a fuller historical account of the transition from the innovative logical theory of the medieval period to the textbook tradition of the early modern period, see Ashworth, "Developments in the Fifteenth and Sixteenth Centuries." It's also important to note that scholars of medieval literature have long recognized in their own period a striking link between advances in the theory of logic and literary representations of reasoning about desire, in this case the forms that structure courtly love. See Hunt, "Aristotle, Dialectic, and Courtly Literature"; Kay, *Courtly Contradictions*, which draws upon medieval debates around the problem of contradiction which are strikingly different from the kinds of debates I survey in this book around the same form of "bad logic," although its argument is less exclusively focused on the erotic; and Rosenfeld, *Ethics and Enjoyment*, which considers the influence of Aristotle's ethics on medieval representations of love and pleasure. Taking their arguments alongside mine, we can begin to see a historical pattern, where new ways of understanding logic might necessarily lead to wide-ranging reconsiderations of how to reason in the first place, and especially how to reason about messy affective and embodied experiences like desire and love. Such major new developments in logic take a long hiatus between the medieval and the Victorian periods.

33. Leibniz, "Preface to a Universal Characteristic," 8–9.

34. Stewart, *Elements of the Philosophy of the Human Mind*, 2:107; Carlyle, *Sartor Resartus*, 53.

35. For background on the influence and longevity of the *Port-Royal Logic* in England, see Wahl, "Arnauld, Antoine," 36.

36. Whewell, "Study of Mathematics," 140.

37. Hamilton, review of "Study of Mathematics," 412.

38. Eliot, *Middlemarch*, 672.

39. Mill, *A System of Logic*, 10.

40. Ibid., 6.

41. Hadley, *Living Liberalism*, 18.

42. Mill, *Utilitarianism*, 12.

43. De Morgan, *Formal Logic*, 46.

44. Rorty, *Contingency, Irony, and Solidarity*, xvi.

45. Sidgwick, *The Methods of Ethics*, 12.

46. Lewes, *Problems of Life and Mind*, 468

47. Carroll, *Symbolic Logic*, xiii.

48. Henderson, "Symbolic Logic and the Logic of Symbolism," 81–82.

49. Kornbluh, "The Realist Blueprint," 204. Kornbluh has in unpublished work expanded this argument in the direction of Lewis Carroll's engagement with symbolic logic as another way to imagine the politics of nonmimetic realism. See Kornbluh, "Realism Redux."

50. Austin, "A Plea for Excuses," 8.

51. Shklovsky, "Art as Device," 6

52. "Contemporary Literature," 575. Although this review was published anonymously, the *Wellesley Index of Victorian Periodicals* concludes that it was likely authored by the philosopher of religion James Martineau.

53. Eliot, "The Natural History of German Life," 128.

54. Ibid.

55. Trollope, *An Autobiography*, 177.

56. Foucault, *The History of Sexuality*, 78.

57. Foucault, *The Hermeneutics of the Subject*, 3, 9, 46.

58. Anderson, *The Powers of Distance*, 5–7, original emphasis.

59. Some of the most important and influential works in this tradition are Bersani, *A Future for Astyanax*; Armstrong, *Desire and Domestic Fiction*; Moretti, *The Way of the World*; and D. A. Miller, *The Novel and the Police*.

60. Hadley, *Living Liberalism*, 14.

61. Frederickson, *The Ploy of Instinct*, 4, 12.

62. Rosenthal, *Good Form*, 1–2.

63. Kurnick, *Empty Houses*, 3.

64. See Kurnick, "Abstraction and the Subject of Novel-Reading" and "An Erotics of Detachment."

65. Cavell, "Must We Mean What We Say?," 12.

66. Ibid., 20–21.

Chapter 1 • Charlotte Brontë's Contradictions

1. Emily Brontë, *Wuthering Heights*, 82, original emphasis. Further citations appear parenthetically within the text.

2. It's beyond the scope of this book to consider more carefully the political meanings of intimacy in Brontë, but as Gayatri Chakravorty Spivak has so influentially argued, in *Jane Eyre*, this limiting of the social world to intimate domestic or erotic relationships also enacts—indeed depends upon—Jane's active extrication of herself from the colonial world with which her life is so entangled, particularly through the violent self-immolation of Bertha Mason, Jane's colonial other. See Spivak, "Three Women's Texts."

3. For a related reading, according to which such refusals of social belonging in Brontë's fiction are part of a complex engagement with hatred as a force both of social disintegration and social cohesion, see Lane, *Hatred and Civility*, 85–106.

4. Charlotte Brontë, *Villette*, 544. Further citations appear parenthetically within the text.

5. For alternative readings of Brontë's engagement with the idea of "abstraction," see Marcus, "The Profession of the Author"; Kreilkamp, "Unuttered"; and Price, *How to Do Things with Books*, 72–106.

6. Several critics have argued for the imperfection, unevenness, or sheer labor of narrative omniscience: see esp. Jaffe, *Vanishing Points*; D. A. Miller, *Jane Austen*; and Culler, "Omniscience."

7. As Sandra Laugier argues, "We could define Quine's 'logical point of view' on the basis of his integration of logic into the learning of everyday language" (Laugier, *Why We Need Ordinary Language Philosophy*, 6). It is this strange integration of the ideal with the everyday, the generic with the particular, that characterizes the irreducible contradiction I'm describing here, which might also be congruous with the relationship between "theory" and "practice" more broadly. Laugier's broader argument is that this contradiction lies at the heart of ordinary language philosophy, which doesn't reject the idea of formal rules but in fact shows how even ordinary language is beholden to such rules.

8. Quine, *From a Logical Point of View*, 5.

9. Wittgenstein, *Philosophical Investigations*, §125.

10. Wittgenstein, *Tractatus*, 41. Further citations appear parenthetically within the text.

11. Wittgenstein, *Philosophical Investigations*, §125, original emphasis.

12. Bersani, *A Future for Astyanax*, 5–6; Gilbert and Gubar, *The Madwoman in the Attic*, 155; Jameson, *The Political Unconscious*, 77; Jameson, *The Antinomies of Realism*, 26; D. A. Miller, *The Novel and the Police*, 99n21; Sedgwick, *Epistemology of the Closet*, 1.

13. I borrow this turn of phrase from the title of Bruno Latour's iconoclastic critique of the available forms of social critique itself, "Why Has Critique Run Out of Steam?" If contradiction has long been taken as an object of critique or a sign of a problem in need of the solutions provided by critique, then Latour's question might be recast in just this way, i.e., as a question about how we approach the form of the contradiction.

14. For a deployment of this form of contradiction as a problem for Brontë, see Carolyn Williams, "Closing the Book." Williams reads contradiction (in the sense of refusal or naysaying) as a structuring principle of *Jane Eyre*, one that might help us make sense of Jane's abdication of the conclusion of her own story to the voice of St. John Rivers. "Other characters," she argues, "other text—the notion of the other world itself—are introduced *in order that* they may in some sense be contradicted, so that the narrating 'I' can distinguish herself from them, defining that 'I' in the process" (67, original emphasis). A similar sense of "contradiction" is at work in Sally Shuttleworth's argument that in *Jane Eyre*, Brontë "explores the contradictions at the heart of theories of unified selfhood" by showing how "Jane dwells repeatedly on her internal divisions, her lack of a unifying, controlling centre of self" (155). For Shuttleworth, this model of internal contradiction as conflict between various faculties of feeling and judgment is drawn from phrenology and its "battleground of warring, autonomous energies, where conflict is inscribed not as an occasional lapse, but as a necessary principle of existence" (155).

15. Charlotte Brontë, *Jane Eyre*, 482. Further citations appear parenthetically within the text.

16. Aristotle, *Metaphysics*, 1005b13-21.

17. Ibid., 1005b24-25.

18. Ibid., 1005b26-34.

19. Hegel, *The Science of Logic*, 51.
20. Sedgwick, *Touching Feeling*, 8, original emphasis.
21. Hegel, *The Encyclopaedia Logic*, 49.
22. Wittgenstein, *Philosophical Investigations*, §125.
23. For a reading of the relationship between Wittgenstein's philosophy of language and the tradition of "social contract" philosophy, see Cavell, *The Claim of Reason*, 3–36.
24. Andrew Miller, *The Burdens of Perfection*, 94.
25. Nagel, *The View from Nowhere*, 173. For a different engagement with Nagel's work as a way to understand the literary problem of point of view, in this case as it relates to the astronomical view from the stars, see Henchman, *The Starry Sky Within*, esp. 1–47. Henchman sees astronomy and literature as two ways of thinking about the same wider problem, that is, the "contradictory impulses found in all aspects of nineteenth-century life: the desire to see things as a whole paired with a growing realization that such a goal is impossible" (39). See also Andrew Miller, *The Burdens of Perfection*, which engages with the philosophical questions posed by Nagel (57–58) and which argues that one way Victorian writers resolve, or at least negotiate, the contradiction between first-person and third-person points of view is through an emphasis on the ethical force of the second-person address. My argument is indebted to Miller's careful consideration of the ethical problems raised by narrative point of view. While his focus is on the third-person perspective and its way of weakening the will and diluting personal convictions in favor of the "agent-neutral" sympathy of utilitarianism (58), and whereas Miller imagines "the cultivation of sympathetic second-person relations" as the result of "that management of perspectives . . . where first- and third-person perspectives are negotiated," I show here that Brontë is interested less in the "management" or "negotiation" of these perspectives than in remaining stubbornly within the first-person perspective, alive to its painful but necessary contradictions (102).
26. Nagel, *The View from Nowhere*, 54.
27. Daston and Galison, *Objectivity*, 37.
28. Ibid., 301–2.
29. Levine, *Dying to Know*, 2.
30. Bernard Williams, *Ethics and the Limits of Philosophy*, 67, 69–70, original emphasis.
31. For a useful survey of early critical responses to this scene, see Yeazell, "More True than Real." "Like all romantic literature," Yeazell argues, "*Jane Eyre* is part dream, but this dream has integrity, coherence, and a logic of its own. Its truth is the truth of the psyche" (128). Justine Pizzo, on the other hand, has recently connected this scene to the historical emergence of climate science, arguing that Brontë draws upon meteorological ideas about the air and its relationship to the body in order to emphasize Jane's "sensitive physicality and acute cognition in relation to the atmosphere," which "allow her to transcend the limits of her first-person point of view and suggest the knowledge of a controlling author" (85). See Pizzo, "Atmospheric Exceptionalism."
32. For a reading of the relationship between authority and narrative voice in *Jane Eyre*, see Bodenheimer, "Jane Eyre in Search of Her Story," 387–402. For a reading of the "erotics of talk" in the novel as a problem for its feminist reception, see Kaplan, *The Erotics of Talk*, 71–98. See Glen, *Charlotte Brontë*, 96–143, for a reading of *Jane Eyre* that links Jane's assumption of authority not to models of feminine morality drawn from conduct books but rather to models of restless aspiration and erotic power drawn from women's poetry. More broadly,

Glen argues that "*Jane Eyre* tells not a single . . . story, but two opposing and incommensurate ones. The self at the centre of each appears in a radically different way: in one, as magically omnipotent, triumphing absolutely; in the other, as insubstantial, the constantly jeopardized object of forces beyond its control" (64).

33. Jaffe, *Vanishing Points*, 19. For other arguments that problematize the relationship between first-person narration and the concept of narrative omniscience, see Culler, "Omniscience," and Royle, "The 'Telepathy Effect.' "

34. This is what the philosopher John Searle (inspired by the earlier work of J. L. Austin and G. E. M. Anscombe) has described as the central difference between idiosyncratic expressions of desire and rational assertions, that is, the "direction of fit" that is presumed in the relationship between "word" and "world." In other words, a desire aims to change the world so that the world comes to "fit" the desired state of affairs; the goal of true assertion is to make the words match the reality of the world as it is. See Searle, *Expression and Meaning*, 4.

35. Sedgwick, *Touching Feeling*, 75.

36. This is a tradition largely filtered through the reception of J. L. Austin's theory of performative language in *How to Do Things with Words* and, even more specifically, Jacques Derrida's deconstructive critique of that theory in his 1972 essay "Signature Event Context" and Derrida's ensuing debate with John Searle. For the full exchange with Searle, see Derrida, *Limited Inc.* For some of the most important examples of how this specific line of thought in the field of ordinary language philosophy enters into literary theory, see Fish, "How to Do Things with Austin and Searle"; Felman, *The Scandal of the Speaking Body*; J. Hillis Miller, *Speech Acts in Literature*; and Sedgwick, *Touching Feeling*, 67–92.

37. Cavell, "Performative and Passionate Utterance," in *Philosophy the Day after Tomorrow*, 185. Further citations appear parenthetically within the text.

38. Anderson, *Powers of Distance*, 53n25; 48.

39. Dames, *Amnesiac Selves*, 120.

40. Kucich, *Repression*, 77. For an earlier and more thoroughly psychoanalytic account of repression in *Villette*, in this case the novel's strained repression of its Romantic influences and its feminist energies, see Jacobus, "The Buried Letter." For a reading of sexual repression as a vexed object of the novel's culture of surveillance, see Shuttleworth, *Charlotte Brontë*, 220–42. Shuttleworth connects Lucy's evasion of "religious, educational, and medical" surveillance to a desire "to render herself illegible" and thereby "to assume control over the processes of her own self-definition" (242). Like Kucich, in other words, Shuttleworth understands Lucy's erotic life as antisocial, whereas I understand it as the foundation of her efforts to go beyond herself, to become socially legible.

41. Kucich, *Repression*, 78.

42. Cohn, *Still Life*, 52, 54, 51.

43. Kucich, *Repression*, 39.

44. Dames, *Amnesiac Selves*, 119. Cohn shares Dames's and Shuttleworth's interest in Brontë's engagement with phrenology and argues that Lucy's periodic abandonment of the phrenological body, an object of intense attention and analysis, in favor of the invention of "dream-bodies" in her states of reverie, allows her to resist, at least momentarily, "the force of social legibility" cultivated by phrenological analysis (*Still Life*, 54).

45. Anderson, *The Powers of Distance*, 47.

46. Andrew Miller, *The Burdens of Perfection*, 192–93.

47. See Matus, *Unstable Bodies*, 131–56, for a reading of these two scenes as together establishing Lucy's gaze as "the gaze of the outsider," a position from which her spectatorship fails to "assert dominance" and rather establishes "a contrast between herself as passive and the others, whom she sees as active players" (133). While my reading of *Villette* in some ways challenges Matus's reading of Lucy's desire as essentially passive, I share her interest in the complex eroticization of Lucy's spectatorship, especially when it comes to her consumption of art and performance.

48. See also Boone, *Libidinal Currents*. Boone's argument is similar to mine in his suggestion that part of the goal of *Villette's* experimental narrative form and its frequent invocation of dreams, fugues, and fantasies, is "to convert . . . psychosexual currents into narratable story" (35). But because Boone wants to position *Villette* as "protomodernist" in its representation of sexuality, he amplifies his argument with the claim that the novel aims for "a radical reenvisioning of subjectivity that . . . is as radically decentered, as unmoored from the commonplaces of a stable or coherent identity, as is the narrative form itself" (37). My argument, on the other hand, presupposes that Brontë's concern with making desire socially intelligible is eminently Victorian and that it demonstrates a deep investment in concepts like sociability, citizenship, and religious and ethical self-examination.

Chapter 2 • Anthony Trollope's Tautologies

1. Trollope, *Can You Forgive Her?*, 233. Further citations appear parenthetically within the text.

2. Barthes, *Mythologies*, 267. Later in his career, in the lecture course published as *The Preparation of the Novel*, Barthes complicated this position, using a Zen parable to demonstrate how the stupidity of tautology might be transformed by interpretation into "the literal." The parable traces three stages to this process: first, the "arrogant, anti-intellectualist tautology" that says "the mountains are mountains"; second, the moment of "initiation" that says "the mountains aren't mountains anymore"; finally, the moment of "interpretation" that "spirals back" to say "the mountains are mountains again" (81). Barthes came around to seeing tautology as something that might be reworked into an object of meaning but maintained to the end of his career that the initial force of tautology, before this particular practice of Zen interpretation, is nothing more than "unthinking certainty" (81).

3. Barthes, *Mythologies*, 106, 107, 108.

4. Trollope, *He Knew He Was Right*, 508.

5. Ibid., 743.

6. Trollope, *Autobiography*, 121.

7. Ibid., 234–35.

8. apRoberts, *Trollope*, 22.

9. Quintilian, *The Orator's Education*, 369.

10. Trollope, *An Autobiography*, 177.

11. Kant, *Logic*, 118.

12. For a fuller exploration of this latter idea about literary representation, see Scarry, *Dreaming by the Book*, esp. 5–9.

13. For an argument that links this kind of freezing, suspension, and isolation to the erotic pleasure of masochism in Trollope, see Jarvis, *Exquisite Masochism*, 56–89.

14. Newman, *Grammar of Assent*, 4. Further citations appear parenthetically within the text.

15. Andrew H. Miller, *Burdens of Perfection*, 146.

16. Ablow, "Reading and Re-reading," 160. For another reading of the representation of falling in love in Victorian fiction and its connection to the discourse of religious faith, see Polhemus, *Erotic Faith*. I share Polhemus's investment in novelists' use of erotic desire as a crucial way of constructing literary character, while diverging from him significantly in his insistence upon the religious and therefore necessarily redemptive force of erotic desire in the novel.

17. Newman, *Grammar of Assent*, 83–84.

18. Hardy, *Life and Work*, 244.

19. Viswanathan, *Outside the Fold*, 44–45.

20. Wittgenstein, *On Certainty*, 2. Further citations appear parenthetically within the text.

21. For "postcritique," see Felski, *The Limits of Critique*, 151–85; for the descriptive turn, see Love, "Close but Not Deep," and Marcus, Love, and Best, "Building a Better Description"; for modesty, see Jeffrey J. Williams, "The New Modesty," and Dancer, "Toward a Modest Criticism."

22. Best and Marcus, "Surface Reading," 4–5.

23. Ibid., 10.

24. Schmitt, "Tidal Conrad (Literally)," 12.

25. Brooks, *Reading for the Plot*, 52, original emphasis. It is worth noting that Brooks's use of the term "desire" as a structuring mechanism of novelistic plotting is very different from this chapter's interest in the difficulties of representing characters' erotic desires.

26. Girard, *Deceit, Desire, and the Novel*, 3, original emphasis.

27. Butler, *Giving an Account of Oneself*, 42, 43.

28. For another reading of Alice's silencing (and her disappearance from the Palliser series) and the relationship of this problem to sexuality and the marriage plot, see Jarvis, *Exquisite Masochism*. As Jarvis puts it, "Alice's transformation at the novel's end, her inscription in a marriage defined by John Grey's oppressive, genital sexuality, all but makes her disappear" (89). Jarvis's goal is to contrast Alice with Glencora, who manages to become the central figure of the Palliser series by investing in a "nonsexual masochism" that directs erotic energy into social life and "affords [her] narrative presence" (89). My reading of this novel (and of *The Way We Live Now*) is in deep sympathy with Jarvis's, even if the terms and theoretical contexts we use to analyze Trollope's odd and shifty engagements with the power of erotic life are quite different.

29. Polhemus, *The Changing World of Anthony Trollope*, 111.

30. Unsigned review of *Can You Forgive Her?*, in Smalley, *Anthony Trollope*, 243.

31. For a different reading of Trollope's marriage plot in relation to the notion of contract, see Marcus, *Between Women*, 193–226. While Marcus links what I call the "abstract, consensual self" to feminist models of equality in marriage, I aim to get at the opposite side of the same coin in focusing upon the potential feminist meanings of the intractable desire that is opposed to just such contractual abstraction.

32. For an extended consideration of Trollope's many uses of this "why should I not?" formulation as a way to represent characters testing the boundaries of norms and ethical systems in fantasy, see Jaffe, *The Victorian Novel Dreams of the Real*, 68–93.

33. Jarvis, *Exquisite Masochism*, 77. For a different reading of the problem of Alice's constrained choice, see Schaffer, *Romance's Rival*, 230–35. Schaffer sees Alice as divided between a model of "familiar marriage"—in this case the "vocational passion" she feels for George—and the "romantic love" that attracts her to Grey, but she also identifies this choice as cruelly structured by the binary conditions of the novel's plot (230). As she puts it, while Trollope depicts these as "parallel feelings of comparable strength," he also "tacitly depicts them as incompatible, for he vests them in different men, associated with divergent futures" (230).

34. Marcus, *Between Women*, 255.

35. Althusser, "Ideology," 116, ellipsis in original.

36. Marcus, *Between Women*, 255.

37. Diamonds have been a major focus of Trollope criticism, particularly in work on *The Eustace Diamonds*. See Andrew H. Miller, *Novels behind Glass*, 159–88; Ben-Yishai, *Common Precedents*, 116–44; William A. Cohen, *Sex Scandal*, 159–90; and Briefel, "Tautological Crimes." But whereas these readings of *The Eustace Diamonds* tend to link the jewels at the heart of that novel to the instability of legal concepts of ownership (in Briefel's and Ben-Yishai's cases) or the problems of the commodity form and the uncertain ownership of female sexuality (in Miller's and Cohen's cases), this moment in *Can You Forgive Her?* makes a different use of diamonds, as a symbol of the impenetrable and dazzling force of certainty.

38. Meredith, *The Egoist*, 142. Further citations appear parenthetically within the text.

39. We might describe Clara's attitude as part of the structure of moral perfectionism described by Andrew H. Miller as central to the nineteenth-century realist novel—a "narrative form" often based upon the consciousness of an "ideal self" or the relationship to "exemplary others" (*Burdens*, 3).

40. Jagose, "Remembering Miss Wade," 448n37.

41. Herman (score and lyrics) and Fierstein (book), *La Cage Aux Folles*.

42. Edith Ellis, *The New Horizon in Love and Life*, 65.

43. D. A. Miller, *Place for Us*, 133.

44. Fuss, *Essentially Speaking*, 20. Discussions of essentialism, and specifically "strategic essentialism," are incredibly wide ranging, but for the origin of the latter concept, see Grosz and Spivak, "Criticism, Feminism, and the Institution." It's also important to note that the essentialism of "I am what I am" is linked to the grammatical structure of predication, not only the logical structure of identity. In "Can the Subaltern Speak?," Spivak argues that subject-predication is a necessary precondition for the positive articulation of a "theory of interests," against poststructuralist theories that see such subject-predication as an illusion of language (273). In other words, responding to those who would theorize "a certain body without predication or without predication-function," so that even a statement such as "I am what I am" would lose its purchase, Spivak confesses in a later essay that she has "been unable to read this as anything but a last-ditch metaphysical longing" and that she remains "bound by the conviction that subject-predication is methodologically necessary" (Spivak, "Scattered Speculations on the Question of Value," 73). We must believe in the reality of predication to believe in the possibility of strategic essentialism, and I follow Spivak here in valuing these structures of self-identity as the basis for the articulation of desire.

45. Here I offer a limited overview of this body of criticism, in addition to the critics discussed presently at greater length. For a reading of the power of language in the central courtship plot of *Can You Forgive Her?* and the capacity of language to disconnect from and even shape "reality," see McMaster, "The Meaning of Words and the Nature of Things." For a

reading of the connection in Trollope between rational deliberation and "irrational" states of desire, instinct, and conviction, see Fessenbecker, "Anthony Trollope on Akrasia, Self-Deception, and Ethical Confusion." For a different reading of Trollope's investment in the force of women's desire, see Morse, *Reforming Trollope*, esp. 91–110. For Trollope's interest in variously reinforcing or critiquing Victorian ideologies of heterosexual marriage, see Fisichelli, "The Language of Law and Love"; Psomiades, "Heterosexual Exchange and Other Victorian Fictions"; Marcus, *Between Women*, 227–56; and Michie, *The Vulgar Question of Money*, 103–41. For readings of women's sexuality in Trollope as related to problems of property, ownership, value, and materiality (one of which makes very different use than I do of the concept of the tautology), see William A. Cohen, *Sex Scandal*, 159–90; Andrew H. Miller, *Novels behind Glass*, 159–88; and Briefel, "Tautological Crimes."

46. Anderson, "Trollope's Modernity," 519.
47. J. Hillis Miller, *Others*, 94, 98.
48. Gagnier, "Gender, Liberalism, and Resentment," 246.
49. Miller, *Others*, 95.
50. Ibid., 93–94.
51. Walkowitz, *Cosmopolitan Style*, 3–4.
52. Miller, *Others*, 100.
53. Muñoz, *Cruising Utopia*, 1.
54. Lacan, *The Ethics of Psychoanalysis*, 319.
55. Žižek, *Interrogating the Real*, 331.
56. Trollope, *The Way We Live Now*, 1:21. Further citations appear parenthetically within the text.
57. Lauren Byler has argued, in "If the Shoe Fits . . . Trollope and the Girl," that "the girl" in Trollope's fiction stands as a paradoxical symbol of both utility (she is required for the smooth functioning of the marriage plot) and uselessness (the marriage plot depends on her "marital impasses that generate narrative and lubricate readerly desires") (268). Her emphasis on the way in which the desires of female characters can "clog" narrative momentum and can bridge the gap between social utility and uselessness complements my own sense of these desires as often refusing linear, communicative language while still signifying resistance.

Chapter 3 • George Eliot's Vagueness

1. Eliot, "The Ilfracombe Journal," 228.
2. Eliot, "Notes on Form in Art," 432. Further citations appear parenthetically within the text.
3. Eliot, *Daniel Deronda*, 157–58.
4. For a wider consideration of Eliot's interest in reverie, lapses in self-awareness, and the problem of development, see Cohn, *Still Life*, 65–110.
5. Eliot, *Middlemarch*, 191. Further citations appear parenthetically within the text.
6. Eliot, *Silas Marner*, 77–78.
7. For a reading of Eliot's attention to the plasticity and "soft matter" (61) of character that also attends to the fuzziness of language and the importance of metaphor, albeit from a different angle than my own, see Brilmyer, "Plasticity."
8. Wittgenstein, *Philosophical Investigations*, §76.
9. Ibid.

10. Ibid., §77.

11. Ibid., §71, §108.

12. Ibid., §108.

13. For a comprehensive (if deeply cynical) précis of the explosion of contemporary academic interest in vagueness, see Rorty, "How Many Grains Make a Heap?" Rorty's review of Scott Soames's multivolume history of analytic philosophy argues that the problem of vagueness is something of a red herring around which the analytic school has developed. Rorty's perspective is particularly useful as an example of a pragmatist's conviction that vagueness is a superficial problem, since as long as language "works" in its social deployment, our investigations of its deep insufficiencies as a representation of an actual world can never actually provide us with any worthwhile or useable insights. For a sustained literary argument that focuses on vagueness and its influence on the modernist novel, see Quigley, *Modernist Fiction and Vagueness*. Quigley argues that "it was not until the end of the nineteenth century with the origins of the analytic tradition that vagueness resurfaced as a key concept" (3). In her account of the philosophical history, therefore, vagueness resurfaces after long neglect as a flashpoint for debate between logical atomists (Russell, Whitehead, early Wittgenstein, etc.) and pragmatists (Peirce, William James, Dewey, etc.). I think that Quigley is right—interest in the problem of vagueness exploded in the late-nineteenth and early-twentieth centuries—however, in my account, this later debate was in fact a further development of an existing nineteenth-century debate between proponents of mathematic logic (de Morgan, Boole, Venn, etc.) and proponents of a traditional logic more fully grounded in ordinary language (Mill, Newman, etc.). I see my account and Quigley's as complementary rather than at odds. See also Bartlett, "Overlooking in Stendhal," for an analysis of Stendhal's techniques of characterization that draws upon recent philosophical work on vagueness. Bartlett argues that Stendhal sees vagueness as a problem of perception and relationality in both time and space, best understood or coped with through concepts such as "overlooking," "approach," "intent," "the not-yet," and "nearness."

14. For a more detailed overview of the history of these different approaches to the sorites paradox, including the origins of the paradox with Eubulides, see Williamson, *Vagueness*, esp. 96–164 and 181–215.

15. Russell, "Vagueness," 85.

16. Kurnick, "An Erotics of Detachment," 584. See also Kurnick, "Abstraction."

17. For a different account of Eliot's interest in the ways in which affect and desire are formed and shaped by the mind, see Chase, *Eros and Psyche*, 136–62. Although our aims are quite dissimilar because of Chase's focus on physiological psychology and the "blind causality" and "unreason" it represents for Eliot (162), I do echo her in her claim that Eliot often pursues "the methods of a philosophical atomism which seeks to understand a phenomenon by analyzing it into smaller and smaller units" and that for Eliot "the secret of the human character . . . lies in the subtle process, the small cause, the gradual change" (159). On the other hand, for an argument for the "insistent segregation of sexuality from the domain of knowledge" (435) in *Middlemarch*, see Shuttleworth, "Sexuality and Knowledge." Like Chase, Shuttleworth is concerned with physiological psychology, its attempt at "a highly involved physiological integration of thought and emotion," and the ways that this presents problems for its attempts to disavow female sexuality as an object of scientific knowledge (435).

18. Moretti, *The Bourgeois*, 128–29, 129–30, 142.

19. Ibid., 144.

20. Eliot, *Daniel Deronda*, 3.

21. Cicero, *Academica* 2.94, trans. in Suzanne Bobzien, "Chrysippus and the Epistemic Theory of Vagueness," 225. Eliot would likely have known this image, at least indirectly, as she was an avid reader of Cicero, and the notebooks she kept during the composition of *Middlemarch* include copious references to Cicero and to secondary works on the history of Stoicism. See Eliot, *George Eliot's* Middlemarch *Notebooks*. Williamson uses this example from Cicero to argue that the Stoics took an epistemicist position on vagueness and that the metaphor of pulling up one's horses before the precipice represents the interlocutor who refuses to continue with the serial questions of the sorites paradox when he realizes he is going to be led to make a false statement, or before the "sharp drop" from true to false, which he is unequipped to locate (13). Bobzien refutes Williamson's reading, and argues that the metaphor represents the philosopher who avoids engaging with the paradox and its series of questions altogether, since he sees in advance that it will lead him down a dangerous road (225–26).

22. For an extended reading of Mr. Brooke's frequent invocation of "things" and "that sort of thing" that recuperates these vague, indirect formulations as mechanisms of novelistic character that extend to the more complex central characters of the novel, see Farina, "*Middlemarch* and 'That Sort of Thing.' "

23. James, "*Middlemarch*," 54, 48.

24. In "Stupid Sensations," Kent Puckett argues that James's description of *Middlemarch* as a novel with a "brain" highlights the particularly important vagueness of the distinction between mind and embodiment in Eliot's fiction. As Puckett puts it, "the brain is not only an organ of intelligence, but also an organ; it is a thing that not only thinks, but 'throbs' " (297). And therefore the centrality of the brain to this reading of *Middlemarch* gets at a host of questions, Puckett suggests, about how we separate the "higher-order" cognitive functions of the brain from its "lower-order" nervous functions.

25. Cohn, *Still Life*, 66, 82.

26. Wittgenstein, *Philosophical Investigations*, §71.

27. Frege, "Scientific Justification," 158.

28. Frege, *Conceptual Notation*, 105.

29. Eliot, *Adam Bede*, 364.

30. For an influential discussion of flowing water as one of Eliot's most ubiquitous metaphors as she develops a "quasi-scientific model to describe the subjective life of the individual, the relations of two persons within the social 'medium,' and the nature of that medium as a whole" (132), see J. Hillis Miller, "Optic and Semiotic." As Hillis Miller puts it, "flowing water is, so to speak, a temporalized web" in *Middlemarch*, a way for Eliot to show how the social web of the novel is "always in movement," and "made up of currents, filaments flowing side by side, intermingling and dividing" (132).

31. For an alternate reading of the problem of desire at the heart of this scene, see Herbert, *Culture and Anomie*. Herbert offers this scene as a striking example of the task he claims for the concept of "culture" as it developed in fields such as anthropology, ethnography, aesthetics, and political thought in the Victorian period. Although Herbert insists that the "culture concept" is fundamentally incoherent, he argues that it took shape as an attempt at "a scientific rebuttal" of "the myth of a state of ungoverned human desire," albeit a rebuttal that "has never succeeded in dispelling" that myth. Herbert reads Maggie's concept of "the seductive guidance of illimitable wants" as presupposing "a polarity of strict renunciation and 'illimitable' libido, with scarcely any intermediate term between the two," so that "ex-

treme self-violence may be the necessary cost of personal moral hygiene" (33). While Herbert tends to imagine Eliot as a champion of the culture concept—especially in what he sees as the reductive dichotomy of "illimitable wants" and desire's negation that is sustained by the structure of *The Mill on the Floss*—I suggest that Eliot's attunement to the affective and erotic experience of vagueness complicates this account.

32. Foucault, "Of Other Spaces," 24–25.

33. Eliot, *Romola*, 502.

34. Ibid., 504.

35. For an important counterargument, see Nancy K. Miller, "Emphasis Added." Miller argues that to equate Maggie's celibacy with an impoverishment of erotic life is to limit our ways of thinking about eroticism (particularly, Miller argues, in women's writing). In other words, if we imagine that Maggie's choice is ultimately reducible to an either-or proposition—either renounce pleasure or give in to it wholeheartedly—then we obscure the fact that she might truly desire neither of these things, that she might in fact desire the preservation and prolonging of erotic excitement in the form of fantasy. I invoke Miller's argument in order to clarify my own position, which is to insist that vagueness, like Miller's concept of subtle variations in "emphasis," is part of an aim to get beyond the logic of the "either-or" in favor of what Miller calls the "both-and," and that even when such an experiment seems to fail or to be limited by the oppressiveness of social norms and scripts (logic included), the very fact that Eliot registers it so frequently as a possibility represents the power of the "both-and" as a conceptual model of desire in her fiction (43). For an argument that responds to and expands upon Miller's argument about women's writing and the inscription of social norms within language, in this case by reading *The Mill on the Floss* alongside the work of Luce Irigaray, see Jacobus, "The Question of Language."

36. Cavell, "Something Out of the Ordinary," in *Philosophy the Day after Tomorrow*, 9.

37. Eliot, letter to Elizabeth Stuart Phelps, Aug. 13, 1875, in *The George Eliot Letters*, 6:163.

38. Entry for "swathe," *Oxford English Dictionary*, 2nd ed.

39. Quigley points out that modernist novelists invested in the vagueness problem consistently play with the connection between the English "vague" and the French *vague*, in ways that Eliot perhaps anticipates here (*Modernist Fiction*, 13–14).

40. Freud, *Civilization and Its Discontents*, 12.

41. Freud, *Three Essays*, 43.

42. Freud, *Civilization and Its Discontents*, 12.

43. Ibid., 13.

44. Bersani, "Sociality and Sexuality," 104.

45. Anderson, *The Way We Argue Now*, 137.

46. Felski and Fraiman, "Introduction," vi.

47. For a reading of this passage with a closer attention to its relationship to Casaubon as a character and his association with the "margin" and the "cluster of signs," see Hertz, *George Eliot's Pulse*, 20–42. The concepts with which Hertz associates Casaubon have to do with his thematic connection to textuality and writing, and their relationship to personhood in Eliot's fiction, and yet the "margin" and the "cluster" have obvious connections as well to the problem of vagueness.

48. See Beer, *Darwin's Plots*, esp. 139–68; and Shuttleworth, *George Eliot and Nineteenth-Century Science*.

49. Dames, *The Physiology of the Novel*, 125.

50. Esty, *Unseasonable Youth*, 56–57.

51. Gallagher, "George Eliot: Immanent Victorian," 62, 70; original emphasis.

52. Venn, *Symbolic Logic*, 427–38. Although Venn's name has by now become synonymous with sets of overlapping circles, he attributes the development of this particular type of diagram to the eighteenth-century Swiss mathematician Leonhard Euler and calls them "Eulerian circles." Venn was, however, largely responsible for adapting this kind of diagram to the field of logic, hence his concern with distinguishing their logical uses and limitations from their mathematical uses. For a useful history of the Venn diagram and its importance to the history of logic and mathematics, see Edwards, *Cogwheels of the Mind*.

53. Venn, *Symbolic Logic*, 438.

54. Frege, "The Thought," 308. In *The Realistic Spirit*, Cora Diamond argues that Frege's distinction between "the mind" and "minds" lies at the heart of a host of problems in the philosophy of language and its connections to ethics and the philosophy of mind (1–12).

Chapter 4 • Henry James's Generality

1. James, *The Awkward Age*, 221. Further citations appear parenthetically within the text.

2. Entry for "everything," *Oxford English Dictionary*, 2nd ed.

3. For a different reading of *everything* as a term through which to understand the construction and deployments of backgrounds, contexts, or worlds in realist description, and in poetry that borrows the techniques of realist description, see Clune, "Whatever Charms Is Alien."

4. The position of "behind" has of course been an important object of discussion for critics interested in Jamesian sexuality. Kaja Silverman, in her Lacanian reading of James in *Male Subjectivity at the Margins*, points to his "predilection for rear subject-positions" (158), which she connects to a structure of "sodomitical identification" (179). In *Touching Feeling*, Eve Kosofsky Sedgwick picks up a similar thread in her analysis of the *New York Edition* prefaces and James's "fussy, immensely productive focus on the sensations, actions and paralyses, accumulations and probings and expulsions of his own lower digestive tract" (49), a reading that explicitly challenges Silverman's assumption of "epistemological privilege" in her analysis of James—her assumption that James couldn't have intended or couldn't have been fully conscious of the sexual meanings in his own writing (54). It's important for our purposes to take note of the idea that the spatial rubric of inside/outside and behind/within map for both critics onto very different epistemological stances, something that is also true of James's invocation of "everything" as a kind of space. I return to both readings of James later on.

5. James, *The Ambassadors*, xxxv–xxxvi. Further citations appear parenthetically within the text.

6. As I've already noted in the introduction, in "The Realist Blueprint," Anna Kornbluh draws upon James's interest in architectural blueprints and this kind of vocabulary of shapes and structural drafts in order to argue for his elaboration of a "nonmimetic realism" (204).

7. Conrad, "Henry James," 15.

8. James, *The Sacred Fount*, 122. Further citations appear parenthetically within the text.

9. See Zubernis, "Henry James's Minimalist Novel," for the argument that we should understand James's style as "minimalist" in just these terms—not in terms of length and tone,

but rather in terms of "a withdrawal from the novel's standard meaning-making functions" in favor of the "unproductive surfaces of Jamesian style" that often reduce his prose to "a dense linguistic fog, a thick blankness" (467).

10. Venn, *Symbolic Logic*, 59.

11. For Russell's first published statement of this paradox and its possible solutions, see *Principles of Mathematics*, 101–5. For helping me to understand this paradox clearly, I am indebted to Irvine and Deutsch, "Russell's Paradox," and to Doxiadis and Papadimitrious, *Logicomix*, 164–68, 335–36.

12. Rayo and Uzquiano, "Introduction," 1.

13. Russell, "On Denoting," 483. Further citations appear parenthetically within the text.

14. Frege, "Sense and Reference," 215.

15. Strawson, "On Referring," 325.

16. James, *What Maisie Knew*, 216.

17. Hegel, *The Science of Logic*, 109, original emphasis, 110.

18. Peirce, "Logic as Semiotic," 98–99; "The Law of Mind," 340. If I seem to push aside Peirce as a figure who would have had a direct influence on James, it's largely because Peirce's work on logic, as I've suggested, echoes many of the preoccupations of the British tradition in logic and epistemology, including its occasional incorporations of Continental ideas as in the work of thinkers such as Carlyle and Eliot. A detailed analysis of his work, in other words, would not add enough to our working vocabulary to make it entirely worthwhile here. Moreover, he doesn't provide us with many interesting accounts either of "everything" or of the infinite, and so it seems appropriate to pay closest attention to the philosophers who do have a great deal to say about these concepts. In other words, a straightforward influence model is not what I pursue in this chapter, nor in this project as a whole, and in any event, the field of direct philosophical influence has been well covered in James criticism. For an excellent recent account of Peirce's influence on James, for example, which pertains specifically to the problem of vagueness, see Quigley, *Modernist Fiction and Vagueness*, 21–62. For one of the most influential readings of Henry James alongside the work of William James and the broader tradition of pragmatism, see Posnock, *The Trial of Curiosity*. For a reading that argues for James's anticipation of ideas in Continental phenomenology, see Cameron, *Thinking in Henry James*.

19. Rayo and Uzquiano, "Introduction," 2. See also Cartwright, "Speaking of Everything," for the observation that the near-consensus among philosophers that such a domain is not really available to logic is a quite recent development. Cartwright begins his essay by pointing out that nineteenth- and early-twentieth-century philosophers such as Frege and Russell, and even Quine at midcentury, were quite comfortable with the idea of unrestricted quantification (1–2).

20. Rayo and Uzquiano, "Introduction," 2n3.

21. Ibid., 1.

22. Sedgwick, *Epistemology of the Closet*, 201.

23. Stevens, *Henry James and Sexuality*, 19.

24. See Mendelssohn, *Henry James, Oscar Wilde, and Aesthetic Culture*. For the most fully worked out reading of James's relationship to aestheticism, which touches upon questions of sexuality in a somewhat more subsidiary way, see Freedman, *Professions of Taste*.

25. Sedgwick, *Touching Feeling*, 61.63.

26. James, *The Portrait of a Lady*, 104. Further citations appear parenthetically within the text.

27. In *The Melodramatic Imagination*, Peter Brooks argues that this is all part of James's strategy for representing what Brooks calls "the melodrama of consciousness." He points out that Isabel's choices become more and more heightened and intensified as the novel goes on, so that her culminating choice to reject Goodwood's advances and return to her unhappy marriage to Osmond "is freighted with the lurid connotations of sacrifice, torture, penance, claustration" (157). This reading tends to minimize the interest of Isabel's early choices, in which she is much more preoccupied with everyday questions of erotic desire than with the very different moral dilemmas and social stigmas associated with committing adultery or ending a marriage. Brooks's reading does, however, help us to see how Isabel begins from a chosen position of naïve and happy self-exclusion, in which "everything" seems a seamless object of knowledge for her, and ends by seeming to choose an unhappy, almost Gothic social exclusion.

28. For an overview of how Isabel's romantic choices have been read and pathologized, including the idea that her decision making demonstrates a general fear of sexuality, see J. Hillis Miller, *Literature as Conduct*, 30–83.

29. Woolf, *To the Lighthouse*, 130, 146, 68–69.

30. Austin, "A Plea for Excuses," 8.

31. For a related argument about ethics and the contingency of the individual point of view in James, see Pippin, *Henry James and Modern Moral Life*. Pippin argues that Ralph's kind of position is typical in James and that it exemplifies his "resistance to skepticism" in questions of ethics (7). At the same time, Pippin argues, "the sorts of worries about contingencies in how we determine what is justifiable or not . . . are frequently raised in James, and are clearly part of his worry about the rigidity and judgmental rigor of the moral point of view" (9). In other words, Pippin's reading of James positions him as someone trying above all to locate stable sources of moral truth in a modernizing world that seems more and more skeptical of the existence of such universal truths.

32. David Kurnick argues against the reading by which James's "major phase" moves away from the "communal and depsychologized vision" of novels such as *The Awkward Age* in favor of "an obsession with point of view" and "the epistemological conundrums this perspectivalism fosters" (*Empty Houses*, 144). Kurnick insists instead that James's late style maintains what he calls a "performative universalism," in which the voices of individual characters are surprisingly interchangeable in their vagueness and abstraction. "One thing Jamesian style wants," he suggests, "is to replace the differentiating energies of the drama of consciousness with an equally compelling vision of collectivity and universalism" (146). This reading of James's style might give us yet another way to think about the erotics of the tension between indefiniteness and particularity in James, although Kurnick's aim is somewhat different than mine in his focus on the theatricality of Jamesian "interiority." For a reading of James's late style that sees its "elusive and multivalent effects of syntax, figure, voice, and tone" as a "queer" disruption of the novel's mimetic aims, and specifically a "systematic challenging of the presumption that desire can be, or ought to be, represented" (2–3), see Ohi, *Henry James and the Queerness of Style*. I share Ohi's sense of James's ambivalence when it comes to the representation of desire, but I would add to his reading that James seems most worried about the representation of desire as a specific, particular object. The elusiveness of "everything," for example, doesn't in-

dicate a disruption of representation but rather a conviction that the object to be represented is best captured by generality rather than mimetic specificity.

33. Wittgenstein, *Tractatus*, 89.

34. James, *The Spoils of Poynton*, 162.

35. See D. A. Miller, *The Novel and the Police*, 192–220.

36. See Sedgwick, *Epistemology of the Closet*, 67–90.

37. François, *Open Secrets*, 3, original emphasis.

38. Ibid., xvi, 32, original emphasis.

39. Silverman, *Male Subjectivity*, 173.

40. For a more optimistic reading of this scene (and of the novel as a whole) as James's first representation of mature love, as opposed to unfulfilled desire, see McWhirter, *Desire and Love in Henry James*, esp. 1–12 and 175–99.

41. Wittgenstein, *Tractatus*, 5.

42. Ahmed, *Queer Phenomenology*, 1.

43. Ibid., 33.

44. For an alternative philosophical history of this kind of desire to reorient oneself in relation to the world "as it is," less focused on the problem of sexuality, see Terada, *Looking Away*.

45. James, *The Spoils of Poynton*, 49.

46. Cavell, *Philosophy the Day after Tomorrow*, 280. For the "contingency" of sexual orientation, see Ahmed, *Queer Phenomenology*, 94–95.

47. In "Homo-Formalism," Stacey Margolis argues that the instability of identity in *The Sacred Fount*, its narrator's confusion about where he ends and Obert begins, mobilizes queer desire as a formal principle of identity. The narrator, as she puts it, "looks at his double and establishes the existence of 'self' by seeing not difference, but sameness" (392). This reading might offer another way to think about the difficulty of detachment in James, another way in which boundaries come to feel deeply uncertain in situations of erotic desire.

Afterword • Queer Fiction and the Law

1. Forster, *Maurice*, 218. Further citations appear parenthetically within the text.

2. Holmes, *The Common Law*, 31.

3. Wilde, *The Picture of Dorian Gray*, 52.

4. Ellis, *New Horizon*, 45–46, 40.

5. Berlant and Warner, "Sex in Public," 553.

6. Hall, *The Well of Loneliness*, 436, 437.

7. Ibid., 437.

Ablow, Rachel. "Reading and Re-reading: Wilde, Newman, and the Fiction of Belief." In *The Feeling of Reading: Affective Experience and Victorian Literature*, edited by Rachel Ablow, 157–78. Ann Arbor: University of Michigan Press, 2010.

Ahmed, Sarah. *Queer Phenomenology: Orientations, Objects, Others*. Durham: Duke University Press, 2006.

Althusser, Louis. "Ideology and Ideological State Apparatuses." In *"Lenin and Philosophy" and Other Essays*, translated by Ben Brewster, 85–126. New York: Monthly Review, 2001.

Anderson, Amanda. *The Powers of Distance: Cosmopolitanism and the Cultivation of Detachment*. Princeton: Princeton University Press, 2001.

———. "Trollope's Modernity." *ELH* 74, no. 3 (Fall 2007): 509–34.

———. *The Way We Argue Now: A Study in the Cultures of Theory*. Princeton: Princeton University Press, 2005.

apRoberts, Ruth. *Trollope, Artist and Moralist*. London: Chatto and Windus, 1971.

Aristotle. *Metaphysics: Books Gamma, Delta, and Epsilon*. 2nd ed. Translated by Christopher Kerman. Edited by J. L. Ackrill and Lindsay Judson. Oxford: Oxford University Press, 1993.

Armstrong, Nancy. *Desire and Domestic Fiction: A Political History of the Novel*. New York: Oxford University Press, 1987.

Ashworth, E. Jennifer. "Developments in the Fifteenth and Sixteenth Centuries." In *Medieval and Renaissance Logic*, 609–44. Vol. 2 of *Handbook of the History of Logic*, edited by Dov M. Gabbay and John Woods. Amsterdam: Elsevier, 2008.

Austin, J. L. *How to Do Things with Words*. Cambridge, MA: Harvard University Press, 1962.

———. "A Plea for Excuses: The Presidential Address." *Proceedings of the Aristotelian Society* 57 (1956–57): 1–30.

Bain, Alexander. *Mental and Moral Science*. 3rd ed. London: Longmans, 1872.

Barthes, Roland. *Mythologies*. Translated by Richard Howard and Annette Lavers. New York: Hill and Wang, 2012.

———. *The Preparation of the Novel: Lecture Courses and Seminars at the Collège de France (1978–1979 and 1979–1980)*. Translated by Kate Briggs. Edited by Nathalie Léger. New York: Columbia University Press, 2011.

Bartlett, Jami. *Object Lessons: The Novel as a Theory of Reference*. Chicago: University of Chicago Press, 2016.

———. "Overlooking in Stendhal." *nonsite.org* 4 (Dec. 2011).

Bauer, Nancy, Sarah Beckwith, Alice Crary, Sandra Laugier, Toril Moi, and Linda Zerilli. Introduction to "Feminist Investigations and Other Essays," edited by Nancy Bauer, Sarah Beckwith, Alice Crary, Sandra Laugier, Toril Moi, and Linda Zerilli. Special issue, *New Literary History* 46, no. 2 (Spring 2015): v–xiii.

Beer, Gillian. *Darwin's Plots: Evolutionary Narrative in Darwin, George Eliot, and Nineteenth-Century Fiction.* London: Routledge, 1985.

Ben-Yishai, Ayelet. *Common Precedents: The Presentness of the Past in Victorian Law and Fiction.* New York: Oxford University Press, 2013.

Berlant, Lauren, and Michael Warner. "Sex in Public." *Critical Inquiry* 24, no. 2 (Winter 1998): 547–56.

Bersani, Leo. *A Future for Astyanax: Character and Desire in Literature.* 1976. Reprint, New York: Columbia University Press, 1984.

———. *Homos.* Cambridge, MA: Harvard University Press, 1996.

———. "Is the Rectum a Grave?" In *Is the Rectum a Grave? and Other Essays*, 3–30. Chicago: University of Chicago Press, 2009.

———. "Sociality and Sexuality." In *Is the Rectum a Grave? and Other Essays*, 102–19. Chicago: University of Chicago Press, 2009.

Best, Stephen, and Sharon Marcus. "Surface Reading: An Introduction." In "The Way We Read Now," edited by Stephen Best and Sharon Marcus. Special issue, *Representations* 108, no. 1 (Fall 2009): 1–21.

Bobzien, Suzanne. "Chrysippus and the Epistemic Theory of Vagueness." *Proceedings of the Aristotelian Society* 102 (2002): 217–38.

Bodenheimer, Rosemarie. "Jane Eyre in Search of Her Story." *Papers on Language and Literature* 16, no. 4 (Fall 1980): 387–402.

Boone, Joseph Allen. *Libidinal Currents: Sexuality and the Shaping of Modernism.* Chicago: University of Chicago Press, 1998.

Briefel, Aviva. "Tautological Crimes: Why Women Can't Steal Jewels." *Novel* 37, nos. 1–2 (Fall 2003–Spring 2004): 135–57.

Brontë, Charlotte. *Jane Eyre.* Edited by Stevie Davies. New York: Penguin, 2006.

———. *Villette.* Edited by Helen Cooper. New York: Penguin, 2004.

Brontë, Emily. *Wuthering Heights.* Edited by Pauline Nestor. New York: Penguin, 2003.

Brooks, Peter. *The Melodramatic Imagination: Balzac, Henry James, Melodrama, and the Mode of Excess.* 1976. Reprint, New Haven: Yale University Press, 1995.

———. *Reading for the Plot: Design and Intention in Narrative.* 1984. Reprint, Cambridge, MA: Harvard University Press, 1992.

Brilmyer, S. Pearl. "Plasticity, Form, and the Matter of Character in *Middlemarch*." *Representations* 130, no. 1 (Spring 2015): 60–83.

Butler, Judith. *Gender Trouble: Feminism and the Subversion of Identity.* 1990. Reprint, New York: Routledge, 2008.

———. *Giving an Account of Oneself.* New York: Fordham University Press, 2005.

Byler, Lauren. "If the Shoe Fits . . . Trollope and the Girl." *Novel* 42, no. 2 (Summer 2009): 268–77.

Cameron, Sharon. *Thinking in Henry James.* Chicago: University of Chicago Press, 1991.

Carlyle, Thomas. *Sartor Resartus.* Edited by Kerry McSweeney and Peter Sabor. Oxford: Oxford University Press, 1999.

Carroll, Lewis. *Symbolic Logic.* London: Macmillan, 1896.

Cartwright, Richard L. "Speaking of Everything." *Noûs* 28 (Mar. 1994): 1–20.

Cavell, Stanley. *The Claim of Reason: Wittgenstein, Skepticism, Morality, and Tragedy*. Oxford: Oxford University Press, 1979.

———. "Must We Mean What We Say?" In *Must We Mean What We Say?*, 1–43. 1969. Reprint, Cambridge: Cambridge University Press, 1989.

———. *Philosophy the Day after Tomorrow*. Cambridge, MA: Harvard University Press, 2005.

Chase, Karen. *Eros and Psyche: The Representation of Personality in Charlotte Brontë, Charles Dickens, and George Eliot*. New York: Methuen, 1984.

Clune, Michael. "'Whatever Charms Is Alien': John Ashbery's Everything." *Criticism* 50, no. 3 (Summer 2008): 447–70.

Cohen, Daniel J. *Equations from God: Pure Mathematics and Victorian Faith*. Baltimore: Johns Hopkins University Press, 2007.

———. "Reason and Belief in Victorian Mathematics." In *The Organisation of Knowledge in Victorian Britain*, edited by Martin Daunton, 159–72. Oxford: Oxford University Press, 2005.

Cohen, William A. *Sex Scandal: The Private Parts of Victorian Fiction*. Durham: Duke University Press, 1996.

Cohn, Elisha. *Still Life: Suspended Development in the Victorian Novel*. New York: Oxford University Press, 2016.

Conrad, Joseph. "Henry James: An Appreciation." In *Notes on Life and Letters*, edited by J. H. Stape, 15–19. Cambridge: Cambridge University Press, 2004.

"Contemporary Literature." *Westminster Review* 61 (Apr. 1854): 564–640.

Culler, Jonathan. "Omniscience." *Narrative* 12, no. 1 (Jan. 2004): 22–34.

Cvetkovich, Ann. *An Archive of Feelings: Trauma, Sexuality, and Lesbian Public Cultures*. Durham: Duke University Press, 2003.

Dames, Nicholas. *Amnesiac Selves: Nostalgia and Forgetting in British Fiction, 1810–1870*. New York: Oxford University Press, 2001.

———. *The Physiology of the Novel: Reading, Neural Science, and the Form of Victorian Fiction*. Oxford: Oxford University Press, 2007.

Dancer, Thom. "Toward a Modest Criticism: Ian McEwan's *Saturday*." *Novel: A Forum on Fiction* 45, no. 2 (Summer 2012): 202–20.

Daston, Lorraine, and Peter Galison. *Objectivity*. New York: Zone, 2007.

De Morgan, Augustus. *Formal Logic: Or, The Calculus of Inference, Necessary and Probable*. London: Taylor and Walton, 1847.

Derrida, Jacques. *Limited Inc*. Translated by Alan Bass. Evanston: Northwestern University Press, 1988.

Diamond, Cora. *The Realistic Spirit: Wittgenstein, Philosophy, and the Mind*. Cambridge, MA: MIT Press, 1991.

Doxiadis, Apostolos, and Christos Papadimitrious. *Logicomix: An Epic Search for Truth*. New York: Bloomsbury, 2009.

Eagleton, Terry. "Wittgenstein's Friends." *New Left Review* 135 (Sept.–Oct. 1982): 64–90.

Edelman, Lee. *No Future: Queer Theory and the Death Drive*. Durham: Duke University Press, 2004.

Edwards, A. W. F. *Cogwheels of the Mind: The Story of Venn Diagrams*. Baltimore: Johns Hopkins University Press, 2004.

Eliot, George. *Adam Bede*. Edited by Stephen Gill. New York: Penguin, 1985.

———. *Daniel Deronda.* Edited by Graham Handley. Oxford: Oxford University Press, 1998.

———. *The George Eliot Letters.* Edited by Gordon S. Haight. 7 vols. New Haven: Yale University Press, 1954–78.

———. *George Eliot's* Middlemarch *Notebooks: A Transcription.* Edited by John Clark Pratt and Victor A. Neufeldt. Berkeley: University of California Press, 1979.

———. "The Ilfracombe Journal." In *Selected Essays, Poems, and Other Writings,* edited by A. S. Byatt and Nicholas Warren, 214–30. New York: Penguin, 1990

———. *Middlemarch.* Edited by Rosemary Ashton. New York: Penguin 1994.

———. *The Mill on the Floss.* Edited by Gordon S. Haight. Oxford: Oxford University Press, 2008.

———. "The Natural History of German Life." In *Selected Essays, Poems, and Other Writings,* edited by A. S. Byatt and Nicholas Warren, 107–39. New York: Penguin, 1990.

———. "Notes on Form in Art." In *Essays of George Eliot,* edited by Thomas Pinney, 431–36. New York: Columbia University Press, 1963.

———. *Romola.* Edited by Dorothea Barrett. New York: Penguin, 1997.

———. *Silas Marner.* Edited by David Carroll. New York: Penguin, 1996.

Ellis, Edith. *The New Horizon in Love and Life.* London: Macmillan, 1921.

Ellis, Havelock. *Studies in the Psychology of Sex.* Vol. 1. New York: Random House, 1942.

Esty, Jed. *Unseasonable Youth: Modernism, Colonialism, and the Fiction of Development.* Oxford: Oxford University Press, 2011.

Farina, Jonathan. "*Middlemarch* and 'That Sort of Thing.'" In "Materiality and Memory," edited by Kate Flint. Special issue, *Romanticism and Victorianism on the Net* 53 (Feb. 2009).

Felman, Shoshana. *The Scandal of the Speaking Body: Don Juan with J. L. Austin, or Seduction in Two Languages.* Translated by Catherine Porter. Stanford: Stanford University Press, 2002.

Felski, Rita. *The Limits of Critique.* Chicago: University of Chicago Press, 2015.

Felski, Rita, and Susan Fraiman. Introduction to "In the Mood," edited by Rita Felski and Susan Fraiman. Special issue, *New Literary History* 43, no. 3 (Summer 2012): v–xii.

Fessenbecker, Patrick. "Anthony Trollope on Akrasia, Self-Deception, and Ethical Confusion." *Victorian Studies* 56, no. 4 (Summer 2014): 649–74.

Fish, Stanley. "How Ordinary Is Ordinary Language?" In *Is There a Text in This Class?,* 97–111. Cambridge, MA: Harvard University Press, 1980.

———. "How to Do Things with Austin and Searle: Speech Act Theory and Literary Criticism." *MLN* 91, no. 5 (Oct. 1976): 983–1025.

Fisichelli, Glynn-Ellen Maria. "The Language of Law and Love: Anthony Trollope's *Orley Farm.*" *ELH* 61, no. 3 (Fall 1994): 635–53.

Forster, E. M. *Maurice.* New York: Penguin, 2000.

Foucault, Michel. *The Hermeneutics of the Subject: Lectures at the Collège de France, 1981–1982.* Translated by Graham Burchell. Edited by Frédéric Gros. New York: Picador, 2005.

———. *The History of Sexuality, Volume 1: An Introduction.* Translated by Robert Hurley. New York: Vintage, 1990.

———. "Of Other Spaces." Translated by Jay Miskowiec. *Diacritics* 16, no. 1 (Spring 1986): 22–27.

François, Anne-Lise. *Open Secrets: The Literature of Uncounted Experience.* Stanford: Stanford University Press, 2008.

Frederickson, Kathleen. *The Ploy of Instinct: Victorian Sciences of Nature and Sexuality in Liberal Governance.* New York: Fordham University Press, 2014.

Freedman, Jonathan. *Professions of Taste: Henry James, British Aestheticism, and Commodity Culture.* Stanford: Stanford University Press, 1990.

Frege, Gottlob. *Conceptual Notation.* In *Conceptual Notation and Related Articles,* edited by Terrell Ward Bynum, 101–203. Translated by Terrell Ward Bynum. Oxford: Clarendon, 1972.

————. "On the Scientific Justification of a Concept-Script." Translated by James M. Bartlett. *Mind* 73, no. 290 (Apr. 1964): 155–60.

————. "Sense and Reference." Translated by Max Black. *Philosophical Review* 57, no. 3 (May 1948): 209–30.

————. "The Thought: A Logical Inquiry." Translated by A. M. Quinton and Marcelle Quinton. *Mind* 65, no. 259 (Jul. 1956): 289–311.

Freud, Sigmund. *Civilization and Its Discontents.* Edited and translated by James Strachey. New York: Norton, 1989.

————. *Introductory Lectures on Psycho-analysis.* Edited and translated by James Strachey. New York: Norton, 1989.

————. *Three Essays on the Theory of Sexuality.* Translated by James Strachey. New York: Basic Books, 2000.

Friedman, Dustin. "Negative Eroticism: Lyric Performativity and the Sexual Subject in Oscar Wilde's 'The Portrait of Mr. W. H.'" *ELH* 80, no. 2 (Summer 2013): 597–626.

Fuss, Diana. *Essentially Speaking: Feminism, Nature, and Difference.* New York: Routledge, 1989.

Gabbay, Dov M., and John Woods, ed. *British Logic in the Nineteenth Century.* Vol. 4 of *Handbook of the History of Logic,* edited by Dov M. Gabbay and John Woods. Amsterdam: Elsevier, 2008.

Gagnier, Regenia. "Gender, Liberalism, and Resentment." In *The Politics of Gender in Anthony Trollope's Novels,* edited by Margaret Marwick, Deborah Denenholz Morse, and Regenia Gagnier, 235–48. Burlington: Ashgate, 2009.

Gallagher, Catherine. "George Eliot: Immanent Victorian." *Representations* 90, no. 1 (Spring 2005): 61–74.

Ganeri, Jonardon. "Introduction: Indian Logic and the Colonization of Reason." In *Indian Logic: A Reader,* edited by Jonardon Ganeri, 1–25. Richmond, UK: Curzon, 2001.

Gilbert, Sandra, and Susan Gubar. *The Madwoman in the Attic: The Woman Writer and the Nineteenth-Century Literary Imagination.* 1979. Reprint, New Haven: Yale University Press, 2000.

Girard, René. *Deceit, Desire, and the Novel: Self and Other in Literary Structure.* Translated by Yvonne Freccero. Baltimore: Johns Hopkins University Press, 1976.

Glen, Heather. *Charlotte Brontë: The Imagination in History.* Oxford: Oxford University Press, 2002.

Grosz, Elizabeth, and Gayatri Chakravorty Spivak. "Criticism, Feminism, and the Institution: An Interview with Gayatri Chakravorty Spivak." *Thesis Eleven,* no. 10 (1984): 175–87.

Hadley, Elaine. *Living Liberalism: Practical Citizenship in Mid-Victorian Britain.* Chicago: University of Chicago Press, 2010.

Halberstam, Jack. *The Queer Art of Failure.* Durham: Duke University Press, 2011.

Hall, Radclyffe. *The Well of Loneliness.* New York: Anchor, 1990.

Hamilton, William. Review of "Thoughts on the Study of Mathematics as Part of a Liberal Education," by William Whewell. *Edinburgh Review* 62, no. 126 (Jan. 1836): 409–55.

Hardy, Thomas. *The Life and Work of Thomas Hardy.* Edited by Michael Millgate. London: Macmillan, 1984.

Hegel, G. W. F. *The Encyclopaedia Logic.* Translated by T. F. Geraets, W. A. Suchting, and H. S. Harris. Indianapolis: Hackett, 1991.

———. *The Science of Logic.* Translated by George di Giovanni. Cambridge: Cambridge University Press, 2010.

Henchman, Anna. *The Starry Sky Within: Astronomy and the Reach of the Mind in Victorian Literature.* New York: Oxford University Press, 2014.

Henderson, Andrea. "Symbolic Logic and the Logic of Symbolism." *Critical Inquiry* 41, no. 1 (Autumn 2014): 78–101.

Herbert, Christopher. *Culture and Anomie: Ethnographic Imagination in the Nineteenth Century.* Chicago: University of Chicago Press, 1991.

Herman, Jerry, and Harvey Fierstein. *La Cage Aux Folles: The Broadway Musical.* Performed by George Hearn, Gene Barry, et al. Recorded 1990. RCA Victor.

Hertz, Neil. *George Eliot's Pulse.* Stanford: Stanford University Press, 2003.

Holmes, Oliver Wendell, Jr. *The Common Law.* In *The Path of the Law and The Common Law,* 31–370. New York: Kaplan, 2009.

Hunt, Tony. "Aristotle, Dialectic, and Courtly Literature." *Viator* 10 (1979): 95–130.

Irvine, Andrew David, and Harry Deutsch. "Russell's Paradox." In *The Stanford Encyclopedia of Philosophy,* edited by Edward N. Zalta. Accessed Jan. 23, 2015. plato.stanford.edu.

Jacobus, Mary. "The Buried Letter: Feminism and Romanticism in *Villette.*" In *Women Writing and Writing about Women,* edited by Mary Jacobus, 42–60. 1979. Reprint, Oxford: Routledge: 2012.

———. "The Question of Language: Men of Maxims and *The Mill on the Floss.*" *Critical Inquiry* 8, no. 2 (Winter 1981): 207–22.

Jaffe, Audrey. *Scenes of Sympathy: Identity and Representation in Victorian Fiction.* Ithaca: Cornell University Press, 2000.

———. *Vanishing Points: Dickens, Narrative, and the Subject of Omniscience.* Berkeley: University of California Press, 1991.

———. *The Victorian Novel Dreams of the Real: Conventions and Ideology.* New York: Oxford University Press, 2016.

Jagose, Annamarie. "Remembering Miss Wade: *Little Dorrit* and the Historicizing of Female Perversity." *GLQ* 4, no. 3 (1998): 423–51.

James, Henry. *The Ambassadors.* Edited by Christopher Butler. Oxford: Oxford University Press, 2008.

———. *The Awkward Age.* Edited by Ronald Blythe. New York: Penguin, 1987.

———. *The Golden Bowl.* Edited by Gore Vidal. New York: Penguin, 1987.

———. "*Middlemarch.*" In *The Art of Criticism: Henry James on the Theory and Practice of Criticism,* edited by William Veeder and Susan M. Griffin, 48–54. Chicago: University of Chicago Press, 1986.

———. *The Portrait of a Lady.* Edited by Geoffrey Moore. New York: Penguin, 2003.

———. *The Sacred Fount.* In *Novels 1901–1902,* edited by Leo Bersani, 1–194. New York: Library of America, 2006.

———. *The Spoils of Poynton.* Edited by David Lodge. New York: Penguin, 1987.

———. *What Maisie Knew.* Edited by Adrian Poole. Oxford: Oxford University Press, 2008.

———. *The Wings of the Dove.* Edited by John Bayley and Patricia Crick. New York: Penguin, 1986.

Jameson, Fredric. *The Antinomies of Realism.* New York: Verso, 2013.

———. *The Political Unconscious: Narrative as a Socially Symbolic Act.* Ithaca: Cornell University Press, 1982.

Jarvis, Claire. *Exquisite Masochism: Marriage, Sex, and the Novel Form.* Baltimore: Johns Hopkins University Press, 2016.

Kant, Immanuel. *Logic.* Translated by Robert S. Hartman and Wolfgang Schwarz. Mineola, NY: Dover, 1988.

Kaplan, Carla. *The Erotics of Talk: Women's Writing and Feminist Paradigms.* Oxford: Oxford University Press, 1996.

Kay, Sarah. *Courtly Contradictions: The Emergence of the Literary Object in the Twelfth Century.* Stanford: Stanford University Press, 2002.

Kornbluh, Anna. "Realism Redux: Symbolic Logic on the Social Plane of *Alice's Adventures in Wonderland.*" Presentation at "Logic and Literary Form," Berkeley, CA, Apr. 14–15, 2017.

———. "The Realist Blueprint." *Henry James Review* 36, no. 3 (Fall 2015): 199–211.

Kreilkamp, Ivan. "Unuttered: Withheld Speech and Female Authorship in *Jane Eyre* and *Villette.*" *Novel: A Forum on Fiction* 32, no. 3 (Summer 1999): 331–54.

Kucich, John. *Repression in Victorian Fiction: Charlotte Brontë, George Eliot, and Charles Dickens.* Berkeley: University of California Press, 1987.

Kurnick, David. "Abstraction and the Subject of Novel-Reading: Drifting through *Romola.*" *Novel: A Forum on Fiction* 42, no. 3 (Fall 2009): 490–96.

———. *Empty Houses: Theatrical Failure and the Novel.* Princeton: Princeton University Press, 2012.

———. "An Erotics of Detachment: *Middlemarch* and Novel-Reading as Critical Practice." *ELH* 74, no. 3 (Fall 2007): 583–608.

Lacan, Jacques. *The Ethics of Psychoanalysis, 1959–60.* Translated by Dennis Porter. Vol. 7 of *The Seminar of Jacques Lacan,* edited by Jacques-Alain Miller. New York: Norton, 1997.

———. "The Instance of the Letter in the Unconscious." In *Écrits: A Selection,* 138–68. Translated by Bruce Fink. New York: Norton, 2004.

Lane, Christopher. *Hatred and Civility: The Antisocial Life in Victorian England.* New York: Columbia University Press, 2004.

Latour, Bruno. "Why Has Critique Run Out of Steam? From Matters of Fact to Matters of Concern." *Critical Inquiry* 30, no. 2 (Winter 2004): 225–48.

Laugier, Sandra. *Why We Need Ordinary Language Philosophy.* Translated by Daniela Ginsburg. Chicago: University of Chicago Press, 2013.

Leibniz, G. W. "Preface to a Universal Characteristic." In *Philosophical Essays,* edited by Roger Ariew and Daniel Garber, 5–9. Translated by Roger Ariew and Daniel Garber. Indianapolis: Hackett, 1989.

LeMahieu, Michael. *Fictions of Fact and Value: The Erasure of Logical Positivism in American Literature, 1945–1975.* New York: Oxford University Press, 2013.

LeMahieu, Michael, and Karen Zumhagen-Yekplé, eds. *Wittgenstein and Modernism.* Chicago: University of Chicago Press, 2017.

Levine, Caroline. *Forms: Whole, Rhythm, Hierarchy, Network.* Princeton: Princeton University Press, 2015.

Levine, George. *Dying to Know: Scientific Epistemology and Narrative in Victorian England.* Chicago: University of Chicago Press, 2002.

Lewes, George Henry. *Problems of Life and Mind, Third Series.* London: Trübner, 1879.

Loesberg, Jonathan. "Wildean Interpretation and Formalist Reading." *Victorian Studies* 58, no. 1 (Autumn 2015): 9–33.

Love, Heather. "Close but Not Deep: Literary Ethics and the Descriptive Turn." *New Literary History* 41, no. 2 (Spring 2010): 371–91.

———. *Feeling Backward: Loss and the Politics of Queer History.* Cambridge, MA: Harvard University Press, 2007.

Mao, Douglas, and Rebecca L. Walkowitz. "Introduction: Modernisms Bad and New." In *Bad Modernisms,* edited by Douglas Mao and Rebecca L. Walkowitz, 1–18. Durham: Duke University Press, 2006.

Marcus, Sharon. *Between Women: Friendship, Desire, and Marriage in Victorian England.* Princeton: Princeton University Press, 2007.

———. "The Profession of the Author: Abstraction, Advertising, and *Jane Eyre.*" *PMLA* 110, no. 2 (Mar. 1995): 206–19.

Marcus, Sharon, Heather Love, and Stephen Best. "Building a Better Description." In "Description across Disciplines," edited by Sharon Marcus, Heather Love, and Stephen Best. Special issue, *Representations* 135, no. 1 (Summer 2016): 1–21.

Margolis, Stacey. "Homo-Formalism: Analogy in *The Sacred Fount.*" *Novel: A Forum on Fiction* 34, no. 3 (Summer 2001): 391–410.

Matus, Jill L. *Unstable Bodies: Victorian Representations of Sexuality and Maternity.* Manchester: Manchester University Press, 1995.

McMaster, Juliet. "'The Meaning of Words and the Nature of Things': Trollope's *Can You Forgive Her?*" *Studies in English Literature, 1500–1900* 14, no. 4 (Autumn 1974): 603–18.

McWhirter, David. *Desire and Love in Henry James: A Study of the Late Novels.* Cambridge: Cambridge University Press, 1989.

Mendelssohn, Michèle. *Henry James, Oscar Wilde, and Aesthetic Culture.* New York: Columbia University Press, 2007.

Meredith, George. *The Egoist.* Edited by Richard C. Stevenson. Peterborough, ON: Broadview, 2010.

Michie, Elsie B. *The Vulgar Question of Money: Heiresses, Materialism, and the Novel of Manners from Jane Austen to Henry James.* Baltimore: Johns Hopkins University Press, 2011.

Mill, John Stuart. *A System of Logic, Ratiocinative and Inductive.* London: John W. Parker, 1843.

———. *Utilitarianism.* 2nd ed. Edited by George Sher. Indianapolis: Hackett, 2001.

Miller, Andrew H. *The Burdens of Perfection: On Ethics and Reading in Nineteenth-Century British Literature.* Ithaca: Cornell University Press, 2008.

———. *Novels behind Glass: Commodity Culture and Victorian Narrative.* Cambridge: Cambridge University Press, 1995.

Miller, D. A. *Jane Austen, or The Secret of Style.* Princeton: Princeton University Press, 2003.

———. *The Novel and the Police.* Berkeley: University of California Press, 1988.

———. *Place for Us: An Essay on the Broadway Musical.* Cambridge, MA: Harvard University Press, 1998.

Miller, J. Hillis. *Literature as Conduct: Speech Acts in Henry James*. New York: Fordham University Press, 2005.

————. "Optic and Semiotic in *Middlemarch*." In *Worlds of Victorian Fiction*, edited by Jerome Buckley, 125–48. Cambridge, MA: Harvard University Press, 1975.

————. *Others*. Princeton: Princeton University Press, 2001.

————. *Speech Acts in Literature*. Stanford: Stanford University Press, 2001.

Miller, Nancy K. "Emphasis Added: Plots and Plausibilities in Women's Fiction." *PMLA* 96, no. 1 (Jan. 1981): 36–48.

Moretti, Franco. *The Bourgeois: Between History and Literature*. New York: Verso, 2013.

————. *The Way of the World: The Bildungsroman in European Culture*. 1987. Reprint, New York: Verso, 2000.

Morse, Deborah Denenholz. *Reforming Trollope: Race, Gender, and Englishness in the Novels of Anthony Trollope*. Burlington: Ashgate, 2013.

Muñoz, José Esteban. *Cruising Utopia: The Then and There of Queer Futurity*. New York: New York University Press, 2009.

Nagel, Thomas. *The View from Nowhere*. 1986. Reprint, New York: Oxford University Press, 1989.

Newman, John Henry. *An Essay in Aid of a Grammar of Assent*. 5th ed. London: Burns and Oates, 1881.

Ngai, Sianne. *Ugly Feelings*. Cambridge, MA: Harvard University Press, 2005.

Ohi, Kevin. *Henry James and the Queerness of Style*. Minneapolis: University of Minnesota Press, 2011.

Peirce, Charles Sanders. "The Law of Mind." In *Philosophical Writings of Peirce*, edited by Justus Buchler, 339–53. Mineola, NY: Dover, 1955.

————. "Logic as Semiotic: The Theory of Signs." In *Philosophical Writings of Peirce*, edited by Justus Buchler, 98–119. Mineola, NY: Dover, 1955.

Perloff, Marjorie. *Wittgenstein's Ladder: Poetic Language and the Strangeness of the Ordinary*. Chicago: University of Chicago Press, 1996.

Pippin, Robert B. *Henry James and Modern Moral Life*. Cambridge: Cambridge University Press, 2001.

Pizzo, Justine. "Atmospheric Exceptionalism in *Jane Eyre*: Charlotte Brontë's Weather Wisdom." *PMLA* 131, no. 1 (Jan. 2016): 84–100.

Polhemus, Robert M. *The Changing World of Anthony Trollope*. Berkeley: University of California Press, 1968.

————. *Erotic Faith: Being in Love from Jane Austen to D. H. Lawrence*. Chicago: University of Chicago Press, 1990.

Posnock, Ross. *The Trial of Curiosity: Henry James, William James, and the Challenge of Modernity*. Oxford: Oxford University Press, 1991.

Price, Leah. *How to Do Things with Books in Victorian Britain*. Princeton: Princeton University Press, 2012.

Psomiades, Kathy Alexis. "Heterosexual Exchange and Other Victorian Fictions: *The Eustace Diamonds* and Victorian Anthropology." *Novel: A Forum on Fiction* 33, no. 1 (Fall 1999): 93–118.

Puckett, Kent. *Bad Form: Social Mistakes and the Nineteenth-Century Novel*. New York: Oxford University Press, 2008.

————. "Stupid Sensations: Henry James, Good Form, and Reading *Middlemarch* without a Brain." *Henry James Review* 28, no. 3 (Fall 2007): 292–98.

Quigley, Megan. *Modernist Fiction and Vagueness: Philosophy, Form, and Language.* Cambridge: Cambridge University Press, 2015.

Quine, Willard Van Orman. *From a Logical Point of View: Nine Logico-Philosophical Essays,* rev. 2nd ed. 1961. Reprint, Cambridge, MA: Harvard University Press, 1980.

Quintilian. *The Orator's Education.* 5 vols. Edited and translated by Donald A. Russell. Cambridge, MA: Loeb Classical Library, 2002.

Rayo, Agustín, and Gabriel Uzquiano. Introduction to *Absolute Generality*, edited by Agustín Rayo and Gabriel Uzquiano, 1–19. New York: Oxford University Press, 2006.

Rorty, Richard. *Contingency, Irony, and Solidarity.* 1989. Reprint, Cambridge: Cambridge University Press, 1999.

———. "How Many Grains Make a Heap?" *London Review of Books* 27, no. 2 (Jan. 20, 2005): 12–13.

Rosenfeld, Jessica. *Ethics and Enjoyment in Late Medieval Poetry: Love after Aristotle.* Cambridge: Cambridge University Press, 2011.

Rosenthal, Jesse. *Good Form: The Ethical Experience of the Victorian Novel.* Princeton: Princeton University Press, 2016.

Royle, Nicholas. "The 'Telepathy Effect': Notes toward a Reconsideration of Narrative Fiction." In *The Uncanny*, 256–76. Manchester: Manchester University Press, 2003.

Russell, Bertrand. "On Denoting." *Mind* 14, no. 56 (Oct. 1905): 479–93.

———. *Principles of Mathematics.* New York: Routledge, 2010.

———. "Vagueness." *Australasian Journal of Psychology and Philosophy* 1, no. 2 (Jan. 1923): 84–92.

Scarry, Elaine. *Dreaming by the Book.* Princeton: Princeton University Press, 2001.

Schaffer, Talia. *Romance's Rival: Familiar Marriage in Victorian Fiction.* New York: Oxford University Press, 2016.

Schmitt, Cannon. "Tidal Conrad (Literally)." *Victorian Studies* 55, no. 1 (Autumn 2012): 7–29.

Scott, Joan W. *Gender and the Politics of History.* Rev. ed. New York: Columbia University Press, 1999.

Searle, John. *Expression and Meaning: Studies in the Theory of Speech Acts.* 1979. Reprint, Cambridge: Cambridge University Press, 1999.

Sedgwick, Eve Kosofsky. *Epistemology of the Closet.* 1990. Reprint, Berkeley: University of California Press, 2008.

———. *Touching Feeling: Affect, Pedagogy, Performativity.* Durham: Duke University Press, 2003.

Shklovsky, Viktor. "Art as Device." In *Theory of Prose*, 1–14. Translated by Benjamin Sher. Normal, IL: Dalkey Archive Press, 1998.

Shuttleworth, Sally. *Charlotte Brontë and Victorian Psychology.* Cambridge: Cambridge University Press, 1996.

———. *George Eliot and Nineteenth-Century Science: The Make-Believe of a Beginning.* Cambridge: Cambridge University Press, 1984.

———. "Sexuality and Knowledge in *Middlemarch.*" *Nineteenth-Century Contexts* 19, no. 4 (1996): 425–41.

Sidgwick, Henry. *The Methods of Ethics.* 7th ed. Indianapolis: Hackett, 1988.

Silverman, Kaja. *Male Subjectivity at the Margins.* New York: Routledge, 1992.

Smalley, Donald, ed. *Anthony Trollope: The Critical Heritage*. London: Routledge, 1969.

Spivak, Gayatri Chakravorty. "Can the Subaltern Speak?" In *Marxism and the Interpretation of Culture*, edited by Cary Nelson and Lawrence Grossberg, 271–316. Urbana: University of Illinois Press, 1988.

———. "Scattered Speculations on the Question of Value." *Diacritics* 15, no. 4 (Winter 1985): 73–93.

———. "Three Women's Texts and a Critique of Imperialism." *Critical Inquiry* 12, no. 1 (Fall 1985): 235–61.

Stevens, Hugh. *Henry James and Sexuality*. Cambridge: Cambridge University Press, 1998.

Stewart, Dugald. *Elements of the Philosophy of the Human Mind*. Vol. 2. Edinburgh: W. Creech, 1814.

Strawson, P. F. "On Referring." *Mind* 59, no. 235 (Jul. 1950): 320–44.

Terada, Rei. *Looking Away: Phenomenality and Dissatisfaction, Kant to Adorno*. Cambridge, MA: Harvard University Press, 2009.

Trollope, Anthony. *An Autobiography*. Edited by Michael Sadleir and Frederick Page. Oxford: Oxford University Press, 2008.

———. *Can You Forgive Her?* Edited by Stephen Wall. New York: Penguin, 2004.

———. *He Knew He Was Right*. Edited by Frank Kermode. New York: Penguin, 2004.

———. *The Way We Live Now*. Edited by John Sutherland. Oxford: Oxford University Press, 2008.

Venn, John. *Symbolic Logic*. London: Macmillan, 1881.

Viswanathan, Gauri. *Outside the Fold: Conversion, Modernity, and Belief*. Princeton: Princeton University Press, 1998.

Wahl, Russell. "Arnauld, Antoine (1612–1694)." In *Philosophy of Education: An Encyclopedia*, edited by J. J. Chambliss, 35–36. New York: Routledge, 1996.

Walkowitz, Rebecca L. *Cosmopolitan Style: Modernism beyond the Nation*. New York: Columbia University Press, 2005.

Whewell, William. "Thoughts on the Study of Mathematics as Part of a Liberal Education." In *On the Principles of English University Education*, 135–77. London: John W. Parker, 1838.

Wilde, Oscar. *De Profundis*. In *De Profundis and Other Prison Writings*, edited by Colm Tóibín, 45–161. New York: Penguin, 2013.

———. *The Picture of Dorian Gray*. Edited by Joseph Bristow. Oxford: Oxford University Press, 2006.

Williams, Bernard. *Ethics and the Limits of Philosophy*. Cambridge, MA: Harvard University Press, 1987.

Williams, Carolyn. "Closing the Book: The Intertextual End of *Jane Eyre*." In *Victorian Connections*, edited by Jerome J. McGann, 60–87. Charlottesville: University of Virginia Press, 1989.

Williams, Jeffrey J. "The New Modesty in Literary Criticism." *Chronicle of Higher Education*, Jan. 5, 2015. chronicle.com/article/The-New-Modesty-in-Literary/150993.

Williamson, Timothy. *Vagueness*. New York: Routledge, 1994.

Wittgenstein, Ludwig. *On Certainty*. Edited by G. E. M. Anscombe and G. H. von Wright. Translated by Denis Paul and G. E. M. Anscombe. Malden, MA: Blackwell, 1975.

———. *Philosophical Investigations*. 4th ed. Translated by G. E. M. Anscombe, P. M. S. Hacker, and Joachim Schulte. Malden, MA: Blackwell, 2009.

————. *Tractatus Logico-Philosophicus*. Translated by D. F. Pears and B. F. McGuinness. London: Routledge, 2003.

Woolf, Virginia. *To the Lighthouse*. Edited by David Bradshaw. Oxford: Oxford University Press, 2008.

Yeazell, Ruth Bernard. "More True than Real: Jane Eyre's 'Mysterious Summons.'" *Nineteenth-Century Fiction* 29, no. 2 (Sep. 1974): 127–43.

Zhang, Dora. "Naming the Indescribable: Woolf, Russell, James, and the Limits of Description." *New Literary History* 45, no. 1 (Winter 2014): 51–70.

Žižek, Slavoj. *Interrogating the Real*. New York: Continuum, 2005.

Zubernis, Emily. "Henry James's Minimalist Novel." *Novel: A Forum on Fiction* 49, no. 3 (Nov. 2016): 467–85.